Betty Crocker's
Great Grilling

Hungry Minds, Inc.

New York, NY ◆ Cleveland, OH ◆ Indianapolis, IN

Hungry Minds™

Published by
Hungry Minds, Inc.
909 Third Avenue
New York, NY 10022
www.hungryminds.com

For general information on Hungry Minds' products and services, please contact our Customer Care Department within the U.S. at 800-762-2974, outside the U.S. at 317-572-3993, or fax 317-572-4002.

For sales inquiries and reseller information, including discounts, premium and bulk quantity sales, and foreign-language translations, please contact our Customer Care Department at 800-434-3422, fax 317-572-4002, or write to Hungry Minds, Inc., Attn: Customer Care Department, 10475 Crosspoint Boulevard, Indianapolis, IN 46256.

Library of Congress Cataloging-in-Publication data

Crocker, Betty
    Betty Crocker's great grilling — great grilling cookbook
        p.   cm.
    Includes index.
    ISBN 0-7645-6642-3
    1. Barbecue cookery   2. Menus   I. Title
TX840.B3C774   1997
641.7'6—dc21

ISBN 0-7645-6642-3

GENERAL MILLS, INC.
Betty Crocker Kitchens
Manager, Publishing: Lois L. Tlusty
Editor: Jean E. Kozar
Recipe Development: Altanette Autry, Joyce K. Battcher-Malchow, Julie Turnbull
Food Stylists: Kate Courtney Condon, Carol Groves
Photographic Services
Photographer: Steve Olson
Hungry Minds, Inc.
Cover design: Michael J. Freeland
Book design: George J. McKeon

For consistent baking results, the Betty Crocker Kitchens recommend Gold Medal Flour.
For more great ideas visit www.bettycrocker.com
Cover photograph by David Bishop

Manufactured in the United States of America
10 9 8 7 6 5 4 3 2 1

Cover photo: Orange-Thyme Marinade (p. 192) shown with steak; Honey-Thyme Grilled Shrimp (p. 81)

INTRODUCTION

We know that everyone loves that smoky aroma of fresh food sizzling on the grill. And since Americans always turn to Betty Crocker for her cooking expertise, we're certain you'll love these great grilling recipes perfect for any occasion, all year round!

Here, in *Betty Crocker's Great Grilling*, you'll find more than 200 luscious recipes for ribs and steaks, burgers, chicken and seafood. What could be more tempting than biting into a well-seasoned juicy burger grilled just the way you like it? Or serving your family moist, tender, marinated chicken breasts hot off the coals?

You know you can trust Betty Crocker to bring you the best in grilling success. That's why we've included helpful, easy-to-follow information such as a glossary with everything you need to know about grilling terms, grilling tools and preparation, plus tips for grilling safety. We also have an illustrated guide to help you select the right grill.

The best part of *Betty Crocker's Great Grilling* are the fabulous recipes. These dishes are not only bursting with flavor but also are a cinch to prepare. Why not try dishes like sweet and smoky Apricot-Glazed Burgers with Apricot Salsa or Peanutty Chicken Kabobs. You can keep your family begging for more with a savory Italian Sausage Spinach Pizza or a Gingery Pepper Steak. There are special recipes to tantalize family and friends, such as Rosemary-Wine Country Ribs, Honey-Pecan Chicken and Spicy Shrimp with Creole Sauce. And don't forget to top it off with sweeter fare. You'll love Pears with Raspberry Sauce or Toasted-Rum Pound Cake— yes, cooked right on the grill!

You'll also find a generous selection of tasty marinades, sauces and rubs, plus chutneys and relishes all packed with flavor. Keep your eye out for a special section called "Flavor Boosters" at the end of many chapters. In it, you'll find all the marinades, sauces, rubs, chutneys, relishes, and flavorings conveniently identified with their page numbers for quick and easy reference. No more bland and boring meals! These sure-fired recipes with a Betty Crocker flare were developed and tested to please your family and friends.

Leave it to Betty Crocker's culinary wisdom to bring you the best in all-time grilling success.

Betty Crocker

CONTENTS

LET'S GET GRILLING!

Nothing is more tantalizing than fresh air filled with the irresistible aroma of grilled food! This combination can go hand in hand any time of the year because grilling is more popular than ever. And it's so convenient with little cleanup. Outdoor grilling not only puts great-tasting food on the table, it also can turn meals into a special event. Visiting with family, friends and neighbors while heating the grill and cooking the food makes mealtime a party.

Selecting and Using a Grill

The variety of types, styles and sizes of grills is endless. Whether you're purchasing your first grill or the third, consider the different types available to best fit your needs. How often you grill, where the cooking is done, which technique you prefer, how many people you feed and how much money you're planning to spend are additional considerations.

Some features to look for include stainless steel grill racks that resist corrosion, nonstick racks that make cleanup easier, and a cover handle designed to be gripped easily and comfortably that's not too close to the firebox. On gas grills, look for an easy-to-replace gas tank that has a fuel gauge so that you won't be caught without.

Types of Outdoor Grills

Although the categories are not clear-cut, we've grouped the many types of grills available by fuel source, shape and size, and function.

Fuel Source

CHARCOAL GRILLS: If there is a tradition in grilling, charcoal is it. For purists who enjoy true charcoal flavor as well as the challenge of starting the fire, this is the grill of choice. Available in all the types and sizes mentioned above, the simplest charcoal grill consists of a firebox with a grate to hold the charcoal, a grill rack to hold the food and possibly a cover or lid.

ELECTRIC GRILLS: Electric outdoor grills are becoming more and more popular, especially for apartment and condominium dwellers for whom charcoal or gas grills are prohibited. Because of the need for an electrical outlet, mobility can be limited. These grills require a separate 110/120-volt grounded outlet, because most require 1,600 to 1,800 watts of cooking power. Most electric grills are designed with a smoking element of some type, such as lava rock, that will give grilled flavor similar to that of charcoal and gas grills. The heating element may be separate under the grill rack or imbedded in the grids of the grill rack.

GAS GRILLS: Convenience is key to the popularity of gas grills—quick starting, accurate heat controls, no charcoal required and more even cooking are a few desirable features. With the flip of a switch, you can heat these grills without attending to them. Gas is used to heat semipermanent ceramic briquettes, or *lava rock*, which are made from natural volcanic stone, that line the grate and radiate heat to cook the food. Gas heat can be controlled more easily than charcoal.

Don't worry about missing the charcoal flavor. Actually, the smoke created when food drippings hit hot lava rock is what accounts for most of the grilled flavor. Although a window in the cover was once a common feature, it is less common now because of heat loss and the difficulty of keeping it clean.

Gas grills come in all shapes, sizes and price ranges, from tabletop models to elaborate wagons complete with side burners, cutting boards and condiment trays. Most often fueled by refillable liquid propane (LP) gas tanks, other models can be fueled by being directly hooked up to a natural gas line. The larger the grill, the higher the BTUs, increasing cooking efficiency. Larger gas grills will have at least two burners.

Shape and Function

OPEN GRILLS OR BRAZIERS: The simplest form of a grill consists of a shallow firebox to hold the charcoal and a metal cooking grill rack for the food. The grill rack is usually just a few inches from the coals so these grills are best for direct-heat grilling of foods such as burgers, chops, steaks and chicken. Braziers can be partially hooded to protect them from wind and retain heat. They can come with either electric or battery-powered rotisserie attachments that require little attention during use.

Charcoal open brazier

Round Kettles and Covered Cookers: *Kettle* describes the round version, whereas *covered cooker* describes the square and rectangular models. They all have deep rounded bottoms and generous lids that allow them to be used for a wide range of cooking methods—grill, roast, steam or smoke. Without their covers, these grills are used for *direct-heat grilling* (grilling foods directly over charcoal). The deep bottoms make them excellent for *indirect-heat grilling*, where a drip pan is placed on the bottom of the grill underneath the food to catch the fat and drippings, and charcoal surrounds the drip pan. Covered, foods can be grilled and lightly smoked at the same time. Draft vents in the bottom and in the cover help control the temperature. Many optional accessories are available.

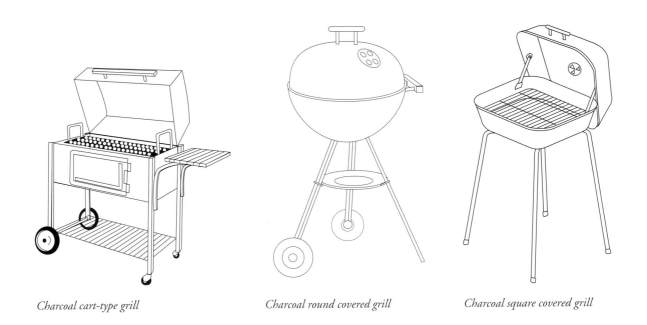

Charcoal cart-type grill   *Charcoal round covered grill*   *Charcoal square covered grill*

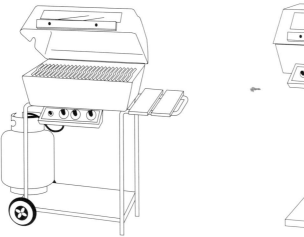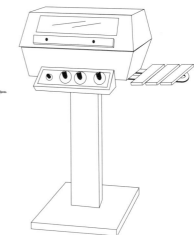

Stand-up LP gas grill   *Permanently installed natural gas grill*

PORTABLE OR TABLETOP GRILLS: Lightweight and portable, these grills are easy to transport, store and clean. They range from uncovered simple cast-metal hibachis of Japanese origin to miniature versions of kettles and covered cookers. They're great for direct-heat cooking for two, limited storage space, beach cookouts, tailgating and picnics. Because the cooking surface is much smaller than that of standard grills, portable grills are not designed for indirect-heat cooking, large cuts of meat, feeding crowds or long cooking times.

Charcoal covered tabletop grill   *Portable electric tabletop grill*   *Portable tabletop gas grill*

WATER SMOKERS: These tall, cylindrical, covered cookers feature a firebox, a water pan, one or two grill racks and a dome-shaped cover. They can be fueled by charcoal, gas or electricity. The food is placed on a grill rack high above the heat. A pan of water or other liquid (beer, fruit juice, wine, cola) is placed between the heat source and the grill rack holding the food. The food cooks very slowly in a dense cloud of smoke and steam. Aromatic wood chips, which have been soaked in water or other liquids can be thrown on the heat to create smoke and add another flavor dimension. Smokers are known for their low, even heat and can re-create the flavors of smokehouse Southern barbecue at home. Foods best suited to smoking include slabs of ribs, beef briskets, roasts, whole turkeys and other poultry, and fish.

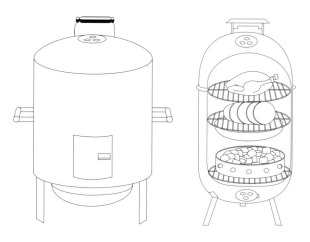

Charcoal, gas or electric water smoker

Grilling Glossary

ALUMINUM FOIL: Use heavy-duty aluminum foil for cleaning, cooking and covering. It is most often found in rolls eighteen inches long. Also see "Aluminum Foil—A Grill's Best Friend" (page 17).

BARBECUE: Definitions vary! For some, this word is interchanged with "grilling," whereas others define barbecue as long, hot-smoke cooking of large meat cuts over low heat that gives fall-off-the-bone tender meat. To others, it describes the entertaining event of outdoor cooking.

BASTE: To brush or spoon liquid over food during grilling.

BRAZIER: An open or partially covered grill used for charcoal cooking.

CERAMIC BRIQUETTES: Similar to lava rock, they are used to line the grate of a gas grill.

CHARCOAL: A porous compound made partly from burned hardwood.

CHARCOAL BRIQUETTES: Compacted, evenly shaped bricks or pieces of charcoal.

CHARCOAL CHIMNEY STARTER: A vented, vertical cylinder-shaped canister that you place in a grill's firebox and into which you crumple newspaper in the bottom, add charcoal briquettes to the top, and light. It's known for quick, even starting of charcoal. Remove the chimney and spread the hot coals before grilling food. It has a large, easy-to-grasp handle for safe handling.

CHARCOAL LIGHTER: A liquid specially formulated to light charcoal quickly, as well as to use in the presence of food.

COAL GRATE OR FIRE GRATE: A rack that holds the charcoal in the firebox.

DIRECT HEAT: Cooking process where food is grilled directly over the heat source.

DRIP PAN: An aluminum foil pan placed under food to catch drippings during cooking while grilling with indirect heat. It also helps prevent flare-ups.

ELECTRIC COIL CHARCOAL STARTER: Charcoal is piled for the heating coil to ignite; the coil is removed after the charcoal has started.

FIRE STARTERS: Convenient tools used to light charcoal: The *charcoal chimney starter* is a vented, vertical cylinder-shaped canister you place in a grill's firebox and into which you crumple newspaper in the bottom, add charcoal briquettes to the top, and light; *charcoal lighter* is a liquid specially formulated to light charcoal quickly, as well as to use in the presence of food; an *electric coil starter* is a device onto which charcoal is piled for the heating coil to ignite—it is removed after the charcoal has started; *cube starters* are made from wax, gel or compressed wood in solid lighter cubes; and *butane charcoal lighter*, six to eight inches long, is designed to keep you at a safe distance from the fire.

FIREBOX, FIRE PAN OR FIRE BOWL: The bottom part of the grill that holds the heat source.

FLARE-UP: When fat drippings hit hot coals or lava rock and catch on fire.

GRILL: The whole cooking unit, whether fueled by charcoal, gas or electricity.

GRILL RACK: The rack on which food is placed for cooking. Also called a *grill grid*.

GRILLING: Cooking foods directly over charcoal, gas or electric heat, most often without the use of a cover. Also see "Barbecue."

GRILLING TOOLS: Long handles are a must for sturdy grilling tools, such as turners, tongs, basting brushes and forks to use for turning food. You may want to have a second set of tongs to use just for moving coals around.

HIBACHI: A small uncovered (usually cast iron) grill of Japanese origin.

HINGED WIRE GRILL BASKET: Flat grilling basket used to easily handle and turn meats (chops, steaks, fish fillets) on the grill. Usually square or rectangular, some are designed with close rungs to hold small foods such as shrimp and vegetable pieces. A fish-shaped basket is also available.

INDIRECT HEAT: Cooking process where food is cooked indirectly and over a drip pan, not directly over the heat source.

LAVA ROCK: Used in place of charcoal, volcanic lava bits are heated in gas and electric grills to cook food.

MARINADE: Mixture of herbs and spices mixed with liquid in which food is soaked to add flavor. If an acid such as lemon juice, vinegar or a tomato-based food is added, it can also tenderize.

MARINATE: Soak a food such as meat or vegetables in a seasoned liquid mixture, called a *marinade,* to add flavor or tenderize.

MEAT THERMOMETER: Using a thermometer is the best way to determine the correct doneness of meat, from burgers to roasts. An *instant-read* thermometer will give an accurate reading about five seconds after being inserted into the food. Keep the thermometer clean and in working order. Insert the thermometer tip into the center of the food or into the largest meat muscle. Keep the tip away from bone, fat or rotisserie rod.

MITTS: Use long, heatproof mitts to protect hands and arms when working with the grill, heat source and food.

MOP: A thin sauce frequently brushed on foods during grilling to help keep foods moist and tender. Clean cloth strips tied together, a clean "dish mop," a cluster of fresh herb sprigs or a barbecue brush can be used as the "mop" to add the sauce.

PAPER TOWELS: Use for cleaning up spills around the grill. Do keep them away from the fire.

ROTISSERIE: A large skewer-type rod (spit) onto which food is threaded and then suspended over the heat source by holders that automatically turn it during grilling. Rotisseries can be electric or powered by batteries. Most often a cover is used for rotisserie grilling.

RUB: A dry or wet mixture of seasonings rubbed into foods before cooking to add flavor.

SKEWERS: Long thin pointed rods (the best are flat or square) made from metal or wood. *Kabob* is the name given to foods threaded on skewers.

SMOKER COOKING: Barrel-shaped grilling equipment, fueled by charcoal, electricity or gas, that allows slow cooking over low heat with hot smoke that flavors as it cooks.

SPIT-ROASTING: See "Rotisserie."

SPRAY BOTTLE: Plastic container that can spray, but preferably squirt, water in a small stream to extinguish flare-ups.

WATER BOTTLE: Keep a water bottle handy with a spray or "spritzer" top to douse grease flare-ups. Recycle a window cleaner bottle or purchase one to locate with your grilling tools. Remove food from the grill before using or clumps of ash may fly up into the food!

WIRE GRILL BRUSH: Long-handled brush used for scraping cooked bits of food off the grill rack and the grill. Follow the grill manufacturer's directions for the type of grill brush to purchase; grill racks vary in material and finish, and some may not withstand brushes that have extremely stiff wire.

WOOD BITS, CHIPS AND CHUNKS: Various sized pieces of aromatic woods soaked in water and then added to the coals to impart their distinctive flavors to the food being grilled.

Fueling the Fire
Charcoal Grilling

Charcoal, or "black magic," is a porous compound made from burned hardwood that's usually compacted and made into the very popular pillow-shaped briquettes or sold in small lumps. Henry Ford is credited with its invention in 1923. Single-use charcoal bags are a premeasured convenience because you light the entire bag.

Damp charcoal can take forever to start, and it burns unevenly. To keep charcoal from becoming damp, store it in a dry place. In humid climates, store charcoal in a tightly closed plastic bag.

Charcoal produces lots of heat, and a little goes a long way. Use enough briquettes to form a solid bed of coals under the grilling area that is a little larger than the area the food will cover. It takes about 30 briquettes to grill one pound of meat. (Each pound of charcoal contains about fifteen to twenty briquettes.) Any food that grills longer than one hour will require about ten additional briquettes per hour. When adding extra briquettes, place them around the edges so that they touch the already burning coals, or give them a head start by lighting them separately (in a can or charcoal chimney starter) before adding.

Start the fire

Arrange the desired number of charcoal briquettes in a slight pyramid shape on the coal grate in the firebox. This shape allows air to circulate, heating the briquettes faster.

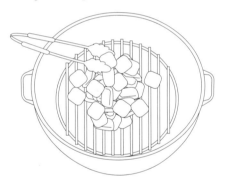

CHARCOAL CHIMNEY STARTERS: Place crumpled newspaper in the bottom of the chimney, add charcoal briquettes and light. Charcoal chimney starters are known for quick, more even starting of charcoal. Remove the chimney and spread the hot coals before grilling food. The chimney has a large, easy-to-grasp handle for safe handling. (You can make a home version by using a two-pound coffee can punched with holes for air circulation.)

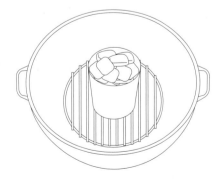

ELECTRIC COIL STARTERS: Arrange the charcoal pyramid over the coil and plug in the starter. After about ten minutes, unplug and remove the starter to a fireproof spot out of the way. The coals will take about twenty minutes before they are ready for grilling.

LIQUID FIRE STARTERS: Look for those specially intended for charcoal and carefully follow the manufacturer's directions. **_Never_** use gasoline or kerosene because it could cause an explosion. Drizzle the charcoal lighter generously (about 1/2 cup) over the charcoal pyramid and wait about one minute to let the liquid soak into the charcoal. Stand back (in case of a possible flare-up) and light the outer edges of the briquettes. The coals will be ready for grilling in about thirty minutes, enough time to allow the charcoal to evenly burn as well as vaporize the fire starter so that any odor is not absorbed by the food.

Coals are ready

- When the coals are 80 percent ashy gray in daylight, they are ready for grilling. (After dark, coals are ready when they have an even red glow.) Bright red coals are too hot, black coals are too cool and a mix of red and black coals gives off uneven heat. Coals that are too cool can cause the food to have an off-flavor from charcoal lighter that has not vaporized.

- Spread a single layer of coals in an even pattern on the coal grate in an area just slightly larger than the area on the cooking grill rack that will be covered by the food.

- Check the temperature of the coals by placing your hand, palm side down, near but not touching the cooking grill rack. If you can keep your hand there for two seconds (one-thousand one, one-thousand two), the temperature is high; three seconds is medium-high; four seconds is medium; five seconds is low.

Check the temperature

Control the heat

- Keep the heat as even as possible throughout the grilling time. If the food does not sizzle, the fire may be too cool.

- Raise the heat by raking the coals closer together and knock off a bit of the ash, lower the cooking grill rack or open the vents.

- Lower the heat by doing the opposite: spread and separate the coals, raise the cooking grill rack or close the vents halfway.

- Occasional flare-ups are a normal part of grilling. Control flare-ups by spacing out the coals or covering the grill. Or keep a spray bottle filled with water handy for spraying; take care not to soak the coals.

Gas Grilling

So convenient, gas grills are instant starters, heat up quickly, are easy to control and can keep temperatures quite even. Generally, heating a gas grill evenly will take about ten minutes.

- Follow the manufacturer's directions for heating the grill for direct- or indirect-heat grilling. (Also see "Direct- and Indirect-Heat Grilling," page 16.)

- Adjust the heat control, reposition the grill rack or cover the grill.

- Most gas grills have faster and slower cooking areas, which can be used effectively when grilling foods with different donenesses. Take the time to learn where these areas are on your grill.

- Lava rock in a gas grill can be used over and over. When lava rock becomes extremely greasy, however, it contributes to flare-ups. Avoid flare-ups and lengthen the life of lava rock by turning the rock over every once in a while (between grilling times) to burn off the grease that accumulates from cooking meat with fat. If flare-ups occur, do not use water on a gas grill. Just close the hood and reduce the heat until it subsides.

Direct- and Indirect-Heat Grilling

DIRECT HEAT GRILLING: Food is cooked on the grill rack directly over the heat source.

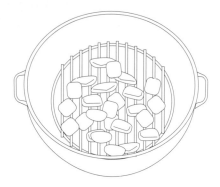

Food is cooked over the evenly distributed hot coals.

Food is cooked directly over the heated burner.

INDIRECT HEAT GRILLING: Food is cooked away from the heat. This is the preferred method for longer-cooking foods, such as whole poultry, whole turkey breasts and roasts.

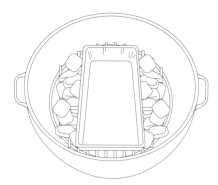

Place a drip pan directly under the grilling area and arrange the coals around the edge of the firebox.

For a dual-burner grill, heat only one side and place food over the burner that is not lit. For a single-burner grill, place food in an aluminum-foil tray or on several layers of aluminum foil and use low heat.

Aluminum Foil— A Grill's Best Friend!

Aluminum foil has many uses for grilling. From using it to line the firebox to making cleanup easier, to using it as a serving "dish," you'll want to keep a roll of heavy-duty aluminum foil handy. In many parts of the country, used aluminum foil can be recycled with aluminum cans. Just give it a good rinsing to remove food particles. Check with your local waste management recycler for details.

Lining the Firebox

Lay a sheet of heavy-duty aluminum foil across the firebox, and press it to mold against the firebox. If necessary, crisscross two sheets. Puncture foil at grill vent openings to allow for air circulation. Add racks, coals and grill as desired. After grill has completely cooled, lift the foil to remove and discard.

Using Aluminum Foil on the Grill

Using foil beats cleaning burned-on grease and smoke from pans! The actual size of the foil sheets used will be determined by the size of the food you are wrapping or the pan size you are making.

Drip Pan or Baking Sheet

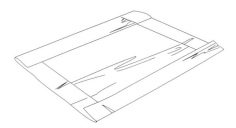

1. Use 2 sheets of heavy-duty aluminum foil 6 inches longer and 6 inches wider than the desired pan size. Fold in all edges 1 1/2 to 2 inches.

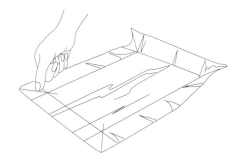

2. Score corners diagonally, corner to corner.

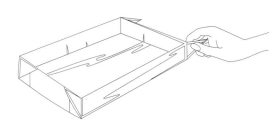

3. Fold edges again, forming 1 1/2- to 2-inch sides; fold at diagonal lines at corners, then fold the angled corners against sides of pan. For drip pan, carefully place between hot coals in the firebox. Let food drippings cool before removing drip pan from grill.

"Saucepan" or Bowl

1. Mold 3 sheets of heavy-duty aluminum foil around a straight-sided bowl, canister or can of desired size that's upside down.

2. Remove bowl. Press edge of foil tightly or crimp edge down to form a tight rim.

3. Turn foil saucepan over, and place on grill rack to use.

Cooking Packet

1. Center food on half of an 18 × 12-inch sheet of heavy-duty aluminum foil. Fold other half over food so edges meet. Seal edges, making a tight 1/2-inch fold. Fold again.

2. Allow space on sides for heat circulation and expansion. Repeat to seal each side.

3. After grilling, place foil packet on plate, using tongs or mitts. To serve, cut a large X across top of packet; fold back foil.

Bundle Wrap

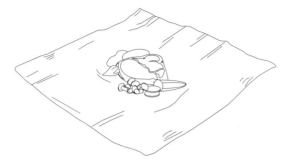

1. *Center food on a square of heavy-duty aluminum foil that's large enough for corners to meet over top.*

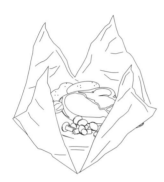

2. *Bring four corners of foil up together in a pyramid shape.*

3. *Allow space on top for heat circulation and expansion. Fold the open edges over 1/2 inch; fold again.*

Other Uses for Aluminum Foil

- Crumple aluminum foil (used foil works well), and use to scrape cooked-on food bits from the grill rack.

- Scoop warm coals onto foil; *cool completely.* Wrap or tightly fold foil around coals before discarding.

- Cover foods after grilling to keep them warm.

- Cover the *outside* of a saucepan or baking pan you plan to use on the grill to keep it from becoming difficult to clean.

- If your grill does not have a cover and a recipe recommends one, shape two sheets of heavy-duty aluminum foil in a dome shape the same size as the grill rack (form foil over bent coat hangers to easily retain the shape).

Grilling Safely

Food Safety Tips

- Trim visible fat from meat to avoid flare-ups.

- Always marinate foods in the refrigerator, never by leaving them on the kitchen counter, and use a nonmetal container.

- Use a long-handled brush for adding sauces or marinades to food before or during grilling. The same brush used for brushing marinades on raw meat should not be used on cooked meat. This prevents transferring any bacteria from the uncooked meat to the cooked meat. Wash the brush in hot, soapy water, and dry thoroughly.

- If a marinade in which raw meat was placed is to be used as a sauce after the meat is cooked, be sure to bring the marinade to boiling and then boil one minute before serving.

- Always served grilled meat on a clean platter. *Never* serve cooked meats on the same unwashed platter on which raw meat was carried to the grill. For example, do not carry raw hamburgers to the grill on a platter and then serve the cooked hamburgers on the same unwashed platter. Dangerous bacteria can be transferred to the cooked meat from the raw meat juices.

- Perishable food should be consumed within two hours; one hour if the outside temperature is over 90°F.

- In case of a flare-up, raise the grill grid and spread the coals to lower the temperature. Remove food from the grill grid before spraying with water or clumps of ash might fly onto the food.

- Open aluminum foil food packets carefully and facing away from you to let out the steam. Steam burns can be painful!

Fire and Fuel Safety Tips

- Place the grill in a well-ventilated area, away from buildings, dry leaves or brush. It can become hot enough to ignite flammable materials.

- Grilling on a wooden deck requires extra precautions; place a metal sheet or several sheets of heavy-duty aluminum foil under the grill to catch any hot ashes that might fall through an open vent.

- *Never* add more liquid fire starter after a charcoal fire is started. The fluid can catch fire as you pour it and can be extremely dangerous. Start three or four more pieces of charcoal separately in a can or on a piece of heavy-duty aluminum foil if needed and then add them using tongs.

- Extinguish coals completely after food is removed and grilling is finished. Close the vents on a covered grill to cut off the supply of oxygen. If there is not a cover, spread the coals or let them burn completely and then cool. Coals can be doused with a heavy layer of ash or water, but clean the grill as soon as it is cool if water was used so that the firebox doesn't rust. After completely dry, partially used coals can be reused.

- Dispose of ashes properly. A covered metal pail works best just in case there is one live coal.

- Don't wear long-sleeved or loose-fitting clothing when grilling.

- Refillable gas tanks of fuel for gas grills have the potential to cause explosions and fires. Fill a portable gas tank to only 80-percent capacity for maximum efficiency and safety. Take care to secure the tank when transporting it so that it can't tip over. Be careful not to tip the tank when it's connected to the regulator. When attaching a refill tank, check the connection by rubbing it with a liquid detergent. If bubbles appear, there is a leak.

- *Never* store spare gas tanks under the grill or in the house.

How Weather Affects Grilling

Check the manufacturer's use-and-care manual of your grill for tips and hints for grilling in different climates and weather conditions. These general tips may be helpful:

■ Place the grill out of the wind. If in the wind, neither the grill nor the food will stay as hot as it should.

■ Charcoal grilling times will be faster on hot, calm days and slower on chilly, windy ones. Cold weather grilling requires more charcoal, a longer time to heat the coals and longer grilling times.

■ Gas grilling will need slightly longer heating times as well as a higher heat setting to speed the cooking if the weather is cool or windy.

Care and Cleaning of Your Grill

Just like other cooking appliances, the better the care, the longer your grill will last. Again, refer to the manufacturer's use-and-care manual for care and cleaning of your grill.

■ The sooner the grill is cleaned after using, the easier cleaning will be!

■ Brushing the grill rack with vegetable oil or spraying with nonstick cooking spray before heating the grill will help prevent foods from sticking and leaving charred food bits.

■ After cooking, scrub or scrape the charred food bits off the grill rack with a wire grill brush or a handful of crumpled aluminum foil. (Some grills have nonstick grill racks, so be sure to check the use-and-care manual to make sure that using foil on your grill is acceptable.) Wear hot mitts if the coals are still hot. The rack of small cooking grills can be soaked in hot, soapy water.

■ Grill racks in gas and electric grills can be cleaned by closing the cover and turning the burner to "high" for about 15 minutes. If the food residue is particularly heavy, brush the grill rack *before* heating.

■ Line the bottom of the firebox in any grill with heavy-duty aluminum foil, shiny side up, to catch the food drippings (and, with charcoal, the ashes). The foil acts as a heat reflector. After cooking and when the ashes are cool, bundle up the remains and toss.

Backyard Grilling Secrets

■ All grills are not created equal! Read the use-and-care manual that comes with your grill for the best tips and recommendations.

■ Get to know *your* grill—whether it has hot spots and where they are, and how long it takes to heat, especially in chilly or windy weather.

■ Brush the grill rack with vegetable oil or spray with nonstick cooking spray *before* heating the grill. This prevents food from sticking, makes cleaning the grill easier and is safer because the grill is not hot.

■ Keep the heat as even as possible throughout the grilling time. For more even cooking, place thicker foods on the center of the grill rack and smaller pieces on the edges.

■ Check the food and fire often, for best results. The type of grill, outdoor temperature and wind, position of food on the grill and temperature of the coals all can affect cooking times.

■ If there isn't a sizzle, the fire might not be hot enough. Increase the heat by raking the coals together, opening the vents, lowering the grill rack and/or adjusting the control on a gas or electric grill.

- If the food is browning too quickly on the outside but the middle is not cooked, the fire is too hot. Spread the coals, close the vents halfway, raise the grill rack and/or adjust the control on a gas or electric grill. Covering the grill also will help control the heat.

- Enhance flavors by using wood chips or chunks to add a smoky taste to grilled foods. A covered grill allows the aroma to penetrate the food.

- Sprinkle the hot coals with soaked and drained dried herbs, fresh herbs or garlic cloves for a different flavor and aroma when grilling.

- Use long-handled barbecue tools to allow for a safe distance between you and the intense heat of the grill.

- Turn foods with tongs instead of piercing them with a fork to retain food juices.

- Brush sauces on foods during the last fifteen to twenty minutes of cooking to prevent overbrowning or burning, especially sauces that contain tomato or sugar.

- To heat sauces or side dishes on the grill without the cleanup job, use an empty coffee can or other can of adequate size, or see "Aluminum Foil—A Grill's Best Friend!" (page 17).

- Use stainless steel flat-bladed skewers to easily turn kabobs. Wooden skewers can be used, but they must be soaked in water at least thirty minutes before using to prevent burning.

Sizzling Backyard Menus

Your backyard is the perfect place to sizzle away a meal. These menus are offered to give you ideas for your next outdoor meal. Whether entertaining, celebrating a special occasion or making a family meal, look to your grill to cook more than just plain old hamburgers!

Burger Bash

Apricot-Glazed Burgers with Apricot Salsa (page 30)
Tortilla chips
Celery, carrot and jicama sticks
Pound Cake S'mores (page 175)

Kabob Buffet

Beef and Corn Kabobs (page 41)
Lemon-Shrimp Kabobs with Squash (page 44)
Tomato-Artichoke Kabobs (page 183)
Mixed-green salad with ranch dressing
Hard rolls
Angel Food Pockets (page 174)

Bon Voyage to the Tropics

Jamaican Jerk Pork Steaks (page 56)
Spicy Potato Planks (page 168)
Sliced cucumbers and tomatoes
Caribbean Curried Bananas (page 184)

Rib Fest

Pork Ribs with Smoky Barbecue Sauce (page 71)
Potato salad
Coleslaw
Texas Toast (page 161)
Watermelon wedges

Southern Nights

Honey-Pecan Chicken (page 94)
Skewered Ratatouille (page 170)
Breadsticks
Crunchy Peach Upside-Down Cake (page 179)

Summer Sea Breezes

Swordfish with Tomato-Basil Butter (page 126)
Herbed Polenta (page 165)
Sliced tomatoes
Summer Cobbler (page 178)

Burrito Barbecue

Barbecued Burritos (page 158)
Red, White and Green Salsa (page 205)
Avocado slices
Pineapple Slices with Ginger Cream (page 185)

Thanksgiving Fiesta

Turkey with Chili-Corn Bread Dressing (page 217)
Sweet Potato Slices (page 168)
Whole green beans
Pear-Cranberry Chutney (page 62)
Pickles and relishes
Pumpkin pie

1

Burgers, Sausage and Kabobs

Caribbean Pork Burger (page 29),
Tomato-Artichoke Kabob (page 183)

Jalapeño Burgers

PREP: 10 MIN; **GRILL:** 12 MIN

MAKES **6** SERVINGS

For a Mexican twist, serve these spunky burgers in flour tortillas accompanied by Fresh Tomato Salsa (page 203), taco sauce or chili sauce, if desired.

1 1/2 pounds lean ground beef or ground buffalo

1 medium onion, finely chopped (1/2 cup)

2 to 3 jalapeño chilies, seeded and finely chopped

1 clove garlic, finely chopped

1. Brush grill rack with vegetable oil. Heat coals or gas grill for direct heat (page 16).

2. Mix all ingredients. Shape mixture into 6 patties, about 1/2 inch thick.

3. Grill patties uncovered about 4 inches from MEDIUM heat 8 to 12 minutes, turning once, until no longer pink in center and juice is clear.

1 Serving: Calories 240 (Calories from Fat 145); Fat 16g (Saturated 7g); Cholesterol 65mg; Sodium 55mg; Carbohydrate 3g (Dietary Fiber 0g); Protein 21g.

Southwestern Cheeseburgers

PREP: 15 MIN; **GRILL:** 16 MIN

MAKES **4** SERVINGS

To toast kaiser rolls—or hamburger buns—grill cut sides down about 4 minutes or until golden brown.

1 1/2 pounds lean ground beef

2 tablespoons onion, finely chopped

2 tablespoons drained canned diced green chilies

1 can (4 ounces) mushroom stems and pieces, well drained and finely chopped

8 slices Monterey Jack cheese with jalapeño peppers, 2 × 1 × 1/4 inch (4 ounces)

4 kaiser rolls, split and toasted

4 slices onion

1/4 cup taco sauce or salsa

1. Brush grill rack with vegetable oil. Heat coals or gas grill for direct heat (page 16).

2. Mix beef, chopped onion and chilies. Shape mixture into 8 thin patties. Mound about 1/4 of the mushrooms on center of 4 of the patties. Top each of these 4 with 2 slices cheese. Place remaining beef patties on top; pinch edges to seal securely.

3. Cover and grill patties 4 to 5 inches from MEDIUM heat 14 to 16 minutes, turning once, until beef is no longer pink in center and juice is clear.

4. Serve cheeseburgers on kaiser rolls with sliced onion and taco sauce.

1 Serving: Calories 605 (Calories from Fat 315); Fat 35g (Saturated 16g); Cholesterol 125mg; Sodium 730mg; Carbohydrate 30g (Dietary Fiber 2g); Protein 44g.

Southwestern Cheeseburger with Spicy Potato Planks (page 168)

Burgundy Burgers

PREP: 10 MIN; GRILL: 15 MIN

MAKES **6** SERVINGS

1 1/2 pounds lean ground beef

1 small onion, finely chopped (1/4 cup)

**1/4 cup Burgundy, other red wine
or nonalcoholic red wine**

1 tablespoon Worcestershire sauce

1 teaspoon salt

1/4 teaspoon pepper

2 cloves garlic, finely chopped

6 rye or whole wheat hamburger buns, split

1. Brush grill rack with vegetable oil. Heat coals or gas grill for direct heat (page 16).

2. Mix all ingredients except buns. Shape mixture into 6 patties, about 3/4 inch thick.

3. Grill patties uncovered about 4 inches from MEDIUM heat 10 to 15 minutes, turning once, until no longer pink in center and juice is clear. Add buns, cut sides down, for last 4 minutes of grilling or until toasted.

4. Serve burgers on buns.

1 Serving: Calories 340 (Calories from Fat 160); Fat 18g (Saturated 7g); Cholesterol 65mg; Sodium 690mg; Carbohydrate 22g (Dietary Fiber 3g); Protein 25g.

Crunchy Teriyaki Burgers

PREP: 10 MIN; MARINATE: 3 HR;
GRILL: 15 MIN

MAKES **6** SERVINGS

Teriyaki Marinade (below)

1 1/2 pounds lean ground beef

1/2 cup finely chopped water chestnuts

4 medium green onions, chopped (1/4 cup)

1. Prepare Teriyaki Marinade in shallow nonmetal dish or resealable plastic bag.

2. Mix beef, water chestnuts and onions. Shape mixture into 6 patties, about 3/4 inch thick. Add patties to marinade, turning to coat with marinade. Cover dish or seal bag and refrigerate, turning patties once, at least 3 hours but no longer than 24 hours.

3. Brush grill rack with vegetable oil. Heat coals or gas grill for direct heat (page 16).

4. Remove patties from marinade; reserve marinade. Grill patties uncovered 4 inches from MEDIUM heat 10 to 15 minutes, brushing frequently with marinade and turning once, until no longer pink in center and juice is clear. Discard any remaining marinade.

TERIYAKI MARINADE

1/4 cup soy sauce

1/4 cup dry sherry or orange juice

1 clove garlic, finely chopped

1 teaspoon molasses or packed brown sugar

1/8 teaspoon ground ginger

Mix all ingredients. About 1/2 cup.

1 Serving: Calories 245 (Calories from Fat 145); Fat 16g (Saturated 7g); Cholesterol 65mg; Sodium 570mg; Carbohydrate 4g (Dietary Fiber 0g); Protein 21g.

Caribbean Pork Burgers

PREP: 20 MIN; GRILL: 18 MIN

MAKES 4 SERVINGS

These zesty burgers pack a spicy punch, pleasantly cooled by the lime peel. When grating the lime, do not include the white membrane—it adds a bitter taste.

1 pound lean ground pork

1 tablespoon grated lime peel

1 teaspoon dried thyme leaves

1/2 teaspoon ground allspice

1/2 teaspoon crushed red pepper

1/4 teaspoon salt

1 medium red onion, cut into 1/2-inch slices

8 slices French bread, 3/4 inch thick

1 tablespoon olive or vegetable oil

1. Brush grill rack with vegetable oil. Heat coals or gas grill for direct heat (page 16).

2. Mix all ingredients except onion, bread and oil. Shape mixture into 4 patties, about 3/4 inch thick.

3. Cover and grill patties 4 to 5 inches from MEDIUM heat 15 to 18 minutes, turning once, until no longer pink in center. Add onion slices for last 8 to 10 minutes of grilling, turning once, until golden brown. Brush both sides of bread slices with oil. Add bread for last 2 to 3 minutes of grilling, turning once, until golden brown.

4. Serve burgers and onion between bread slices.

1 Serving: Calories 390 (Calories from Fat 190); Fat 21g (Saturated 7g); Cholesterol 70mg; Sodium 490mg; Carbohydrate 28g (Dietary Fiber 2g); Protein 24g.

Apricot-Glazed Burgers with Apricot Salsa

PREP: 20 MIN; GRILL: 15 MIN

MAKES **4** SERVINGS

There's a generous amount of the tasty Apricot Salsa here, so you can serve it on leafy greens.

Apricot Salsa (right)

1 pound ground turkey breast

2 teaspoons chopped fresh or 1/2 teaspoon dried thyme leaves

1/2 teaspoon salt

1/2 cup apricot jam

1. Prepare Apricot Salsa (right).

2. Brush grill rack with vegetable oil. Heat coals or gas grill for direct heat (page 16).

3. Mix turkey, thyme and salt. Shape mixture into 4 patties, about 3/4 inch thick.

4. Cover and grill patties 4 to 5 inches from MEDIUM heat 12 to 15 minutes, turning and brushing patties with apricot jam after 6 minutes, until no longer pink in center. Discard any remaining jam.

5. Serve burgers with Apricot Salsa.

APRICOT SALSA

4 medium apricots, pitted and chopped, or 3 cups frozen sliced peaches, thawed and chopped

1 medium red bell pepper, chopped (1 cup)

1 small red onion, finely chopped

2 tablespoons chopped fresh parsley

2 tablespoons white vinegar

1 tablespoon vegetable oil

1/4 teaspoon salt

Salad greens, if desired

Mix all ingredients. Cover and refrigerate until serving. Serve salsa generously on salad greens. About 4 cups.

1 Serving: Calories 355 (Calories from Fat 135); Fat 15g (Saturated 4g); Cholesterol 75mg; Sodium 520mg; Carbohydrate 33g (Dietary Fiber 2g); Protein 24g.

Apricot-Glazed Burgers with Apricot Salsa

Pita Pocket Burgers

PREP: 15 MIN; GRILL: 16 MIN

MAKES **4** SERVINGS

Cucumber-Yogurt Dressing (right)

1/2 pound ground lamb

1/2 pound lean ground beef

2 tablespoons finely chopped onion

1/2 teaspoon salt

1/4 teaspoon ground cinnamon

1/8 teaspoon pepper

1 clove garlic, finely chopped

2 pita breads (6 inches in diameter), cut in half to form pockets

1 small tomato, chopped (1/2 cup)

1/2 cup coarsely chopped cucumber

2 medium green onions, sliced (1/4 cup)

1. Prepare Cucumber-Yogurt Dressing.

2. Brush grill rack with vegetable oil. Heat coals or gas grill for direct heat (page 16).

3. Mix lamb, beef, 2 tablespoons onion, the salt, cinnamon, pepper and garlic. Shape mixture into 4 patties, about 3/4 inch thick. Wrap pita breads in heavy-duty aluminum foil.

4. Cover and grill patties 4 to 5 inches from MEDIUM heat 14 to 16 minutes, turning once, until no longer pink in center and juice is clear. Add pocket of pita breads to side of grill for last 10 minutes of grilling, turning occasionally, until warm.

5. To serve, place patties in pita breads. Top with tomato, cucumber, green onions and dressing.

CUCUMBER-YOGURT DRESSING

1/2 cup plain yogurt

2 tablespoons finely chopped cucumber

1/2 teaspoon chopped fresh or 1/8 teaspoon dried dill weed

1 small clove garlic, finely chopped

Mix all ingredients. Cover and refrigerate until serving. About 2/3 cup.

1 Serving: Calories 335 (Calories from Fat 155); Fat 17g (Saturated 7g); Cholesterol 70mg; Sodium 530mg; Carbohydrate 22g (Dietary Fiber 1g); Protein 24g.

Dijon and Wild Rice Turkey Burgers

PREP: 15 MIN; GRILL: 16 MIN

MAKES 6 SERVINGS

Dilled Dijon Sauce (below)

1 pound ground turkey

4 medium green onions, chopped (1/4 cup)

1 cup cooked wild rice

1 tablespoon chopped fresh or 1 teaspoon dried dill weed

2 tablespoons Dijon mustard

6 hamburger buns, split

1. Prepare Dilled Dijon Sauce (below).

2. Brush grill rack with vegetable oil. Heat coals or gas grill for direct heat (page 16).

3. Mix remaining ingredients except buns. Shape mixture into 6 patties, about 3/4 inch thick.

4. Grill patties uncovered 4 to 6 inches from MEDIUM heat 14 to 16 minutes, turning once, until no longer pink in center. Add buns, cut sides down, for last 4 minutes of grilling or until toasted.

5. Serve burgers on buns. Top with Dilled Dijon Sauce.

DILLED DIJON SAUCE

1/3 cup mayonnaise or salad dressing

1 teaspoon chopped fresh or 1/4 teaspoon dried dill weed

1 teaspoon Dijon mustard

Mix all ingredients. Cover and refrigerate until serving. About 1/3 cup.

1 Serving: Calories 365 (Calories from Fat 180); Fat 20g (Saturated 5g); Cholesterol 60mg; Sodium 430mg; Carbohydrate 28g (Dietary Fiber 2g); Protein 20g.

Italian Burgers on Focaccia

PREP: 20 MIN; GRILL: 15 MIN

MAKES 4 SERVINGS

Tomato Cream (below)

1 pound ground chicken

2 tablespoons tomato paste

3 tablespoons chopped fresh or 1 teaspoon dried basil leaves

1 clove garlic, finely chopped

1 medium tomato, sliced

1 loaf focaccia bread (8 to 9 inches in diameter)

1. Prepare Tomato Cream.

2. Brush grill rack with vegetable oil. Heat coals or gas grill for direct heat (page 16).

3. Mix chicken, tomato paste, basil and garlic. Shape mixture into 8 patties, about 1/2 inch thick. Place tomato slice between 2 patties; press edges to seal. Repeat with remaining patties.

4. Cover and grill patties 4 to 5 inches from MEDIUM heat 12 to 15 minutes, turning once, until chicken is no longer pink in center.

5. Cut focaccia into 4 wedges; cut wedges horizontally in half. Serve burgers between focaccia slices with Tomato Cream.

TOMATO CREAM

1/2 cup sour cream

1 tablespoon tomato paste

Mix ingredients. Cover and refrigerate until serving. About 1/2 cup.

1 Serving: Calories 630 (Calories from Fat 215); Fat 24g (Saturated 7g); Cholesterol 85mg; Sodium 1340mg; Carbohydrate 71g (Dietary Fiber 3g); Protein 35g.

Great Grilling Gadgets!

Whether you call them *accessories*, *gadgets* or *gizmos*, an endless number of them awaits you beyond the true grilling necessities. Some accessories are truly helpful, whereas others just take up space. Only you know which ones will work for you. Most cooking accessories are available with a nonstick finish for easy cleanup.

For the Fire

CHARCOAL HOLDERS OR RAILS: Metal charcoal boxes that keep charcoal piled against sides of the grill to provide a larger cooking area when indirect heat is used.

GAS GRILL SMOKER BOX: Vented small metal box into which wood chips are placed so that a smoked flavor is added to foods during grilling.

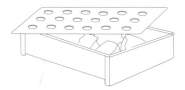

HOOD HOLDER: Props the hood open to three different heights to allow better temperature control and easy access for turning and basting foods.

For the Food

HINGED WIRE GRILL BASKET: A flat, wire basket with hinges so that it can be adjusted to the thickness of the food such as fish fillets, steaks or ribs. It is used to turn foods easily during grilling.

GRILLING SCREEN OR GRID: A flat, metal screen (or metal sheet with holes) to use with delicate foods, such as fish or shellfish, or small pieces of food such as cut-up vegetables. It is used to keep foods from falling through the grill rack.

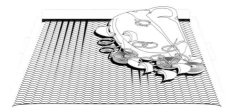

GRILL OR SMOKER THERMOMETER: Metal thermometer that magnetically attaches to the outside of any steel grill or that can be placed directly on the grill rack or cooking surface to indicate temperature of the coals.

KABOB OR SKEWER RACK: Evenly spaces kabobs and holds them off the grill rack to prevent them from sticking and to make them easy to turn.

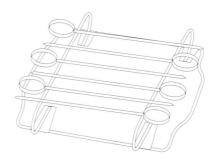

ROTISSERIE: A large skewer-type rod (spit) onto which food is threaded and then suspended over the heat source by holders that automatically turn it during grilling.

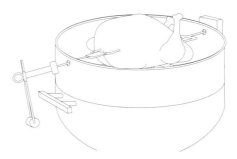

Continued on next page

VERTICAL RIB RACK: Space-efficient vertical cooking rack designed for slow-cooking slabs of ribs, ears of corn, chicken pieces, chops and potatoes.

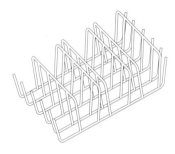

SKEWERS: Great for kabobs, these small diameter, long thin rods are usually made from stainless steel. Lengths vary from about 8 to 16 inches. We recommend flat skewers because food on round skewers can "spin" when turned, making it difficult to cook the other side. Bamboo or wooden skewers are also available but must be soaked in water at least 30 minutes before using to avoid burning during grilling.

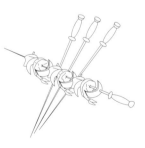

TUMBLE BASKET: A drum-shaped wire basket that attaches to the spit rod of a rotisserie and allows grilling without frequent attention. Great for chicken pieces, large vegetable chunks and shellfish (whole lobster, crab legs, clams, mussels).

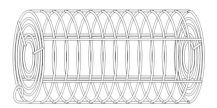

Kielbasa and Cabbage

PREP: 10 MIN; GRILL: 20 MIN

MAKES 4 SERVINGS

Convenient coleslaw mix makes this recipe extra-easy.

**1 ring (1 pound) fully cooked kielbasa
   sausage**

3 cups coleslaw mix (8 ounces)

**1/2 medium green bell pepper, cut into
   1-inch pieces**

1/2 teaspoon celery seed

1/2 teaspoon salt

Dash of pepper

1 tablespoon margarine or butter

3 tablespoons water

Bratwurst buns, if desired

1. Heat coals or gas grill for direct heat (page 16).

2. Place sausage ring in 8-inch square aluminum foil pan. Mix coleslaw mix, bell pepper, celery seed, salt and pepper. Mound cabbage mixture in center of sausage ring. Dot with margarine; sprinkle with water. Cover with aluminum foil, sealing edges securely.

3. Cover and grill sausage mixture 4 to 5 inches from MEDIUM heat 15 to 20 minutes or until cabbage is crisp-tender and sausage is hot.

4. Serve sausage and cabbage mixture on buns.

1 Serving: Calories 390 (Calories from Fat 315); Fat 35g (Saturated 13g); Cholesterol 65mg; Sodium 1480mg; Carbohydrate 6g (Dietary Fiber 1g); Protein 14g.

Bratwurst with Caraway Kraut

PREP: 10 MIN; MICROWAVE: 12 MIN;
GRILL: 15 MIN

MAKES 4 SERVINGS

4 fresh bratwurst (1 pound)

3/4 cup beer

1 small onion, chopped (1/4 cup)

1 teaspoon packed brown sugar

1/4 teaspoon caraway seed

1 can (8 ounces) sauerkraut, undrained

4 bratwurst buns, split

1. Brush grill rack with vegetable oil. Heat coals or gas grill for direct heat (page 16).

2. Arrange bratwurst in single layer in square microwavable dish, 8×8×2 inches. Add beer and onion. Cover with plastic wrap, folding back one corner to vent. Microwave on HIGH 5 minutes. Turn over and rearrange bratwurst. Re-cover and microwave on MEDIUM-HIGH (70%) 3 to 4 minutes or until bratwurst are no longer pink in center. Discard beer and onion.

3. Grill bratwurst uncovered 4 to 5 inches from MEDIUM heat 12 to 15 minutes, turning once or twice, until brown.

4. While bratwurst are grilling, mix brown sugar, caraway seed and sauerkraut in 9-inch round aluminum foil pan. Cover pan with aluminum foil, sealing edges securely. Add to side of grill for last 10 minutes of grilling, stirring once, until hot.

5. Serve bratwurst on buns with sauerkraut mixture.

1 Serving: Calories 530 (Calories from Fat 325); Fat 36g (Saturated 13g); Cholesterol 80mg; Sodium 1690mg; Carbohydrate 34g (Dietary Fiber 3g); Protein 21g.

Mustard Grilled Italian Sausage

PREP: 25 MIN; GRILL: 20 MIN

MAKES 6 SERVINGS

Two-Tomato Relish (below)

1/4 cup Dijon mustard

2 teaspoons chopped fresh or 1/2 teaspoon dried oregano leaves

6 fresh sweet Italian turkey sausages (about 1 1/4 pounds)

6 bratwurst buns, split

1. Brush grill rack with vegetable oil. Heat coals or gas grill for direct heat (page 16).

2. Prepare Two-Tomato Relish. Mix mustard and oregano.

3. Cover and grill sausages 4 to 5 inches from MEDIUM heat 10 minutes, turning occasionally. Continue grilling 8 to 10 minutes longer, turning and brushing occasionally with mustard mixture, until no longer pink in center. Discard any remaining mustard mixture.

4. Serve sausages on buns with Two-Tomato Relish.

TWO-TOMATO RELISH

2 medium tomatoes, finely chopped (1 1/2 cups)

2 medium yellow pear tomatoes, finely chopped (1/2 cup)

1 tablespoon red wine vinegar

1 teaspoon chopped fresh or 1/4 teaspoon dried oregano leaves

Mix all ingredients. Cover and refrigerate until serving. About 2 cups.

1 Serving: Calories 335 (Calories from Fat 115); Fat 13g (Saturated 4g); Cholesterol 70mg; Sodium 1270mg; Carbohydrate 31g (Dietary Fiber 2g); Protein 26g.

Pork Sausages with Apples and Onions

PREP: 20 MIN; GRILL: 20 MIN

MAKES 8 SERVINGS

These sausages make an easy summer brunch or breakfast—just add fresh fruit and muffins for an outdoor feast.

1/4 cup maple-flavored syrup

2 tablespoons packed brown sugar

2 large apples, sliced

1 large sweet onion (Vidalia, Walla Walla), sliced

2 packages (8 ounces each) pork sausages

1. Brush grill rack with vegetable oil. Heat coals or gas grill for direct heat (page 16).

2. Mix maple syrup and brown sugar. Place apples and onion on 18-inch square of aluminum foil. Brush with half of the syrup mixture. Wrap foil securely around apples and onion.

3. Cover and grill sausages and foil packet 4 to 5 inches from MEDIUM heat 15 minutes, turning sausages occasionally. Continue grilling about 5 minutes longer, brushing sausages with remaining syrup mixture, until sausages are no longer pink in center. Discard any remaining syrup mixture.

1 Serving: Calories 175 (Calories from Fat 80); Fat 9g (Saturated 3g); Cholesterol 20mg; Sodium 350mg; Carbohydrate 20g (Dietary Fiber 2g); Protein 5g.

Pork Sausages with Apples and Onions

Italian Mixed Grill

PREP: 15 MIN; STAND: 1 HR; MICROWAVE: 12 MIN; GRILL: 25 MIN

MAKES 8 SERVINGS

The meats in this zesty grill take different times to cook, so grill the ones that take the most time first. Grill the beef about 4 minutes, then add the chicken and grill both 2 minutes—add the sausages last, grilling all the meat for 12 to 14 minutes longer.

Herbed Lemon Oil (right)

4 fresh Italian sausages (about 1 pound)

1/2 cup water

1 small onion, chopped (1/4 cup)

4 skinless boneless chicken breast halves or thighs (about 1 pound)

1-pound beef boneless top loin steak, about 1 inch thick

1. Prepare Herbed Lemon Oil.

2. Place sausages, water and onion in 2-quart microwavable casserole. Cover and microwave on High 5 minutes; rearrange sausages. Re-cover and microwave on MEDIUM (50%) 5 to 7 minutes or until sausages are done. Remove sausages; discard onion and water.

3. Brush grill rack with vegetable oil. Heat coals or gas grill for direct heat (page 16).

4. Brush all sides of chicken, beef and sausages with oil mixture.

5. Grill meats uncovered 4 to 5 inches from MEDIUM heat, brushing frequently with oil mixture and turning once: beef 18 to 25 minutes for medium doneness; chicken 14 to 16 minutes or until no longer pink when centers of thickest pieces are cut; sausages 12 to 14 minutes or until brown. Discard any remaining oil mixture.

6. To serve, cut sausages and chicken pieces in half, and cut beef into slices.

HERBED LEMON OIL

1/2 cup olive or vegetable oil

3 tablespoons lemon juice

3 tablespoons chopped fresh parsley

1 tablespoon chopped fresh or 1 teaspoon dried oregano leaves

2 teaspoons chopped fresh or 1/2 teaspoon dried thyme leaves

1/2 teaspoon salt

1/4 teaspoon pepper

2 large cloves garlic, finely chopped

Mix all ingredients. Cover and let stand at least 1 hour to blend flavors. About 1 cup.

1 Serving: Calories 380 (Calories from Fat 235); Fat 26g (Saturated 8g); Cholesterol 105mg; Sodium 650mg; Carbohydrate 1g (Dietary Fiber 0g); Protein 35g.

Beef and Corn Kabobs

PREP: 15 MIN; MARINATE: 4 HR;
GRILL: 20 MIN

MAKES 6 SERVINGS

Spicy Wine Marinade (below)

1 1/2 pounds beef boneless top round steak, cut into 1-inch cubes

4 small ears corn, husks removed

2 green or red bell peppers, cut into 1 1/2-inch pieces

1. Prepare Spicy Wine Marinade in shallow non-metal dish or resealable plastic bag. Add beef, stirring to coat with marinade. Cover dish or seal bag and refrigerate, stirring beef occasionally, at least 4 hours but no longer than 24 hours.

2. Brush grill rack with vegetable oil. Heat coals or gas grill for direct heat (page 16).

3. Cut each ear of corn into 3 pieces. Remove beef from marinade; reserve marinade. Thread beef, corn and bell peppers alternately on each of six 10- to 12-inch metal skewers, leaving space between each. Brush with marinade.

4. Cover and grill kabobs 4 to 5 inches from MEDIUM heat 15 to 20 minutes for medium beef doneness, brushing with marinade and turning frequently. Discard any remaining marinade.

SPICY WINE MARINADE

1/2 cup vegetable oil

1/4 cup red wine vinegar

1 teaspoon dried thyme leaves

1/2 teaspoon ground red pepper (cayenne)

1 clove garlic, finely chopped

Mix all ingredients. About 3/4 cup.

1 Serving: Calories 240 (Calories from Fat 115); Fat 13g (Saturated 3g); Cholesterol 55mg; Sodium 45mg; Carbohydrate 10g (Dietary Fiber 1g); Protein 22g.

Sausage and Potato Kabobs

PREP: 30 MIN; GRILL: 25 MIN

MAKES 4 SERVINGS

8 new potatoes (3/4 pound)

1 pound fully cooked smoked Polish sausage, cut into 12 pieces

12 baby dill pickles

1/4 cup margarine or butter, melted

2 teaspoons chopped fresh or 1/2 teaspoon dried dill weed

1. Heat 1 inch water to boiling in 2-quart saucepan. Add potatoes. Boil about 15 minutes or until almost tender; drain. Cool slightly.

2. Brush grill rack with vegetable oil. Heat coals or gas grill for direct heat (page 16).

3. Cut potatoes in half. Thread sausage pieces, potatoes and pickles alternately on each of four 15-inch metal skewers, leaving space between each.

4. Grill kabobs uncovered 4 to 5 inches from MEDIUM heat 20 to 25 minutes, turning frequently, until sausage is hot.

5. While kabobs are grilling, mix margarine and dill weed; brush over potatoes for last 5 minutes of grilling.

1 Serving: Calories 565 (Calories from Fat 350); Fat 39g (Saturated 13g); Cholesterol 80mg; Sodium 2490mg; Carbohydrate 37g (Dietary Fiber 3g); Protein 19g.

Ginger-Spice Beef Kabobs

PREP: 15 MIN; MARINATE: 1 HR; GRILL: 15 MIN

MAKES 4 SERVINGS

Not a beef lover? Then try these kabobs with chicken. Use 1 pound skinless boneless chicken breast meat, cut into 1×1×1/4-inch pieces.

Ginger-Spice Marinade (right)

1-pound beef sirloin steak or beef round steak, 1 1/4 inches thick

2 bunches green onions

1. Prepare Ginger-Spice Marinade in shallow non-metal dish or resealable plastic bag.

2. Trim fat and bone from beef. Cut beef into 1 1/4-inch strips; cut each strip into 1/4-inch pieces. Add beef to marinade, stirring to coat with marinade. Cover dish or seal bag and refrigerate at least 1 hour but no longer than 24 hours.

3. Brush grill rack with vegetable oil. Heat coals or gas grill for direct heat (page 16).

4. Trim green tops from onions and reserve for another use. Cut onions into 1-inch pieces. Remove beef from marinade; reserve marinade. Thread beef and onion pieces alternately on each of four 15-inch metal skewers, leaving space between each.

5. Grill kabobs uncovered 4 to 5 inches from MEDIUM heat 10 to 15 minutes for medium beef doneness, turning frequently and brushing occasionally with marinade.

6. To serve, heat remaining marinade to boiling; boil and stir 1 minute. Spoon marinade over kabobs.

GINGER-SPICE MARINADE

1/4 cup soy sauce

1/4 cup water

2 tablespoons honey

1/2 teaspoon grated gingerroot or 1/4 teaspoon ground ginger

1/4 teaspoon ground allspice

1 clove garlic, finely chopped

Mix all ingredients. About 2/3 cup.

1 Serving: Calories 140 (Calories from Fat 25); Fat 3g (Saturated 1g); Cholesterol 55mg; Sodium 560mg; Carbohydrate 8g (Dietary Fiber 1g); Protein 21g.

Peanutty Chicken Kabobs

PREP: 15 MIN; GRILL: 20 MIN

MAKES 4 SERVINGS

1 pound skinless boneless chicken breast halves or thighs, cut into 1 1/2-inch pieces

Spicy Peanut Sauce (right)

Chopped peanuts, if desired

1. Brush grill rack with vegetable oil. Heat coals or gas grill for direct heat (page 16).

2. Thread chicken pieces on four 10- to 12-inch metal skewers, leaving space between each.

3. Prepare Spicy Peanut Sauce; reserve 1/2 cup sauce to serve with cooked kabobs. Brush chicken with half of the remaining sauce.

4. Cover and grill kabobs 4 to 5 inches from MEDIUM heat 15 to 20 minutes, turning and brushing occasionally with remaining sauce, until chicken is no longer pink in center.

5. Serve kabobs with reserved sauce and the peanuts.

SPICY PEANUT SAUCE

1/3 cup crunchy peanut butter

1/3 cup boiling water

1 tablespoon grated gingerroot or 1 teaspoon ground ginger

1 tablespoon lemon juice

1/8 teaspoon crushed red pepper

Mix all ingredients. About 3/4 cup.

1 Serving: Calories 260 (Calories from Fat 125); Fat 14g (Saturated 3g); Cholesterol 60mg; Sodium 160mg; Carbohydrate 5g (Dietary Fiber 1g); Protein 30g.

Lemon-Shrimp Kabobs with Squash

PREP: 20 MIN; MARINATE: 30 MIN; GRILL: 12 MIN

MAKES 6 SERVINGS

Grilling shrimp in the shells helps shrimp to stay moist during cooking.

3 tablespoons honey

1/4 cup lemon juice

1 teaspoon chopped fresh or 1/2 teaspoon crushed dried rosemary leaves

1 1/2 pounds fresh or frozen uncooked large shrimp in shells

3 medium zucchini, cut into 1-inch slices

2 medium yellow summer squash, cut into 1-inch slices

1 small green bell pepper, cut into 1-inch wedges

1 small lemon, cut into wedges, if desired

1. Mix honey, lemon juice and rosemary in shallow nonmetal bowl or resealable plastic bag. Add shrimp, stirring to coat with marinade. Cover and refrigerate 30 minutes.

2. Brush grill rack with vegetable oil. Heat coals or gas grill for direct heat (page 16).

3. Remove shrimp from marinade; reserve marinade. Thread shrimp, zucchini, yellow squash and bell pepper alternately on each of six 15-inch metal skewers.

4. Cover and grill kabobs 5 to 6 inches from MEDIUM heat about 12 minutes, turning and brushing 2 or 3 times with marinade, until shrimp are pink and firm. Discard any remaining marinade.

5. To serve, peel shrimp. Squeeze juice from lemon wedges over shrimp and vegetables.

1 Serving: Calories 115 (Calories from Fat 10); Fat 1g (Saturated 0g); Cholesterol 105mg; Sodium 130mg; Carbohydrate 15g (Dietary Fiber 2g); Protein 13g.

Lemon-Shrimp Kabobs with Squash

Shrimp and Scallop Kabobs

PREP: 10 MIN; GRILL: 15 MIN

MAKES 4 SERVINGS

Lemon-Thyme Marinade (right)

3/4 pound sea scallops

12 uncooked large shrimp in shells, thawed if frozen

8 medium whole mushrooms (about 6 ounces)

8 cherry tomatoes

1 medium zucchini (about 1 inch in diameter), cut into 1-inch slices

1. Prepare Lemon-Thyme Marinade.

2. Brush grill rack with vegetable oil. Heat coals or gas grill for direct heat (page 16).

3. Cut scallops in half if over 1 inch in diameter. Thread scallops, shrimp and vegetables alternately on each of four 10- to 12-inch metal skewers, leaving space between each. Brush with marinade.

4. Grill kabobs uncovered 4 inches from MEDIUM heat 10 to 15 minutes, brushing frequently with marinade and turning once, until scallops are white and shrimp are pink and firm. Discard any remaining marinade.

LEMON-THYME MARINADE

1/4 cup lemon juice

1/4 cup vegetable oil

1 tablespoon chopped fresh or 1 teaspoon dried thyme leaves

1/4 teaspoon salt

1/4 teaspoon pepper

Mix all ingredients. About 1/2 cup.

1 Serving: Calories 210 (Calories from Fat 80); Fat 9g (Saturated 2g); Cholesterol 65mg; Sodium 350mg; Carbohydrate 8g (Dietary Fiber 1g); Protein 25g.

Provençal Fish Kabobs

**PREP: 20 MIN; MARINATE: 20 MIN;
GRILL: 12 TO 15 MIN**

MAKES 6 SERVINGS

1/2 cup red wine vinegar

1 tablespoon vegetable oil

**2 teaspoons chopped fresh or 1/2 teaspoon
dried tarragon leaves**

**2 teaspoons chopped fresh or 1/2 teaspoon
dried thyme leaves**

**1 pound tuna or swordfish steaks,
cut into 2-inch pieces**

1 small eggplant (1 pound)

2 cups cherry tomatoes

1/2 pound medium whole mushrooms

6 large cloves garlic, peeled

1. Mix vinegar, oil, tarragon and thyme in shallow nonmetal dish or resealable plastic bag. Add fish, stirring to coat with marinade. Cover dish or seal bag and refrigerate 20 minutes.

2. Brush grill with vegetable oil. Heat coals or gas heat for direct heat (page 16).

3. Remove fish from marinade; reserve marinade. Cut eggplant into 1-inch slices; cut slices into fourths. Thread fish, eggplant, tomatoes and mushrooms alternately on each of six 15-inch skewers, leaving space between each. Thread 1 clove garlic on end of each skewer.

4. Cover and grill kabobs 5 to 6 inches from MEDIUM heat 12 to 15 minutes, turning and brushing 2 to 3 times with marinade, until fish flakes easily with fork. Discard any remaining marinade.

1 Serving: Calories 170 (Calories from Fat 65); Fat 7g (Saturated 2g); Cholesterol 30mg; Sodium 40mg; Carbohydrate 11g (Dietary Fiber 3g); Protein 19g.

Flavor Boosters

For your convenience, here is a list of great-tasting marinades and sauces in this chapter.

Teriyaki Marinade 28

Apricot Salsa 30

Cucumber-Yogurt Dressing 32

Dilled Dijon Sauce 33

Tomato Cream 33

Two-Tomato Relish 38

Herbed Lemon Oil 40

Spicy Wine Marinade 41

Ginger-Spice Marinade 42

Spicy Peanut Sauce 43

Lemon-Thyme Marinade 46

2

Steaks and Chops

Pesto-Stuffed Steaks with
Peppered Tomatoes (page 50)

Pesto-Stuffed Steaks with Peppered Tomatoes

PREP: 20 MIN; GRILL: 14 MIN

MAKES **4** SERVINGS

Pesto adds a delicious herbed flavor to this steak. You can also use your favorite pesto variations—they'll work equally as well.

1/4 cup Pesto (page 199) or prepared pesto

2 tablespoons finely shredded Parmesan cheese

1/2 teaspoon salt

Peppered Tomatoes (right)

2 beef rib eye steaks, 1 1/2 inches thick (about 2 pounds)

1 tablespoon olive or vegetable oil

1/3 cup finely shredded Parmesan cheese

1. Prepare Pesto. Mix 1/4 cup Pesto, 2 tablespoons cheese and the salt.

2. Brush grill rack with vegetable oil. Heat coals or gas grill for direct heat (page 16).

3. Make a horizontal cut in side of each beef steak, forming a pocket (do not cut through to opposite side). Spread pesto mixture evenly on insides of pockets; press pockets closed. Drizzle oil over beef. Roll beef in 1/3 cup cheese until well coated.

4. Cover and grill beef 4 to 5 inches from MEDIUM heat 12 to 14 minutes for medium doneness, turning once.

5. While beef is grilling, prepare Peppered Tomatoes. Place tomatoes, cut sides up, on grill with beef for last 3 to 4 minutes of grilling or until hot.

6. To serve, cut each beef steak in half or into thick strips. Serve with tomatoes.

PEPPERED TOMATOES

2 firm medium tomatoes, cut in half

1 1/2 teaspoons olive or vegetable oil

1/8 teaspoon garlic pepper or other seasoned pepper

Coat bottoms and sides of tomatoes lightly and drizzle cut sides with oil. Sprinkle all sides evenly with garlic pepper.

1 Serving: Calories 635 (Calories from Fat 440); Fat 49g (Saturated 17g); Cholesterol 135mg; Sodium 620mg; Carbohydrate 4g (Dietary Fiber 1g); Protein 46g.

Gingery Pepper Steak

PREP: 15 MIN; MARINATE: 1 HR;
GRILL: 16 MIN

MAKES 4 SERVINGS

Look for the freshest gingerroot you can find; it should not be shriveled or cracked, and cut surfaces shouldn't be dried out. Sniff it—gingerroot should smell freshly piquant, not musty.

1-pound beef boneless top sirloin steak, 3/4 inch thick

1/4 cup red wine vinegar

1 1/2 tablespoons chopped fresh or 1 1/2 teaspoons dried oregano leaves

1 tablespoon grated gingerroot

2 tablespoons olive or vegetable oil

2 tablespoons water

2 teaspoons cracked black pepper

4 large cloves garlic, crushed

1. Cut beef into 4 pieces. Mix remaining ingredients in shallow nonmetal dish or resealable plastic bag. Add beef, turning to coat with marinade. Cover dish or seal bag and refrigerate, turning once, at least 1 hour but no longer than 24 hours.

2. Brush grill rack with vegetable oil. Heat coals or gas grill for direct heat (page 16).

3. Remove beef from marinade; discard marinade. Cover and grill beef 4 to 5 inches from MEDIUM heat 14 to 16 minutes for medium doneness, turning once.

1 Serving: Calories 220 (Calories from Fat 125); Fat 14g (Saturated 5g); Cholesterol 65mg; Sodium 55mg; Carbohydrate 1g (Dietary Fiber 0g); Protein 22g.

Deviled Steaks

PREP: 10 MIN; STAND: 30 MIN; GRILL: 11 MIN

MAKES 4 SERVINGS

1/4 cup Dijon mustard

2 teaspoons chopped fresh or 1/2 teaspoon dried rosemary leaves, crushed

1 teaspoon coarsely ground pepper

2 cloves garlic, finely chopped

4 beef boneless top loin steaks, about 1 inch thick (about 1 pound)

1. Mix mustard, rosemary, pepper and garlic. Cover and let stand 30 minutes.

2. Brush grill rack with vegetable oil. Heat coals or gas grill for direct heat (page 16).

3. Spread mustard mixture on both sides of beef.

4. Grill beef uncovered 4 to 5 inches from MEDIUM heat 1 minute on each side to seal in juices. Cover and grill 8 to 9 minutes longer for medium doneness, turning once.

1 Serving: Calories 190 (Calories from Fat 80); Fat 9g (Saturated 4g); Cholesterol 65mg; Sodium 250mg; Carbohydrate 2g (Dietary Fiber 0g); Protein 25g.

Fiesta Steak

PREP: 15 MIN; MARINATE: 6 HR; GRILL: 25 MIN

MAKES 8 SERVINGS

Have a party! Serve rice and beans, a salad of sliced oranges, avocado and red onion rings, and Corn with Chili-Lime Spread (page 173).

**1 cup Fresh Tomato Salsa (page 203)
or prepared salsa**

**2-pound beef boneless top round steak,
about 1 inch thick**

Tequila Marinade (right)

1/2 cup sour cream

**1 container (6 ounces) frozen avocado dip,
thawed**

1. Prepare Fresh Tomato Salsa.

2. Pierce beef with fork several times on both sides. Prepare Tequila Marinade in shallow nonmetal dish or resealable plastic bag. Add beef, turning to coat with marinade. Cover dish or seal bag and refrigerate, turning beef occasionally, at least 6 hours but no longer than 24 hours.

3. Brush grill rack with vegetable oil. Heat coals or gas grill for direct heat (page 16).

4. Remove beef from marinade; reserve marinade. Cover and grill beef 4 to 5 inches from MEDIUM heat 20 to 25 minutes for medium doneness, brushing occasionally with marinade and turning once. Discard any remaining marinade.

5. Cut beef across grain into thin slices. Serve with Fresh Tomato Salsa, sour cream and avocado dip.

TEQUILA MARINADE

1/4 cup lime juice

2 tablespoons vegetable oil

2 tablespoons tequila or lime juice

1/2 teaspoon salt

1/2 teaspoon ground cumin

1/2 teaspoon ground red pepper (cayenne)

2 cloves garlic, finely chopped

Mix all ingredients. About 1/2 cup.

1 Serving: Calories 185 (Calories from Fat 90); Fat 10g (Saturated 4g); Cholesterol 65mg; Sodium 320mg; Carbohydrate 4g (Dietary Fiber 1g); Protein 21g.

Barbecued London Broil

PREP: 15 MIN; MARINATE: 8 HR;
GRILL: 12 MIN

MAKES 4 TO 6 SERVINGS

By grilling to medium-rare and cutting steak into thin diagonal slices across the grain, this less tender cut can taste like the very best!

1/3 cup white vinegar

1/3 cup olive or vegetable oil

3 tablespoons packed brown sugar

3 tablespoons soy sauce

1/2 teaspoon coarsely ground pepper

2 medium onions, sliced

1 clove garlic, finely chopped

1 1/2-pound beef flank steak

1. Mix all ingredients except beef in shallow non-metal dish or resealable plastic bag. Add beef, turning to coat with marinade. Cover dish or seal bag and refrigerate, turning beef occasionally, at least 8 hours but no longer than 24 hours.

2. Brush grill rack with vegetable oil. Heat coals or gas grill for direct heat (page 16).

3. Remove beef and onions from marinade; discard marinade. Place onions in 9-inch round aluminum foil pan. Grill beef uncovered 2 inches from MEDIUM heat about 12 minutes for medium-rare doneness, turning once. At same time, add pan of onions to grill, stirring occasionally, until tender.

4. Cut beef diagonally across grain into very thin slices. To serve, top with onions.

1 Serving: Calories 300 (Calories from Fat 145); Fat 16g (Saturated 5g); Cholesterol 90mg; Sodium 105mg; Carbohydrate 5g (Dietary Fiber 1g); Protein 35g.

Italian Flank Steak

PREP: 10 MIN; MARINATE: 1 HR;
GRILL: 10 MIN

MAKES 6 SERVINGS

Open food cans can be heated directly on the grill. If they have paper labels, be sure to remove them before placing the can on the grill.

**2-pound beef flank or round steak,
1/2 inch thick**

1 tablespoon chopped fresh or 1 teaspoon dried oregano leaves

3 tablespoons olive or vegetable oil

2 tablespoons white vinegar or lemon juice

1 teaspoon salt

2 cloves garlic, finely chopped

1 can (8 ounces) tomato sauce

1. Make cuts about 1/2 inch apart and 1/8 inch deep in diamond pattern in both sides of beef. Mix remaining ingredients except tomato sauce in shallow nonmetal dish or resealable plastic bag. Add beef, turning to coat with marinade. Cover dish or seal bag and refrigerate at least 1 hour but no longer than 24 hours.

2. Brush grill rack with vegetable oil. Heat coals or gas grill for direct heat (page 16).

3. Open can of tomato sauce and place at edge of grill to warm. Grill beef uncovered 4 inches from MEDIUM heat about 10 minutes for medium doneness, brushing frequently with tomato sauce and turning once.

4. Heat any remaining tomato sauce to boiling; boil and stir 1 minute. Cut beef diagonally across grain into thin slices. Serve beef with remaining tomato sauce.

1 Serving: Calories 240 (Calories from Fat 110); Fat 12g (Saturated 5g); Cholesterol 80mg; Sodium 280mg; Carbohydrate 2g (Dietary Fiber 0g); Protein 31g.

Flank Steak with Chimichurri Sauce

PREP: 15 MIN; MARINATE: 4 HR; GRILL: 16 MIN

MAKES 4 OR 5 SERVINGS

The spunky Chimichurri Sauce often is described as "the sauce of life" in Argentina, where barbecue bashes are common. It is used both as a marinade before grilling and as a sauce for serving.

1 1/2-pound beef flank steak

Chimichurri Sauce (right)

1. Make cuts about 1/2 inch apart and 1/8 inch deep in diamond pattern in both sides of beef. Place beef in shallow nonmetal dish or resealable plastic bag.

2. Prepare Chimichurri Sauce. Pour 1 cup of the sauce over beef; turn beef to coat with sauce. Cover remaining sauce and set aside to serve with beef. Cover dish or seal bag and refrigerate beef, turning occasionally, at least 4 hours but no longer than 24 hours.

3. Brush grill rack with vegetable oil. Heat coals or gas grill for direct heat (page 16).

4. Remove beef from marinade; reserve marinade. Grill beef uncovered 4 to 5 inches from MEDIUM heat 12 to 16 minutes for medium doneness, brushing with marinade and turning once. Discard any remaining marinade.

5. Cut beef diagonally across grain into thin slices. Serve with remaining sauce.

CHIMICHURRI SAUCE

1/4 cup chopped fresh parsley

1 cup vegetable oil

1/2 cup white wine vinegar

1/2 cup lemon juice

1 teaspoon crushed red pepper

4 cloves garlic, finely chopped

Shake all ingredients in tightly covered container. About 1 1/4 cups.

1 Serving: Calories 500 (Calories from Fat 351); Fat 39g (Saturated 9g); Cholesterol 90mg; Sodium 85mg; Carbohydrate 3g (Dietary Fiber 0g); Protein 34g.

Flank Steak with Chimichurri Sauce

Jamaican Jerk Pork Steaks

PREP: 20 MIN; MARINATE: 30 MIN; GRILL: 14 MIN

MAKES 4 SERVINGS

Fresh sage on the coals and on the pork gives a Jamaican country-style touch of "jerking," or roasting over an herb-and-wood fire. However, you can add 1/4 teaspoon crushed dried sage leaves to the seasoning mixture and omit the fresh sage.

Jamaican Jerk Seasoning (right)

3 sprigs (6 inches each) sage

**4 pork boneless blade or butt steaks,
   3/4 inch thick (about 1 pound)**

Fresh sage leaves, if desired

**Warm Fruit Medley (page 62) or Tropical
   Fruit Salsa (page 205), if desired**

1. Prepare Jamaican Jerk Seasoning. Rub seasoning into pork. Cover and refrigerate at least 30 minutes but no longer than 1 hour.

2. While pork is marinating, reserve 12 leaves from sage sprigs. Cover sprigs with water and set aside.

3. Brush grill rack with vegetable oil. Heat coals or gas grill for direct heat (page 16).

4. Drain sage sprigs and place directly on hot coals. Immediately cover and grill pork 4 to 5 inches from MEDIUM heat 4 minutes. Turn pork and place 3 of the reserved sage leaves on each pork steak. Cover and grill 4 to 8 minutes longer or until slightly pink in center.

5. To serve, remove sage leaves from pork. Garnish pork with fresh sage leaves. Serve pork with Warm Fruit Medley.

JAMAICAN JERK SEASONING

2 teaspoons dried thyme leaves

1 teaspoon ground allspice

1 teaspoon packed brown sugar

1/2 teaspoon salt

1/2 teaspoon cracked black pepper

**1/4 to 1/2 teaspoon ground red pepper
   (cayenne)**

4 cloves garlic, finely chopped

Mix all ingredients. About 2 tablespoons.

1 Serving: Calories 280 (Calories from Fat 190); Fat 21g (Saturated 8g); Cholesterol 80mg; Sodium 320mg; Carbohydrate 3g (Dietary Fiber 0g); Protein 20g.

Herbed Pork Steaks

PREP:10 MIN; MARINATE: 1 HR;
GRILL: 16 MIN

MAKES 4 SERVINGS

Herbed Marinade (below)

**4 pork boneless sirloin steaks, about
3/4 inch thick (about 1 pound)**

1. Prepare Herbed Marinade in shallow nonmetal dish or resealable plastic bag. Add pork, turning to coat with marinade. Cover dish or seal bag and refrigerate at least 1 hour but no longer than 24 hours.

2. Brush grill rack with vegetable oil. Heat coals or gas grill for direct heat (page 16).

3. Remove pork from marinade; discard marinade. Cover and grill pork 4 to 5 inches from MEDIUM heat 14 to 16 minutes, turning once, until slightly pink in center.

HERBED MARINADE

1/4 cup olive or vegetable oil

**1 tablespoon chopped fresh or 1 teaspoon
dried oregano leaves**

**1 teaspoon chopped fresh or 1/4 teaspoon
dried thyme leaves**

3/4 teaspoon salt

1/4 teaspoon pepper

1 clove garlic, finely chopped

Mix all ingredients. About 1/3 cup.

1 Serving: Calories 150 (Calories from Fat 65); Fat 7g
(Saturated 2g); Cholesterol 60mg; Sodium 160mg;
Carbohydrate 0g (Dietary Fiber 0g); Protein 22g.

Honey-Mustard Pork Chops

PREP: 10 MIN; GRILL: 16 MIN

MAKES 4 SERVINGS

The sweet honey glaze on these chops browns easily, so watch the chops carefully and make sure the coals aren't too hot.

Honey-Mustard Glaze (below)

**4 pork butterfly loin chops, 1 inch thick
(about 1 pound)**

1. Brush grill rack with vegetable oil. Heat coals or gas grill for direct heat (page 16).

2. Prepare Honey-Mustard Glaze.

3. Cover and grill pork 4 to 5 inches from MEDIUM heat 14 to 16 minutes, brushing occasionally with glaze and turning once, until slightly pink in center. Discard any remaining glaze.

HONEY-MUSTARD GLAZE

1/4 cup honey

2 tablespoons Dijon mustard

1 tablespoon orange juice

**1 teaspoon chopped fresh or 1/4 teaspoon
dried tarragon leaves**

1 teaspoon balsamic or cider vinegar

1/2 teaspoon white Worcestershire sauce

Dash of onion powder

Mix all ingredients. About 1/2 cup.

1 Serving: Calories 195 (Calories from Fat 70); Fat 8g
(Saturated 3g); Cholesterol 65mg; Sodium 90mg;
Carbohydrate 9g (Dietary Fiber 0g); Protein 22g.

Mesquite Pork Chops with Apples and Onions

PREP: 25 MIN; MARINATE: 1 HR; GRILL: 12 MIN

MAKES 6 SERVINGS

To turn apples and onions easily, skewer them with water-soaked, thin wooden skewers, putting skewers through to center of onions to hold the layers together.

Jalapeño Marinade (right)

6 pork boneless loin chops, 3/4 to 1 inch thick (about 2 pounds)

2 cups mesquite wood chips

2 medium Granny Smith apples, cored and cut crosswise into 1/2-inch slices

2 medium yellow onions, cut crosswise into 1/2-inch slices

1. Prepare Jalapeño Marinade; reserve 1/2 cup for brushing on pork, apples and onions during grilling. Pour remaining marinade over pork in shallow nonmetal dish or resealable plastic bag; turn pork to coat with marinade. Cover dish or seal bag and refrigerate at least 2 hours but no longer than 24 hours.

2. Cover wood chips with water; soak 30 minutes.

3. Brush grill rack with vegetable oil. Heat coals or gas grill for direct heat (page 16).

4. Drain pork; discard marinade. Drain wood chips and place directly on hot coals. Immediately cover and grill pork 4 to 5 inches from MEDIUM heat 10 to 12 minutes, turning once and brushing with reserved marinade, until slightly pink in center. Add apples and onions for last 4 to 5 minutes of grilling, turning and brushing 2 or 3 times with reserved marinade, until crisp-tender.

5. Serve pork with apples and onions.

JALAPEÑO MARINADE

1/2 cup red jalapeño jelly

1/4 cup chopped fresh or 4 teaspoons dried thyme leaves

1/3 cup olive or vegetable oil

Place jelly and thyme in microwavable 2-cup measure. Microwave uncovered on High 45 to 60 seconds, stirring every 15 seconds, until jelly is melted; or heat jelly and thyme in 1-quart saucepan over medium heat, stirring constantly, until jelly is melted. Gradually stir in oil, stirring until smooth.

1 Serving: Calories 390 (Calories from Fat 205); Fat 23g (Saturated 7g); Cholesterol 90mg; Sodium 60mg; Carbohydrate 18g (Dietary Fiber 2g); Protein 30g.

Wild Rice- and Almond-Stuffed Pork Chops

PREP: 20 MIN; GRILL: 45 MIN

MAKES 4 SERVINGS

Quick-cooking wild rice is faster to prepare than regular wild rice and is equally delicious. If you can't find wild rice, try a wild rice blend or brown rice instead.

Wild Rice and Almond Stuffing (right)

1/3 cup apricot preserves

1 tablespoon dry white wine or apple juice

1/8 teaspoon ground cinnamon

4 pork loin chops, 1 inch thick (about 2 1/2 pounds)

1. Prepare Wild Rice and Almond Stuffing. Mix apricot preserves, wine and cinnamon.

2. Make a horizontal cut in side of each pork chop on the meatiest side of the bone, forming a pocket (do not cut through to opposite side). Press about 1/3 cup stuffing mixture into each pocket. Secure openings with toothpicks.

3. Brush grill rack with vegetable oil. Heat coals or gas grill for direct heat (page 16).

4. Cover and grill pork 4 to 5 inches from MEDIUM-LOW heat 40 to 45 minutes, brushing occasionally with apricot mixture and turning 2 or 3 times, until pork is slightly pink when cut near bone on the unstuffed sides of chops. Remove toothpicks; discard any remaining apricot mixture.

WILD RICE AND ALMOND STUFFING

1 teaspoon margarine or butter

1/3 cup finely chopped celery

1 medium green onion, finely chopped (1 tablespoon)

1 cup cooked wild rice

1 tablespoon sliced almonds

1/4 teaspoon salt

1/8 teaspoon pepper

Melt margarine in 8-inch skillet over medium heat. Cook celery and onion in margarine, stirring frequently, until celery is crisp-tender. Stir in remaining ingredients. About 1 1/3 cups.

1 Serving: Calories 295 (Calories from Fat 90); Fat 10g (Saturated 4g); Cholesterol 65mg; Sodium 220mg; Carbohydrate 27g (Dietary Fiber 1g); Protein 25g.

Basil-Lemon Pork Chops with Melon

PREP: 20 MIN; MARINATE: 1 HR; GRILL: 16 MIN

MAKES 4 SERVINGS

To sliver basil easily, stack about 5 large leaves at a time; roll lengthwise and cut with a sharp knife into thin slices.

Basil-Lemon Marinade (right)

4 pork loin or rib chops, 1 inch thick (about 2 pounds)

1/4 honeydew melon, peeled and cut into 4 wedges

1/4 cantaloupe, peeled and cut into 4 wedges

Salt and white pepper, to taste

1. Prepare Basil-Lemon Marinade; reserve 3/4 cup for brushing on pork and melon during grilling. Pour remaining marinade over pork in shallow nonmetal dish or resealable plastic bag; turn pork to coat with marinade. Cover dish or seal bag and refrigerate, turning once, at least 1 hour but no longer than 2 hours.

2. Brush grill rack with vegetable oil. Heat coals or gas grill for direct heat (page 16).

3. Drain pork; discard marinade. Cover and grill pork 4 to 5 inches from MEDIUM heat 12 to 16 minutes, turning once and brushing with reserved marinade, until slightly pink when cut near bone. Add melon and cantaloupe wedges for last 3 to 4 minutes of grilling, turning and brushing 2 to 3 times with reserved marinade, until hot.

4. Sprinkle pork with salt and white pepper. Serve pork with melon.

BASIL-LEMON MARINADE

1 can (12 ounces) frozen lemonade concentrate, thawed

1/2 cup slivered fresh basil leaves or 2 1/2 tablespoons dried basil leaves

1/4 cup olive or vegetable oil

Mix all ingredients. About 1 1/4 cups.

1 Serving: Calories 450 (Calories from Fat 215); Fat 24g (Saturated 8g); Cholesterol 105mg; Sodium 370mg; Carbohydrate 23g (Dietary Fiber 1g); Protein 37g.

Basil-Lemon Pork Chops with Melon

Curried Lamb Chops with Pear-Cranberry Chutney

PREP: 25 MIN; MARINATE: 1 HR; GRILL: 14 MIN

MAKES 4 SERVINGS

1/2 cup plain yogurt

1 small onion, finely chopped (1/4 cup)

2 1/2 teaspoons curry powder

1/2 teaspoon salt

4 lamb shoulder blade chops, 3/4 inch thick (about 1 1/2 pounds)

Pear-Cranberry Chutney (right) or Warm Fruit Medley (page 208)

1. Mix yogurt, onion, curry powder and salt in shallow nonmetal dish or resealable plastic bag. Add lamb, turning to coat with marinade. Cover dish or seal bag and refrigerate at least 1 hour but no longer than 2 hours.

2. Prepare Pear-Cranberry Chutney.

3. Brush grill rack with vegetable oil. Heat coals or gas grill for direct heat (page 16).

4. Remove lamb from marinade; discard marinade. Cover and grill lamb 4 to 5 inches from MEDIUM heat 14 to 16 minutes for medium doneness, turning once.

5. Serve lamb with chutney.

PEAR-CRANBERRY CHUTNEY

3 medium firm ripe pears, peeled, cored and coarsely chopped (3 cups)

1 cup dried or fresh cranberries

3/4 cup sugar

1/2 cup cider vinegar

2 teaspoons finely chopped gingerroot

1/2 teaspoon ground cinnamon

1/4 teaspoon ground cloves

1. Mix all ingredients in 2-quart saucepan. Heat to boiling; reduce heat to low. Simmer uncovered about 1 hour, stirring frequently, until thickened.

2. Cool 1 hour, stirring occasionally. Serve chutney at room temperature for best flavor. Serve with grilled beef, pork or poultry. Cover and refrigerate up to 2 weeks. Makes about 2 1/2 cups chutney.

1 Serving: Calories 495 (Calories from Fat 90); Fat 10g (Saturated 4g); Cholesterol 85mg; Sodium 380mg; Carbohydrate 85g (Dietary Fiber 13g); Protein 29g.

Curried Lamb Chops with Pear-Cranberry Chutney

Southwestern Pork Chops

PREP: 10 MIN; **MARINATE:** 30 MIN; **GRILL:** 12 MIN

MAKES 8 SERVINGS

Because this rub has oil in it, is it's known as a "wet" rather than the more typical "dry" rub. It's also delicious!

Southwestern Rub (right)

8 pork loin or rib chops, about 1/2 inch thick (about 2 1/2 pounds)

1. Prepare Southwestern Rub.

2. Cut outer edge of fat on pork diagonally at 1-inch intervals to prevent curling (do not cut into meat). Spread rub evenly on both sides of pork. Cover and refrigerate at least 30 minutes but no longer than 24 hours.

3. Brush grill rack with vegetable oil. Heat coals or gas grill for direct heat (page 16).

4. Cover and grill pork 4 to 5 inches from MEDIUM heat 10 to 12 minutes, turning frequently, until slightly pink when cut near bone.

SOUTHWESTERN RUB

1 tablespoon chili powder

1 tablespoon vegetable oil

1 teaspoon ground cumin

1/4 teaspoon salt

1/4 teaspoon ground red pepper (cayenne)

1 large clove garlic, finely chopped

Mix all ingredients. About 3 tablespoons.

1 Serving: Calories 220 (Calories from Fat 125); Fat 14g (Saturated 5g); Cholesterol 65mg; Sodium 120mg; Carbohydrate 1g (Dietary Fiber 0g); Protein 22g.

Mint-Smoked Lamb Chops

PREP: 10 MIN; GRILL: 12 MIN

MAKES 4 SERVINGS

To capture the wonderful fresh mint smoke, quickly cover the grill after adding the mint and the lamb chops.

2 tablespoons dry white wine or chicken broth

2 tablespoons honey

1 tablespoon margarine or butter, melted

1 teaspoon chopped fresh mint leaves

1/4 teaspoon salt

1/8 teaspoon pepper

1 cup whole fresh mint leaves

8 lamb rib or loin chops, about 1 inch thick (about 2 pounds)

1. Brush grill rack with vegetable oil. Heat coals or gas grill for direct heat (page 16).

2. Mix all ingredients except 1 cup mint and the lamb.

3. Sprinkle 1 cup mint over hot coals or lava rock. Immediately cover and grill lamb 4 to 5 inches from HOT heat 6 minutes. Brush with wine mixture. Turn lamb; brush with wine mixture. Cover and grill about 6 minutes longer for medium doneness. Discard any remaining wine mixture.

1 Serving: Calories 380 (Calories from Fat 200); Fat 22g (Saturated 8g); Cholesterol 140mg; Sodium 290mg; Carbohydrate 4g (Dietary Fiber 0g); Protein 41g.

Sesame Pork with Garlic Cream Sauce

PREP: 15 MIN; GRILL: 15 MIN

MAKES 6 SERVINGS

The sesame seeds toast while grilling and impart a wonderful aroma, as well as flavor.

1 1/2 pounds pork tenderloin

2 tablespoons vegetable oil

1/4 cup sesame seed

Garlic Cream Sauce (right)

1. Brush grill rack with vegetable oil. Heat coals or gas grill for direct heat (page 16).

2. Cut pork crosswise into 12 slices. Flatten slices between plastic wrap or waxed paper with a meat mallet or rolling pin to 1/2-inch thickness. Brush pork with oil; coat with sesame seed.

3. Cover and grill pork 5 to 6 inches from MEDIUM heat 12 to 15 minutes, turning once, until no longer pink in center.

4. While pork is grilling, prepare Garlic Cream Sauce. Serve sauce with pork.

GARLIC CREAM SAUCE

1 tablespoon margarine or butter

2 cloves garlic, finely chopped

1 package (3 ounces) cream cheese, cut into cubes

1/3 cup milk

1 tablespoon chopped fresh or 1 teaspoon freeze-dried chives

Melt margarine in 10-inch skillet over medium heat. Cook garlic in margarine about 2 minutes, stirring occasionally; until golden; reduce heat to low. Add cream cheese and milk. Cook, stirring constantly, until smooth and hot. Stir in chives. Serve warm. About 2/3 cup.

1 Serving: Calories 285 (Calories from Fat 170); Fat 19g (Saturated 7g); Cholesterol 85mg; Sodium 120mg; Carbohydrate 2g (Dietary Fiber 0g); Protein 27g.

Balsamic Pork with Mixed-Herb Brush

PREP: 15 MIN; **MARINATE:** 1 HR; **GRILL:** 15 MIN

MAKES **6** SERVINGS

To prevent overcooking, the thin ends of the tender-loin are coiled into round filets and secured with toothpicks.

2 pork tenderloin (about 1 1/2 pounds)
8 large sprigs rosemary
8 large sprigs thyme
1/2 cup balsamic vinegar
1/4 cup olive or vegetable oil

1. Cut each pork tenderloin crosswise into 6 pieces. Press each piece, cut side down, to form a round, about 1 1/2 inches thick. If end pieces are thin, coil into round fillets; secure with toothpicks.

2. Place rosemary and thyme sprigs in nonmetal dish or resealable plastic bag. Stir in vinegar and oil. Add pork, turning to coat with marinade. Cover dish or seal bag and refrigerate, turning pork 2 to 3 times, at least 1 hour but no longer than 24 hours.

3. Brush grill rack with vegetable oil. Heat coals or gas grill for direct heat (page 16).

4. Remove pork and herbs from marinade; reserve marinade. Place herbs directly on hot coals. Immediately cover and grill pork 4 to 5 inches from MEDIUM heat 7 minutes, turning and brushing frequently with marinade. Discard any remaining marinade. Cover and grill pork 6 to 8 minutes longer, turning frequently, until slightly pink in center. Remove toothpicks.

1 Serving: Calories 180 (Calories from Fat 80); Fat 9g (Saturated 2g); Cholesterol 70mg; Sodium 50mg; Carbohydrate 1g (Dietary Fiber 0g); Protein 24g.

Flavor Boosters

For your convenience, here is a list of great-tasting marinades, seasonings and sauces in this chapter.

3

Ribs and Roasts

Contest Winners from the Grill

Lemony Thai Ribs (page 75)

Rosemary-Wine Country Ribs

PREP: 10 MIN; COOK: 5 MIN; MARINATE: 4 HR; GRILL: 70 MIN

MAKES 4 SERVINGS

Rosemary-Wine Marinade (right)

3 pounds pork country-style ribs, cut into serving pieces

1. Prepare Rosemary-Wine Marinade.

2. Place pork in shallow nonmetal dish or heat-proof resealable plastic bag. Pour marinade over pork; turn pork to coat with marinade. Cover dish or seal bag and refrigerate, turning pork occasionally, at least 4 hours but no longer than 24 hours.

3. Brush grill rack with vegetable oil. Heat coals or gas grill for indirect heat (page 16).

4. Remove pork from marinade; reserve marinade. Cover and grill pork, meaty sides up, over drip pan and 4 to 5 inches from MEDIUM heat 60 to 70 minutes, turning and brushing occasionally with marinade, until no longer pink when cut near bone. Discard any remaining marinade.

ROSEMARY-WINE MARINADE

2 tablespoons vegetable oil

1 tablespoon chopped fresh or 1 teaspoon dried rosemary leaves, crushed

1 clove garlic, finely chopped

1/2 cup dry red wine or grape juice

1 teaspoon sugar

1/2 teaspoon salt

1/4 teaspoon pepper

Heat oil in 1 1/2-quart saucepan over medium heat. Cook rosemary and garlic in oil, stirring frequently, until garlic is tender; remove from heat. Stir in wine, sugar, salt and pepper.

1 Serving: Calories 640 (Calories from Fat 460); Fat 51g (Saturated 18g); Cholesterol 170mg; Sodium 350mg; Carbohydrate 2g (Dietary Fiber 0g); Protein 43g.

Pork Ribs with Smoky Barbecue Sauce

PREP: 10 MIN; GRILL: 70 MIN; COOK: 20 MIN

MAKES 4 SERVINGS

Because these smoky ribs are not precooked, they'll be winners for folks who like their ribs chewy and firm.

**4 pounds pork loin back ribs
   (not cut into serving pieces)**

1 tablespoon vegetable oil

**4 teaspoons chopped fresh or
   1 1/2 teaspoons dried thyme leaves**

Smoky Barbecue Sauce (right)

1. Brush grill rack with vegetable oil. Heat coals or gas grill for indirect heat (page 16).

2. Brush meaty sides of pork with oil. Sprinkle with thyme.

3. Cover and grill pork, meaty sides up, over drip pan and 4 to 5 inches from MEDIUM heat 60 to 70 minutes or until no longer pink when cut near bone.

4. While pork is grilling, prepare Smoky Barbecue Sauce. Brush pork with sauce 2 or 3 times during the last 15 minutes of grilling. Heat any remaining sauce to boiling; boil and stir 1 minute.

5. To serve, cut pork into serving pieces. Serve with sauce.

SMOKY BARBECUE SAUCE

1/2 cup ketchup

1/4 cup water

3 tablespoons packed brown sugar

2 tablespoons white vinegar

2 teaspoons celery seed

1/4 teaspoon liquid smoke

1/4 teaspoon red pepper sauce

Heat all ingredients to boiling in 1-quart saucepan; reduce heat to low. Simmer uncovered 15 minutes, stirring occasionally. About 1 cup.

1 Serving: Calories 960 (Calories from Fat 630); Fat 70g (Saturated 25g); Cholesterol 260mg; Sodium 570mg; Carbohydrate 19g (Dietary Fiber 0g); Protein 64g.

Cajun Pork Loin Ribs

PREP: 10 MIN; GRILL: 60 MIN; COOK: 5 MIN

MAKES 6 SERVINGS

2 teaspoons chili powder

2 teaspoons ground mustard (dry)

1 teaspoon ground red pepper (cayenne)

1/4 teaspoon salt

4 pounds pork loin back ribs (not cut into serving pieces)

Sweet and Spicy Glaze (below)

1. Brush grill rack with vegetable oil. Heat coals or gas grill for indirect heat (page 16).

2. Mix chili powder, mustard, red pepper and salt. Sprinkle evenly over meaty sides of pork.

3. Cover and grill pork, meaty sides up, over drip pan and 4 to 5 inches from MEDIUM heat 50 to 60 minutes or until pork is no longer pink when cut near bone.

4. While pork is grilling, prepare Sweet and Spicy Glaze. Brush pork with glaze 2 or 3 time during the last 15 minutes of grilling. Discard any remaining glaze.

5. To serve, cut pork into serving pieces.

SWEET AND SPICY GLAZE

1 tablespoon vegetable oil

2 cloves garlic, finely chopped

1/2 cup chili sauce

3 tablespoons packed brown sugar

1/4 teaspoon ground red pepper (cayenne)

Heat oil in 1-quart saucepan over medium heat. Cook garlic in oil, stirring frequently, until golden. Stir in remaining ingredients; heat just to boiling. About 3/4 cup.

1 Serving: Calories 645 (Calories from Fat 425); Fat 47g (Saturated 18g); Cholesterol 175mg; Sodium 480mg; Carbohydrate 13g (Dietary Fiber 0g); Protein 43g.

Glazed Country Ribs

PREP: 15 MIN; MICROWAVE: 18 MIN; GRILL: 12 MIN

MAKES 4 SERVINGS

Microwave precooking means faster grilling! Because ribs are precooked, the sweet sauce can be added right at the beginning of grilling.

3 pounds pork country-style ribs, cut into serving pieces

1/2 cup orange juice

3/4 cup cocktail sauce

1/2 cup orange marmalade

1. Brush grill rack with vegetable oil. Heat coals or gas grill for direct heat (page 16).

2. While grill is heating, arrange pork, meatiest pieces to outside edge, in 3-quart microwavable casserole. Add orange juice. Cover and microwave on HIGH 5 minutes. Rearrange and turn over pork, so less-cooked pieces are to outside edge of casserole. Re-cover and microwave 3 minutes; rearrange pork. Re-cover and microwave on MEDIUM (50%) 8 to 10 minutes or until very little pink remains.

3. While pork is microwaving, mix cocktail sauce and marmalade; reserve 1/2 cup to serve with pork.

4. Drain pork; discard cooking liquid. Cover and grill pork 5 to 6 inches from MEDIUM heat 10 to 12 minutes, turning and brushing generously with sauce mixture 2 or 3 times, until pork is glazed, browned and no longer pink when cut near bone.

5. Serve pork with reserved sauce mixture.

1 Serving: Calories 740 (Calories from Fat 405); Fat 45g (Saturated 17g); Cholesterol 170mg; Sodium 600mg; Carbohydrate 41g (Dietary Fiber 1g); Protein 44g.

Glazed Country Ribs

Sweet Lemon Spareribs

PREP: 15 MIN; COOK: 1 3/4 HR;
MARINATE: 4 HR; GRILL: 30 MIN

MAKES 6 TO 8 SERVINGS

6 pounds pork spareribs, cut into serving pieces

1 can (6 ounces) frozen lemonade concentrate, thawed

3/4 cup barbecue sauce

1. Place pork in Dutch oven. Add enough water to cover pork. Heat to boiling; reduce heat to low. Cover and simmer about 1 1/2 hours or until tender.

2. Remove pork to rectangular 13×9×2-inch baking dish. Mix lemonade concentrate and barbecue sauce. Pour over pork; turn pork to coat with marinade. Cover and refrigerate, turning pork occasionally, at least 4 hours but no longer than 24 hours.

3. Brush grill rack with vegetable oil. Heat coals or gas grill for direct heat (page 16).

4. Remove pork from marinade; reserve marinade. Grill pork, meaty sides up, uncovered 4 inches from MEDIUM-HOT heat about 30 minutes, turning and brushing frequently with marinade, until glazed and heated through. Discard any remaining marinade.

1 Serving: Calories 740 (Calories from Fat 485); Fat 54g (Saturated 20g); Cholesterol 215mg; Sodium 340mg; Carbohydrate 12g (Dietary Fiber 0g); Protein 52g.

Lemony Thai Ribs

PREP: 20 MIN; **MICROWAVE:** 12 MIN; **GRILL:** 12 MIN

MAKES 4 SERVINGS

For the most authentic flavor, use fish sauce and substitute peeled and thinly sliced (white part only) lemongrass for the grated lemon peel. Fish sauce and lemongrass can be found in Asian markets and Asian sections of many large supermarkets.

Lemony Thai Sauce (right)

4 pounds pork back loin ribs, cut into serving pieces

1/2 cup water

1. Prepare Lemony Thai Sauce; set aside.

2. Brush grill rack with vegetable oil. Heat coals or gas grill for direct heat (page 16).

3. While grill is heating, arrange pork, meatiest pieces to outside edge, in 3-quart microwavable casserole. Add water. Cover and microwave on High 5 minutes. Rearrange and turn over pork, so less-cooked pieces are to outside edge of casserole. Re-cover and microwave 5 to 7 minutes or until very little pink remains.

4. Drain pork; discard cooking liquid. Return pork to casserole. Pour sauce over ribs, turning to coat each rib completely. Cover and grill pork 5 to 6 inches from MEDIUM heat 10 to 12 minutes, turning and brushing generously with remaining sauce 2 or 3 times, until brown and no longer pink when cut near bone. Discard any remaining sauce.

LEMONY THAI SAUCE

1/3 cup lemon juice

1/3 cup fish sauce or soy sauce

2 tablespoons vegetable oil

4 teaspoons grated lemon peel

4 teaspoons ground coriander

2 teaspoons sugar

1/4 to 1/2 teaspoon ground red pepper (cayenne)

1/4 teaspoon pepper

2 cloves garlic, crushed

Mix all ingredients. About 3/4 cup.

1 Serving: Calories 880 (Calories from Fat 610); Fat 68g (Saturated 25g); Cholesterol 265mg; Sodium 550mg; Carbohydrate 3g (Dietary Fiber 0g); Protein 64g.

Beer-Marinated Rump Roast

PREP: 15 MIN; COOK: 5 MIN; MARINATE: 8 HR; GRILL: 2 HR

MAKES 8 SERVINGS

2 tablespoons vegetable oil

1 medium onion, chopped (1/2 cup)

1 clove garlic, finely chopped

1/2 cup chili sauce

1/2 teaspoon salt

1/4 teaspoon pepper

1 can or bottle (12 ounces) beer or nonalcoholic beer

3 1/2- to 4-pound beef rolled rump roast

2 cups hickory wood chips

1. Heat oil in 1-quart saucepan over medium-high heat. Cook onion and garlic in oil, stirring frequently, until onion is tender; remove from heat. Stir in chili sauce, salt, pepper and beer.

2. Place beef in shallow nonmetal dish or resealable plastic bag. Pour beer mixture over beef; turn beef to coat with marinade. Cover dish or seal bag and refrigerate, turning beef occasionally, at least 8 hours but no longer than 24 hours.

3. Cover wood chips with water; soak 30 minutes.

4. Brush grill rack with vegetable oil. Heat coals or gas grill for indirect heat (page 16).

5. Remove beef from marinade; reserve marinade. Insert spit rod lengthwise through center of beef; hold firmly in place with adjustable holding forks. Insert barbecue meat thermometer so tip is near center of beef but not touching spit rod. Drain wood chips. Add about 1/2 cup wood chips to MEDIUM-LOW coals or rock.

6. Cover and grill beef on rotisserie over drip pan and 4 inches from MEDIUM-LOW heat about 2 hours for medium doneness (160°F on meat thermometer), brushing occasionally with marinade and adding 1/2 cup wood chips to coals or rock every 30 minutes. Remove spit rod, holding forks and thermometer. Discard any remaining marinade. Cover beef with aluminum foil and let stand 15 minutes before slicing.

1 Serving: Calories 225 (Calories from Fat 65); Fat 7g (Saturated 3g); Cholesterol 95mg; Sodium 230mg; Carbohydrate 4g (Dietary Fiber 0g); Protein 37g.

Barbecued Chuck Roast

PREP: 15 MIN; MARINATE: 8 HR; GRILL: 1 1/4 HR

MAKES 6 TO 8 SERVINGS

California Marinade (right)

**3- to 4-pound beef chuck roast,
2 1/2 to 3 inches thick**

2 tablespoons ketchup

1. Prepare California Marinade in shallow non-metal dish or resealable plastic bag.

2. Add beef to marinade, turning to coat with marinade. Cover dish or seal bag and refrigerate, turning beef frequently, at least 8 hours but no longer than 24 hours.

3. Brush grill rack with vegetable oil. Heat coals or gas grill for direct heat (page 16).

4. Remove beef from marinade. Insert barbecue meat thermometer so tip is in center of beef and not touching bone. Place marinade in heat-proof container; stir in ketchup. Heat marinade mixture on grill, stirring occasionally, until heated through; brush over beef.

5. Grill beef uncovered 4 to 5 inches from MEDIUM heat 1 to 1 1/4 hours, turning and brushing every 10 minutes with hot marinade, until medium doneness (155°F on meat thermometer). Discard any remaining marinade.

CALIFORNIA MARINADE

2 cloves garlic, crushed

1 tablespoon chopped fresh or 1 teaspoon dried rosemary leaves, crushed

1/2 teaspoon ground mustard (dry)

2 teaspoons soy sauce

1/4 cup olive or vegetable oil

1/4 cup red wine or cider vinegar

1/4 cup sherry or apple juice

Mix all ingredients. About 3/4 cup.

1 Serving: Calories 495 (Calories from Fat 370); Fat 41g (Saturated 15g); Cholesterol 105mg; Sodium 250mg; Carbohydrate 2g (Dietary Fiber 0g); Protein 29g.

Contest Winners from the Grill

Everybody loves a winner, and a winning recipe is no exception! Many barbecue societies sponsor contests and events nationwide, both local and national, where folks compete with the best barbecuers and grillers. Some contests are for individuals, and others focus on competition from local and national restaurants known for their barbecue. Barbecue newsletters share information about the contests and provide barbecuing tips. Some contests are held only once, but others are held every year.

We contacted some national organizations and asked to print these great, prizewinning recipes from grilling contests. The recipes were created by people just like you who love to grill and cook. So fire up the grill and get ready for your own rave reviews!

Peachy Smoked Pork Roast

PREP: 15 MIN; GRILL: 60 MIN

MAKES 8 SERVINGS

You'll win raves with this new recipe for pork from the "Fresh Ideas with Boneless Pork Recipe Contest," sponsored by the National Pork Producers Council.

1/2 cup packed brown sugar

1 tablespoon salt

3 tablespoons chili sauce

2 tablespoons vegetable oil

2 tablespoons cider vinegar

1 teaspoon ground ginger

1/2 teaspoon pepper

1 can (29 ounces) sliced peaches in heavy syrup, undrained

2-pound pork boneless loin roast

2 cups hickory wood chips

Place all ingredients except pork and wood chips in blender or food processor. Cover and blend on medium speed until smooth. Place pork in resealable plastic bag. Pour half of the peach sauce over pork; turn pork to coat with marinade. Seal bag and refrigerate at least 8 hours but no longer than 24 hours. Cover and refrigerate remaining peach sauce to serve with pork.

Cover wood chips with water; soak 30 minutes. Brush grill rack with vegetable oil. Heat coals or gas grill for indirect heat (page 16). Drain wood chips and add to MEDIUM-HOT coals or MEDIUM lava rock.

Cover and grill pork over drip pan and 4 to 6 inches from heat about 1 hour, turning and brushing frequently with marinade, until meat thermometer reads 155°F to 160°F when tip is inserted in center of pork. Discard any remaining marinade.

Remove pork to carving board; let stand 10 minutes. Heat reserved peach sauce. Cut pork into thin slices. Serve with sauce.

1 Serving: Calories 340 (Calories from Fat 125); Fat 14g (Saturated 5g); Cholesterol 55mg; Sodium 980mg; Carbohydrate 36g (Dietary Fiber 1g); Protein 19g.

Margarita Beef with Orange Salsa

PREP: 30 MIN; MARINATE: 4 HR; GRILL: 22 TO 26 MIN

MAKES 5 TO 6 SERVINGS

This wining beef recipe comes from the "National Beef Cook-Off®," sponsored by the National Livestock and Meat Board. It adds a taste of the tropics any time you grill.

2/3 cup frozen (thawed) orange juice concentrate

1/2 cup tequila

1/2 cup fresh lime juice

2 tablespoons finely chopped gingerroot

2 tablespoons olive or vegetable oil

1 teaspoon salt

1 teaspoon dried oregano leaves

1/4 teaspoon ground red pepper (cayenne)

2 medium cloves garlic, crushed

1/2-pound well-trimmed beef boneless top round steak, 1 inch thick

Orange Salsa (right)

Cilantro sprigs, if desired

Lime wedges, if desired

Mix juice concentrate, tequila, lime juice, gingerroot, oil, salt, oregano, red pepper and garlic in resealable plastic bag. Add beef, turning to coat with marinade. Seal bag and refrigerate at least 4 hours but no longer than 24 hours. Prepare Orange Salsa.

Brush grill rack with vegetable oil. Heat coals or gas grill for direct heat (page 16). Remove beef from marinade; discard marinade. Insert barbecue meat thermometer so tip is in center of beef and not touching bone. Grill beef uncovered 4 to 6 inches from MEDIUM heat 22 to 26 minutes for medium-rare (150°F) to medium (160°F) doneness, turning once.

Remove beef to carving board; let stand 10 minutes. Cut beef crosswise into thin slices; place on serving platter. Garnish with cilantro sprigs and lime wedges. Serve with Orange Salsa.

ORANGE SALSA

2 medium oranges, cut into 1/2-inch pieces

1/2 cup red or white chopped onion

1 medium jalapeño chili, seeded and finely chopped

1/4 cup chopped fresh cilantro

2 to 3 tablespoons fresh lime juice

2 tablespoons olive or vegetable oil

1/2 teaspoon salt

1/2 teaspoon dried oregano leaves

Mix all ingredients in nonmetal bowl. Cover and refrigerate at least 1 hour. About 1 1/2 cups.

1 Serving: Calories 245 (Calories from Fat 100); Fat 11g (Saturated 3g); Cholesterol 65mg; Sodium 280mg; Carbohydrate 13g (Dietary Fiber 2g); Protein 25g.

Continued on next page

Caribbean "Jerk" Turkey Burgers

PREP: 30 MIN; GRILL: 10 MIN

MAKES **4** SERVINGS

Jolt your burgers into a new level of flavor with this prizeworthy recipe from the "Turkey Lover's Recipe Contest," sponsored by the National Turkey Federation.

1/2 cup boiling water

1/3 cup uncooked couscous

1 tablespoon canola or vegetable oil

1 small red bell pepper, diced (1/2 cup)

1 teaspoon dried thyme leaves

1 teaspoon curry powder

1/2 teaspoon salt

1/2 teaspoon ground allspice

1/2 teaspoon ground cumin

1/2 teaspoon ground ginger

1/4 teaspoon pepper

1/4 teaspoon paprika

1/4 teaspoon ground red pepper (cayenne)

1 pound ground turkey

4 tablespoons reduced-fat mayonnaise

4 large kaiser buns, split, toasted and buttered

4 lettuce leaves

1 mango*, peeled and thinly sliced

Spray grill rack with nonstick cooking spray. Heat coals or gas grill for direct heat (page 16). Mix water and couscous in small bowl; cover and let stand 15 to 20 minutes or until water is absorbed.

Heat oil in 8-inch nonstick skillet over medium heat. Cook bell pepper, thyme, curry powder, salt, allspice, cumin, ginger, pepper, paprika and red pepper in oil 1 to 2 minutes, stirring constantly, until bell pepper is tender; cool.

Mix turkey, bell pepper mixture and couscous. Shape mixture into 4 patties, about 4 1/2 inches in diameter. Grill patties uncovered about 10 minutes, turning once, until no longer pink in center.

To serve, spread 1 tablespoon mayonnaise on bottom of each bun. Place lettuce leaf and burger on bottom half of each bun. Top with 3 slices mango and top of bun.

*Peach or tomato slices can be substituted for the mango.

1 Serving: Calories 565 (Calories from Fat 205); Fat 23g (Saturated 5g); Cholesterol 80mg; Sodium 840mg; Carbohydrate 61g (Dietary Fiber 4g); Protein 32g.

Honey-Thyme Grilled Shrimp

PREP: 30 MIN; BAKE: 45 MIN; MARINATE: 2 HR; GRILL: 10 MIN

MAKES 6 SERVINGS

These shrimp swim in a sophisticated marinade, then leap on the grill as a no-fuss kabob. This champion comes from the "Marvelous Marinade Recipe Contest," sponsored by Zip-Loc® Bags, Dow Brands.

Roasted Garlic Marinade (right)

2 pounds fresh or frozen uncooked large shrimp in shells

1 medium red bell pepper, cut into 1-inch squares and blanched

1 medium yellow bell pepper, cut into 1-inch squares and blanched

1 medium red onion, cut into fourths and separated into chunks

Prepare Roasted Garlic Marinade. Peel shrimp. (If shrimp are frozen, do not thaw; peel in cold water.) Make a shallow cut lengthwise down back of each shrimp; wash out vein.

Pour 1/2 cup of the marinade into small resealable plastic bag; seal bag and refrigerate until serving. Pour remaining marinade into large resealable plastic bag. Add shrimp, bell peppers and onion, turning to coat with marinade. Seal bag and refrigerate at least 2 hours but no longer than 24 hours.

Brush grill rack with vegetable oil. Heat coals or gas grill for direct heat (page 16). Remove shrimp and vegetables from marinade; drain well. Discard marinade. Thread shrimp and vegetables alternately on each of six 15-inch metal skewers, leaving space between each.

Grill kabobs uncovered 4 to 6 inches from HOT heat 7 to 10 minutes, turning once, until shrimp are pink and firm. Place kabobs on serving tray. Cut a tiny corner from small plastic bag of reserved marinade, using scissors. Drizzle marinade over shrimp and vegetables.

ROASTED GARLIC MARINADE

1 medium bulb garlic

1/3 cup olive or vegetable oil

2/3 cup orange juice

1/4 cup spicy honey mustard

3 tablespoons honey

3/4 teaspoon dried thyme leaves, crushed

Heat oven to 375°F. Cut one-third off top of unpeeled garlic bulb, exposing cloves. Place garlic in small baking dish; drizzle with oil. Cover tightly and bake 45 minutes; cool. Squeeze garlic pulp from papery skin. Place garlic and remaining ingredients in blender. Cover and blend on high speed until smooth. About 1 1/2 cups.

1 Serving: Calories 135 (Calories from Fat 45); Fat 5g (Saturated 1g); Cholesterol 140mg; Sodium 200mg; Carbohydrate 7g (Dietary Fiber 1g); Protein 16g.

Continued on next page

Grilled Mushrooms and Colored Pepper Fajitas

PREP: 25 MIN; GRILL: 24 MIN

MAKES 6 SERVINGS

Straight from the computer screen to the grill screen, this cutting-edge recipe was the winner of the very first recipe contest held on the internet—the "Cyberspace Mushroom Lover's Challenge," sponsored by The Mushroom Council.

Chipotle Cream Sauce (right)

1 teaspoon cumin seed

2 tablespoons olive or vegetable oil

1 tablespoon finely chopped garlic

1 1/2 pounds assorted whole fresh mushrooms (such as portobello caps, shiitake and crimini)

1/2 pound fresh regular white mushrooms

1 medium red bell pepper, cut in half and stem and seeds removed

1 medium green bell pepper, cut in half and stem and seeds removed

1 medium sweet onion, cut in half

12 flour tortillas (6 inches in diameter), warmed

8 ounces crumbled feta cheese

Chopped fresh cilantro, if desired

Prepare Chipotle Cream Sauce. Heat cumin seed in 8-inch skillet over medium heat about 1 minute, stirring constantly, until fragrant. Toss cumin seed, oil, garlic and mushrooms in large bowl.

Heat coals or gas grill for direct heat (page 16). Place mushrooms, bell peppers and onion in batches on grill screen. Grill uncovered 2 to 3 inches from MEDIUM heat 5 to 8 minutes, stirring or turning occasionally, until mushrooms are cooked through.

Cut vegetables into strips. Divide vegetables among tortillas. Sprinkle with cheese. Drizzle with Chipotle Cream Sauce. Garnish with cilantro.

CHIPOTLE CREAM SAUCE

1 container (8 ounces) sour cream

1 canned chipotle chili, stem and seeds removed

1/2 teaspoon salt

Place all ingredients in food processor. Cover and process 15 to 30 seconds or until chili is finely chopped. About 1 cup.

1 Serving: Calories 495 (Calories from Fat 235); Fat 26g (Saturated 12g); Cholesterol 60mg; Sodium 980mg; Carbohydrate 54g (Dietary Fiber 5g); Protein 16g.

Grilled Mushrooms and Colored Pepper Fajitas

Grilled Roast Stuffed with Smoked Sausage

PREP: 15 MIN; MARINATE: 12 HR; GRILL: 1 HR; STAND: 15 MIN

MAKES 8 SERVINGS

The smoked sausage and marinade add a delicious flavor to this popular Spanish stuffed beef roast, known as Boliche.

2 1/2-pound beef eye round roast

1 fully cooked smoked sausage link, 1 inch in diameter and 8 to 9 inches long (about 1/2 pound)*

1/4 cup olive or vegetable oil

1/4 cup orange juice

1 tablespoon chopped fresh or 1 teaspoon dried tarragon leaves

1 tablespoon chopped fresh or 1 teaspoon dried basil leaves

2 tablespoons red wine vinegar

1/2 teaspoon garlic pepper seasoning

Orange-Jicama Salsa (page 203)

1. Cut 2-inch-wide slit lengthwise through the center of beef roast. Cut sausage the same length as the roast; insert sausage in slit.

2. Mix remaining ingredients except Orange-Jicama Salsa in shallow nonmetal dish or resealable plastic bag. Add beef, turning to coat with marinade. Cover dish or seal bag and refrigerate, turning beef 3 or 4 times, at least 6 hours but no longer than 12 hours.

3. Prepare Orange-Jicama Salsa.

4. Brush grill rack with vegetable oil. Heat coals or gas grill for direct heat (page 16).

5. Remove beef from marinade; reserve marinade. Cover and grill beef 4 to 5 inches from MEDIUM heat about 1 hour for medium doneness (155°F on meat thermometer), turning and brushing every 15 minutes with marinade. (If using a barbecue meat thermometer, insert so tip is in center of beef about 1/2 inch from sausage.) Remove beef from grill. Cover with a tent of aluminum foil and let stand 15 minutes before cutting. Discard any remaining marinade.

6. Serve beef with Orange-Jicama Salsa.

*2 or 3 sausage links or half of a ring sausage can be substituted.

1 Serving: Calories 325 (Calories from Fat 190); Fat 21g (Saturated 8g); Cholesterol 95mg; Sodium 360mg; Carbohydrate 1g (Dietary Fiber 0g); Protein 33g.

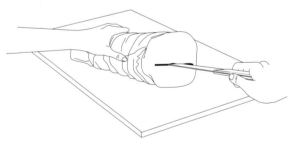

Cut 2-inch-wide slit lengthwise through center of roast using sharp long-bladed knife. Insert sausage in slit.

Grilled Roast Stuffed with Smoked Sausage, Dilled Baby Carrots (page 173), Orange-Jicama Salsa (page 203)

Spit-Roasted Porketta

PREP: 20 MIN; MARINATE: 8 HR; GRILL: 3 HR

MAKES **12** SERVINGS

Rolled into the meat, herbs flavor the meat throughout.

3-pound pork boneless shoulder roast

1/2 cup chopped fresh parsley

1 tablespoon chopped fresh or 1 teaspoon dried oregano leaves

1 tablespoon chopped fresh or 1 teaspoon dried rosemary leaves, crushed

1 1/2 teaspoons fennel seed, crushed

1/2 teaspoon salt

1/4 teaspoon ground red pepper (cayenne)

2 large cloves garlic, finely chopped

Paprika Coating (right)

1. Remove strings from pork roast. Unroll pork; trim excess fat. Mix remaining ingredients except Paprika Coating. Rub parsley mixture evenly on inside surface of pork. Reroll pork; tie with string. Cover and refrigerate at least 8 hours but no longer than 24 hours.

2. Brush grill rack with vegetable oil. Heat coals or gas grill for indirect heat (page 16).

3. Prepare Paprika Coating. Insert spit rod lengthwise through center of pork; hold firmly in place with adjustable holding forks. Sprinkle coating evenly on pork.

4. Cover and grill pork on rotisserie over drip pan and about 4 inches from MEDIUM heat 2 1/2 to 3 hours or until meat thermometer reads 160°F. Remove spit rod, holding forks and thermometer. Cover pork with aluminum foil tent and let stand 15 minutes before slicing.

5. Remove string. To serve, cut pork into slices.

PAPRIKA COATING

1 tablespoon paprika

1 teaspoon chopped fresh or 1/4 teaspoon dried oregano leaves

1/2 teaspoon salt

1/4 teaspoon pepper

Mix all ingredients. About 5 teaspoons.

1 Serving: Calories 245 (Calories from Fat 155); Fat 17g (Saturated 7g); Cholesterol 80mg; Sodium 250mg; Carbohydrate 1g (Dietary Fiber 0g); Protein 22g.

Pork Loin Roast with Rosemary Brush

PREP: 15 MIN; GRILL: 2 1/2 HR

MAKES **16** SERVINGS

If fresh rosemary sprigs aren't available to use as a brush for the marinade, use an ordinary basting brush.

3 tablespoons vegetable oil

1 tablespoon chopped fresh or 1 teaspoon dried rosemary leaves, crushed

1 large clove garlic, finely chopped

1/3 cup dry sherry, dry white wine or nonalcoholic white wine

1/2 teaspoon salt

1/4 teaspoon coarsely ground pepper

4-pound pork boneless top loin roast

Fresh rosemary sprigs

1. Heat oil in 10-inch skillet over medium heat. Cook chopped rosemary and garlic in oil, stirring frequently, until garlic is golden; remove from heat. Stir in sherry, salt and pepper.

2. Brush grill rack with vegetable oil. Heat coals or gas grill for indirect heat (page 16).

3. Insert spit rod lengthwise through center of pork; hold firmly in place with adjustable holding forks.

4. Cover and grill pork on rotisserie over drip pan and 4 inches from MEDIUM-LOW heat 2 to 2 1/2 hours, brushing frequently with sherry mixture using rosemary sprigs as a "brush," until meat thermometer reads 160°F. Remove spit rod, holding forks and thermometer. Discard any remaining sherry mixture. Cover pork with a tent of aluminum foil and let stand 15 minutes before slicing.

1 Serving: Calories 200 (Calories from Fat 100); Fat 11g (Saturated 4g); Cholesterol 70mg; Sodium 115mg; Carbohydrate 0g (Dietary Fiber 0g); Protein 25g.

Teriyaki Pork Tenderloins

PREP: 10 MIN; MARINATE: 8 HR; GRILL: 30 MIN

MAKES **6** SERVINGS

2 pork tenderloins (each about 3/4 pound)

Peppery Teriyaki Marinade (below)

1. Fold thin end of each pork tenderloin under so pork is an even thickness; secure with toothpicks.

2. Mix Peppery Teriyaki Marinade in shallow non-metal dish or resealable plastic bag. Add pork, turning to coat with marinade. Cover dish or seal bag and refrigerate, turning pork occasionally, at least 8 hours but no longer than 24 hours.

3. Brush grill rack with vegetable oil. Heat coals or gas grill for indirect heat (page 16).

4. Remove pork from marinade; reserve marinade. Cover and grill pork over drip pan and 4 to 5 inches from MEDIUM heat 25 to 30 minutes, brushing occasionally with marinade and turning once, until pork is slightly pink in center. Discard any remaining marinade.

5. Remove toothpicks. To serve, cut pork across grain into thin slices.

PEPPERY TERIYAKI MARINADE

1/4 cup soy sauce

2 tablespoons water

1 tablespoon lemon juice

1 tablespoon vegetable oil

1 teaspoon packed brown sugar

1/4 teaspoon coarsely ground pepper

1 clove garlic, finely chopped

Mix all ingredients. About 1/2 cup.

1 Serving: Calories 175 (Calories from Fat 65); Fat 7g (Saturated 2g); Cholesterol 70mg; Sodium 740mg; Carbohydrate 2g (Dietary Fiber 0g); Protein 26g.

Rack of Lamb

PREP: 15 MIN; GRILL: 45 MIN

MAKES 8 SERVINGS

Mopping or brushing the lamb with the zesty Wine Mop keeps the meat very moist, as well as making it tasty.

3-pound rack of lamb

2 teaspoons dried marjoram leaves (not fresh)

1 teaspoon salt

1 clove garlic

2 tablespoons olive or vegetable oil

Wine Mop (right)

1. Have butcher saw backbone between center rib bones of lamb so lamb can be cut apart for serving. Trim excess fat.

2. Brush grill rack with vegetable oil. Heat coals or gas grill for direct heat (page 16).

3. Grind marjoram, salt and garlic in a mortar with pestle or small bowl with back of spoon; add oil to make a paste. Rub marjoram mixture on cut surfaces of lamb.

4. Prepare Wine Mop.

5. Grill lamb, fat side down, uncovered about 4 inches from HOT heat 25 minutes, mopping or brushing frequently with wine mixture. Turn lamb; grill uncovered 15 to 20 minutes longer or until medium. Discard any remaining wine mixture.

6. To serve, cut lamb apart between ribs.

WINE MOP

2 tablespoons lemon juice

2 tablespoons Worcestershire sauce

3/4 cup dry red wine, nonalcoholic red wine or apple cider

Mix all ingredients. About 1 cup.

1 Serving: Calories 370 (Calories from Fat 290); Fat 32g (Saturated 14g); Cholesterol 95mg; Sodium 400mg; Carbohydrate 1g (Dietary Fiber 0g); Protein 20g.

Lamb Roast with Creamy Mint Sauce

PREP: 25 MIN; GRILL: 30 MIN

MAKES **8** SERVINGS

The easy Creamy Mint Sauce can be served cool or heated over low heat until hot if desired.

1/2 cup chicken broth

1 tablespoon vegetable oil

1 clove garlic, finely chopped

1/4 teaspoon salt

1/4 teaspoon pepper

2 1/2- to 3-pound butterfly leg of lamb*

Creamy Mint Sauce (below)

1. Brush grill rack with vegetable oil. Heat coals or gas grill for direct heat (page 16).

2. Prepare Creamy Mint Sauce.

3. Mix broth, oil, garlic, salt and pepper. Mop or brush broth mixture over lamb.

4. Cover and grill lamb 4 to 6 inches from MEDIUM heat 30 to 35 minutes for medium doneness (160°F on meat thermometer), turning lamb and mopping with broth mixture every 10 minutes.

5. Serve lamb with sauce.

CREAMY MINT SAUCE

2/3 cup firmly packed fresh mint leaves

1 package (3 ounces) cream cheese, softened

2 tablespoons chicken broth

1/8 teaspoon pepper

Place all ingredients in blender or food processor. Cover and blend on medium speed about 1 minute or process until smooth. About 2/3 cup.

*If a butterflied leg of lamb is not available, purchase a lamb center leg roast and remove the bone: Using a sharp knife, make a long cut through meat to bone, directly in line with bone and along length of bone. Carefully cut meat away from bone, leaving meat in one piece; discard bone. Meat will appear lumpy.

1 Serving: Calories 315 (Calories from Fat 190); Fat 21g (Saturated 9g); Cholesterol 115mg; Sodium 260mg; Carbohydrate 1g (Dietary Fiber 0g); Protein 31g.

Flavor Boosters

For your convenience, here is a list of great-tasting marinades, seasonings and sauces in this chapter.

Rosemary-Wine Marinade 70

Smoky Barbecue Sauce 71

Sweet and Spicy Glaze 72

Lemony Thai Sauce 75

California Marinade 77

Orange Salsa 79

Roasted Garlic Marinade 81

Chipotle Cream Sauce 82

Paprika Coating 86

Peppery Teriyaki Marinade 87

Wine Mop 88

Creamy Mint Sauce 89

4

Chicken and Turkey

Cranberry Chicken (page 99)

Asian Kumquat Chicken

PREP: 20 MIN; GRILL: 1 1/2 HR; COOK: 5 MIN

MAKES **6** SERVINGS

This tantalizing chicken is brushed with sherry and soy sauce during grilling, then served with an exotic Kumquat Sauce for Oriental flavor.

3- to 3 1/2-pound whole broiler-fryer chicken

3 tablespoons sherry or orange juice

2 tablespoons soy sauce

1/2 teaspoon garlic powder

Kumquat Sauce (right)

1. Brush grill rack with vegetable oil. Heat coals or gas grill for indirect heat (page 16).

2. Fold wings of chicken across back with tips touching. Tie or skewer drumsticks to tail. Insert barbecue meat thermometer so tip is in thickest part of inside thigh muscle and does not touch bone.

3. Cover and grill chicken, breast side up, over drip pan and 4 to 6 inches from MEDIUM heat 45 minutes.

4. While chicken is grilling, mix sherry, soy sauce and garlic powder; brush over chicken. Cover and grill about 45 minutes longer, brushing once or twice with sherry mixture, until thermometer reads 180°F and juice of chicken is no longer pink when center of thigh is cut. Discard any remaining sherry mixture.

5. About 20 minutes before chicken is done, prepare Kumquat Sauce. Serve chicken with sauce.

KUMQUAT SAUCE

1/3 cup thinly sliced preserved kumquats (from 10-ounce jar) or chopped dried peaches or apricots

1/2 cup orange juice

3 tablespoons orange marmalade

1 tablespoon lemon juice

1/4 teaspoon ground ginger

1 tablespoon cold water

2 teaspoons cornstarch

2 tablespoons slivered almonds, toasted

1 tablespoon orange-flavored liqueur, if desired.

Remove seeds from kumquats. Mix orange juice, orange marmalade, lemon juice and ginger in 1-quart saucepan. (If using dried peaches or apricots, add them to saucepan.) Heat to boiling. Mix water and cornstarch; stir into orange juice mixture. Heat to boiling, stirring constantly. Boil and stir about 1 minute or until thickened. Stir in kumquats, almonds and liqueur. About 1 1/4 cups.

1 Serving: Calories 275 (Calories from Fat 115); Fat 13g (Saturated 5g); Cholesterol 85mg; Sodium 420mg; Carbohydrate 13g (Dietary Fiber 1g); Protein 28g.

Chicken with Sweet Pepper Sauce

PREP: 40 MIN; GRILL: 2 HR

MAKES **6** SERVINGS

Hot cooked pasta is great with this chicken, as it soaks up the tasty Sweet Pepper Sauce.

Sweet Pepper Sauce (right)

1/3 cup cider vinegar

2 tablespoons water

2 tablespoons margarine or butter

1 clove garlic, finely chopped

1/4 teaspoon pepper

3- to 3 1/2-pound whole broiler-fryer chicken

1. Prepare Sweet Pepper Sauce.

2. Mix vinegar, water, margarine, garlic and pepper in small 1-quart saucepan. Cook over low heat 5 minutes, stirring occasionally. Cool completely.

3. Brush grill rack with vegetable oil. Heat coals or gas grill for indirect heat (page 16).

4. Fold wings of chicken across back with tips touching. Tie or skewer drumsticks to tail. Brush chicken with vinegar mixture. Insert barbecue meat thermometer so tip is in thickest part of inside thigh muscle and does not touch bone.

5. Cover and grill chicken, breast side up, over drip pan and 4 inches from LOW heat 1 3/4 to 2 1/4 hours, turning every 20 minutes and brushing with vinegar mixture, until thermometer reads 180°F and juice of chicken is no longer pink when center of thigh is cut. Discard any remaining vinegar mixture.

6. Serve chicken with Sweet Pepper Sauce.

SWEET PEPPER SAUCE

2 medium red bell peppers

12 to 15 fresh basil leaves or 2 teaspoons dried basil leaves

8 whole Kalamata or ripe olives, pitted

1 clove garlic

1 tablespoon balsamic or cider vinegar

1/8 teaspoon salt

1/8 teaspoon pepper

Heat coals or gas grill for direct heat (page 16). Cut bell peppers lengthwise in half; remove stems and seeds. Flatten pepper halves with hand. Cover and grill peppers, skin sides down, 4 to 6 inches from HIGH heat 10 to 15 minutes or until skin is charred. Place charred peppers in paper or plastic bag; cool. Remove and discard skins. Place peppers and remaining ingredients in food processor or blender. Cover and process about 1 minute or until smooth. Cover and let stand until serving. About 1 cup.

1 Serving: Calories 265 (Calories from Fat 145); Fat 16g (Saturated 5g); Cholesterol 85mg; Sodium 220mg; Carbohydrate 3g (Dietary Fiber 1g); Protein 28g.

Honey-Pecan Chicken

PREP: 15 MIN; COOK: 5 MIN; GRILL: 1 HR 20 MIN

MAKES 4 SERVINGS

Pecans can be toasted in a small skillet over medium-low heat about 5 minutes, stirring frequently until browning begins. Toast extra to keep on hand in the freezer.

Honey-Pecan Sauce (right)

1/4 cup margarine or butter, melted

2 tablespoons lemon juice

2 tablespoons water

1/2 teaspoon Worcestershire sauce

1/4 teaspoon salt

1/8 teaspoon pepper

3- to 3 1/2-pound whole broiler-fryer chicken, cut into fourths

1. Brush grill rack with vegetable oil. Heat coals or gas grill for direct heat (page 16).

2. Prepare Honey-Pecan Sauce.

3. Mix remaining ingredients except chicken in small 1-quart saucepan. Cook over low heat 5 minutes, stirring occasionally. Mop or brush margarine mixture over chicken.

4. Cover and grill chicken, skin sides up, 5 to 6 inches from MEDIUM heat 25 to 35 minutes; turn. Mop with margarine mixture. Cover and grill 35 to 45 minutes longer, turning and mopping 2 or 3 times with margarine mixture, until juice of chicken is no longer pink when centers of thickest pieces are cut. Discard any remaining margarine mixture.

5. Serve chicken with Honey-Pecan Sauce.

HONEY-PECAN SAUCE

3 tablespoons honey

2 tablespoons margarine or butter, melted

2 tablespoons chopped pecans, toasted

2 teaspoons lemon juice

1 teaspoon mustard

Mix all ingredients. About 1/2 cup.

1 Serving: Calories 510 (Calories from Fat 290); Fat 32g (Saturated 8g); Cholesterol 130mg; Sodium 340mg; Carbohydrate 14g (Dietary Fiber 0g); Protein 42g.

Honey-Pecan Chicken

Mexican Citrus Chicken

PREP: 15 MIN; MARINATE: 3 HR; GRILL: 1 HR

MAKES **6** SERVINGS

The combination of flavors in the Mexican-inspired marinade will make everyday chicken seem like a fiesta!

Mexican Citrus Marinade (right)

3- to 3 1/2-pound cut-up broiler-fryer chicken

1. Prepare Mexican Citrus Marinade. Add chicken, turning to coat with marinade. Cover and refrigerate at least 3 hours but no longer than 24 hours.

2. Brush grill rack with vegetable oil. Heat coals or gas grill for direct heat (page 16).

3. Remove chicken from marinade; reserve marinade. Cover and grill chicken, skin sides up, 4 to 5 inches from MEDIUM heat 15 to 20 minutes; turn. Cover and grill 20 to 40 minutes longer, turning and brushing 2 or 3 times with marinade, until juice of chicken is no longer pink when centers of thickest pieces are cut. Discard any remaining marinade.

MEXICAN CITRUS MARINADE

1/4 cup orange juice

1/4 cup lime juice

1/4 cup olive or vegetable oil

2 tablespoons chopped fresh cilantro or parsley

2 teaspoons chili powder

1 teaspoon ground cumin

1/2 teaspoon salt

1/4 teaspoon red pepper sauce

1/2 small onion, chopped

Mix all ingredients in shallow nonmetal dish or resealable plastic bag. About 1 cup.

1 Serving: Calories 260 (Calories from Fat 145); Fat 16g (Saturated 4g); Cholesterol 85mg; Sodium 180mg; Carbohydrate 1g (Dietary Fiber 0g); Protein 28g.

Great Grilling Flavorizers

Enhance the traditional grilled flavor of foods by adding aromatic woods, herbs or other seasonings right to the fire or heat source. These flavorizers should smolder and smoke, not immediately burn to a crisp. Ideally, they enhance and add a new dimension to the food, not mask the true flavor of the food.

It is important to soak all wood pieces, herbs (dried or fresh) and spices, and all other flavorings in water for at least 30 minutes before draining and scattering on the hot coals or lava rock. For most gas grills, place in a drip pan or open-ended aluminum foil packet and place directly on the grill rack, or sprinkle directly on the lava rock. For electric grills, place flavorings on the bottom of the grill, under the heating element.

A handful of wood chips usually will be enough for direct grilling. Two handfuls, one added at the beginning of grilling and the second added halfway through, will work well for indirect grilling. Replenish as necessary, and adjust amounts according to the package directions and your personal preference.

Wood Flavors

Wood is the most popular added flavor when grilling. Use only hardwoods. Do not use softwoods, such as cedar, pine or spruce, because they contain resin or sap that gives off fumes that impart an "off" flavor to foods. Hardwoods are available in bits, chips and chunks. Bits or sawdust are used for a subtle flavor. Chips give true wood-smoke flavor. Can be soaked in liquid (water, coffee, beer) for at least thirty minutes, then drained and sprinkled over hot coals or lava rock for rich flavor. Chunks are ideal for longer-cooking foods, such as ribs, roasts and whole poultry. Soak chunks at least three hours in liquid before using on hot coals.

Type	Flavor	Use with
Alder	Light, delicate mildly sweet smoky flavor; associated with Pacific Northwest. If not available, substitute fruitwoods.	Salmon and other fish, scallops, chicken, pork
Fruit (apple, apricot, pork, cherry, peach)	Light, slightly sweet, fragrant smoke.	Poultry and game, veal, ham, vegetables, fish and shellfish
Grapevine cuttings (or grapevine wreaths)	Sweet and subtle, winelike flavor. Popular in wine-producing regions.	Poultry, veal, lamb, fish, vegetables
Hickory	Most popular wood flavor; pungent, smoky, robust, sweet and baconlike. Associated with southern cooking.	Ham, ribs, pork, beef
Mesquite	Smoky but sweeter, tangy and more delicate than hickory. Rich and woody. Burns very hot and can become bitter with long cooking times. This wild, scrubby tree grows in the Southwest.	Steak, beef, lamb, poultry
Nut (walnut, pecan)	Sweet, delicate.	Poultry and game, fish
Oak	Smoky but pleasant, robust and tangy.	Beef, pork, ham, poultry
Sugar maple	Mildly smoky and sweet.	Ham, poultry, vegetables

Other Flavor Enhancers

Here are some additional enticing flavor enhancers; however, feel free to create your own special, exciting blends.

Type	Flavor	Use with
Flavored charcoals	Varied flavors such as hardwood, bourbon.	See suggestions on package
Cinnamon sticks, whole nutmeg, whole cloves	Spicy, slightly sweet.	Poultry, pork
Citrus peel	Tangy, sharp.	Beef, poultry, pork, ribs, duck
Coffee grounds	Rich, musty; too much can become bitter.	Beef, pork
Corn cobs, dried	Mellow, slightly sweet.	Beef, pork
Garlic cloves	Mellow, nutty.	Beef, poultry
Herbs (fresh or dried)	Basil, bay leaves, cilantro, dill, fennel leaves, rosemary, tarragon, thyme. Flavor varies with the herb.	Poultry, fish, shellfish, beef
Herb packets	Special herb blends available in tea-bag form.	Poultry, fish, shellfish, beef, vegetables
Nut shells	From hardwood trees, such as almonds, hazelnuts, pecans, pistachios, walnuts. Flavor varies with the nut.	Poultry, pork, fish
Seaweed (washed and dried)	Somewhat tangy.	Shellfish, mild-flavored fish

Cranberry Chicken

PREP: 15 MIN; MARINATE: 8 HR; GRILL: 45 MIN

MAKES **6** SERVINGS

Most of this thick marinade will cling to the chicken, giving it a glazed look after grilling.

Tangy Cranberry Marinade (right)

3- to 3 1/2-pound cut-up broiler-fryer chicken

1. Prepare Tangy Cranberry Marinade.

2. Place chicken in shallow nonmetal dish or re-sealable plastic bag. Pour marinade over chicken; turn chicken to coat with marinade. Cover dish or seal bag and refrigerate at least 8 hours but no longer than 24 hours.

3. Brush grill rack with vegetable oil. Heat coals or gas grill for direct heat (page 16).

4. Remove chicken from marinade; discard marinade. Cover and grill chicken, skin sides up, 4 to 6 inches from MEDIUM heat 20 minutes; turn. Cover and grill 25 to 40 minutes longer or until juice is no longer pink when centers of thickest pieces are cut.

TANGY CRANBERRY MARINADE

1/2 cup dried cranberries

1 one-inch piece peeled gingerroot

3 cloves garlic

1 small serrano chili or 1 tablespoon chopped green chilies

1/3 cup vegetable oil

1/4 cup lime juice

3 tablespoons soy sauce

1/2 teaspoon salt

Place all ingredients in blender or food processor. Cover and blend on high speed 1 minute. About 1 1/4 cups.

1 Serving: Calories 250 (Calories from Fat 135); Fat 15g (Saturated 4g); Cholesterol 85mg; Sodium 330mg; Carbohydrate 1g (Dietary Fiber 0g); Protein 28g.

Lemonade-Ginger Chicken

PREP: 20 MIN; COOK: 15 MIN; MARINATE: 1 HR; GRILL: 55 MIN

MAKES **6** SERVINGS

**1 can (6 ounces) frozen lemonade
concentrate, thawed**

3/4 cup water

2 tablespoons finely chopped gingerroot

2 tablespoons vegetable oil

1 1/2 teaspoons fennel seed

1/2 teaspoon salt

1/4 teaspoon pepper

2 cloves garlic, finely chopped

1 tablespoon cornstarch

1 tablespoon water

**3- to 3 1/2-pound cut-up broiler-fryer
chicken**

1. Mix all ingredients except cornstarch, 1 table-spoon water and the chicken in 1-quart sauce-pan. Heat to boiling; reduce heat to low. Simmer uncovered 5 minutes, stirring frequently. Mix cornstarch and 1 tablespoon water; stir into lemonade mixture. Heat to boiling; reduce heat to low. Simmer uncovered about 1 minute, stirring frequently, until sauce is slightly thickened; remove from heat.

2. Place chicken in shallow nonmetal dish or resealable heatproof plastic bag. Pour lemonade mixture over chicken; turn chicken to coat with marinade. Cover and refrigerate, turning chicken occasionally, at least 1 hour but no longer than 24 hours.

3. Brush grill rack with vegetable oil. Heat coals or gas grill for direct heat (page 16).

4. Remove chicken from marinade; reserve marinade. Place chicken, skin sides up, on grill; brush with marinade. Cover and grill 5 to 6 inches from MEDIUM heat 15 minutes; turn. Cover and grill 20 to 40 minutes longer, turning and brushing with marinade occasionally, until juice of chicken is no longer pink when centers of thickest pieces are cut.

5. Heat remaining marinade to boiling; boil and stir 1 minute. Serve with chicken.

1 Serving: Calories 285 (Calories from Fat 135); Fat 15g (Saturated 4g); Cholesterol 85mg; Sodium 210mg; Carbohydrate 10g (Dietary Fiber 0g); Protein 28g.

Chicken with Caramelized Onions

PREP: 15 MIN; GRILL: 55 MIN; COOK: 20 MIN

MAKES **6** SERVINGS

The sweet, smooth taste of honey is a perfect match for the indulgent flavor of caramelized onions—one bite, and you'll be hooked. These onions also are great with grilled steaks, baked ham or piled high on juicy hamburgers.

**3- to 3 1/2-pound cut-up broiler-fryer
chicken**

1/8 teaspoon pepper

1 tablespoon margarine or butter, melted

1 tablespoon vegetable oil

1 tablespoon honey

Honey-Caramelized Onions (right)

1. Brush grill rack with vegetable oil. Heat coals or gas grill for direct heat (page 16).

2. Sprinkle chicken with pepper. Mix melted margarine and oil. Place chicken, skin sides up, on grill; brush with margarine mixture. Cover and grill 5 to 6 inches from MEDIUM heat 15 minutes. Turn chicken; brush with margarine mixture. Cover and grill 20 to 40 minutes longer, turning occasionally, until juice of chicken is no longer pink when centers of thickest pieces are cut. Brush with 1 tablespoon honey.

3. While chicken is grilling, prepare Honey-Caramelized Onions.

4. Serve onions with chicken.

HONEY-CARAMELIZED ONIONS

2 tablespoons margarine or butter

3 large onions, thinly sliced

2 tablespoons honey

1 teaspoon ground mustard (dry)

**1/4 cup sweet white wine or nonalcoholic
white wine**

Melt 2 tablespoons margarine in 10-inch skillet over medium-high heat. Cook onions in margarine about 8 minutes, stirring frequently, until transparent. Stir in 2 tablespoons honey. Cook about 3 minutes, stirring frequently, until onions are caramel colored. Mix mustard and wine; pour over onions. Cook over medium heat about 2 minutes, stirring frequently, until liquid is absorbed. About 1 1/2 cups.

1 Serving: Calories 350 (Calories from Fat 180); Fat 20g (Saturated 5g); Cholesterol 85mg; Sodium 145mg; Carbohydrate 15g (Dietary Fiber 1g); Protein 28g.

Peppery Horseradish Chicken

PREP: 5 MIN; GRILL: 55 MIN

MAKES 6 SERVINGS

A perfect choice for picnics, this zesty chicken is great paired with cool, creamy potato salad from the deli and crisp carrot sticks for an easy, no-fuss meal.

1/4 cup prepared horseradish

1/4 cup sour cream

1/4 teaspoon pepper

3- to 3 1/2-pound cut-up broiler-fryer chicken

1. Brush grill rack with vegetable oil. Heat coals or gas grill for direct heat (page 16).

2. Mix horseradish, sour cream and pepper.

3. Place chicken, skin sides up, on grill; brush with horseradish mixture. Cover and grill 5 to 6 inches from MEDIUM heat 15 minutes. Turn chicken; brush with horseradish mixture. Cover and grill 20 to 40 minutes longer, turning and brushing with horseradish mixture occasionally, until juice of chicken is no longer pink when centers of thickest pieces are cut. Discard any remaining horseradish mixture.

1 Serving: Calories 235 (Calories from Fat 115); Fat 13g (Saturated 4g); Cholesterol 90mg; Sodium 80mg; Carbohydrate 1g (Dietary Fiber 0g); Protein 28g.

Orange-Tarragon Chicken

PREP: 15 MIN; MARINATE: 8 HR; GRILL: 45 MIN

MAKES 4 SERVINGS

Orange-Tarragon Marinade (below)

4 chicken breast halves (about 1 pound)

Chopped tomato, if desired

Chopped fresh tarragon leaves, if desired

1. Prepare Orange-Tarragon Marinade. Add chicken, turning to coat with marinade. Cover dish or seal bag and refrigerate at least 8 hours but no longer than 24 hours.

2. Brush grill rack with vegetable oil. Heat coals or gas grill for direct heat (page 16).

3. Remove chicken from marinade; reserve marinade. Cover and grill chicken, skin sides up, 4 to 6 inches from MEDIUM heat 20 minutes; turn. Brush with marinade. Cover and grill 25 to 40 minutes longer or until juice of chicken is no longer pink when centers of thickest pieces are cut.

4. Heat remaining marinade to boiling; boil and stir 1 minute. Serve with chicken. Garnish with tomato and fresh tarragon.

ORANGE-TARRAGON MARINADE

1/2 cup orange juice

1/4 cup vegetable oil

1/4 cup white wine vinegar

2 tablespoons chopped shallots

1 teaspoon dried tarragon leaves

2 teaspoons grated orange peel

1/2 teaspoon salt

Mix all ingredients in shallow nonmetal dish or resealable plastic bag. About 1 1/4 cups.

1 Serving: Calories 345 (Calories from Fat 205); Fat 23g (Saturated 5g); Cholesterol 80mg; Sodium 360mg; Carbohydrate 5g (Dietary Fiber 0g); Protein 29g.

Chicken and Confetti Rice

PREP: 10 MIN; GRILL: 65 MIN

MAKES 6 SERVINGS

A level grill helps to ensure best results with this recipe. If your grill isn't perfectly level, be sure to turn the skillet occasionally.

3- to 3 1/2-pound cut-up broiler-fryer chicken or 6 chicken breast halves

1/4 teaspoon salt

1/8 teaspoon pepper

2 tablespoons olive or vegetable oil

1 small bell pepper, chopped (1/2 cup)

1 medium onion, chopped (1/2 cup)

1 clove garlic, finely chopped

1 cup uncooked regular long grain rice

2 1/2 cups chicken broth

1 can (14 1/2 ounces) whole tomatoes, drained

1/2 teaspoon saffron or 1/4 teaspoon ground turmeric

1/2 teaspoon salt

1/2 cup frozen green peas, thawed

1 tablespoon diced pimiento

1. Brush grill rack with vegetable oil. Heat coals or gas grill for direct heat (page 16).

2. Sprinkle chicken with 1/4 teaspoon salt and the pepper. Cover and grill chicken, skin sides down, 4 to 5 inches from MEDIUM heat 10 minutes; turn. Cover and grill 10 minutes longer. Remove chicken from grill; keep warm.

3. Heat oil in 14-inch ovenproof skillet or paella pan on grill. Cook bell pepper, onion and garlic in oil about 5 minutes, stirring frequently, until onion is tender. Stir in rice. Cook 5 minutes, stirring occasionally. Stir in broth, tomatoes, saffron and 1/2 teaspoon salt, breaking up tomatoes.

4. Place chicken in rice mixture. Cover and grill 20 to 30 minutes or until liquid is absorbed and juice of chicken is no longer pink when centers of thickest pieces are cut. (Add additional broth if liquid is absorbed before rice is tender.) Sprinkle peas and pimiento over rice for last few minutes of grilling.

1 Serving: Calories 405 (Calories from Fat 155); Fat 17g (Saturated 5g); Cholesterol 85mg; Sodium 810mg; Carbohydrate 32g (Dietary Fiber 2g); Protein 33g.

Cheddar-Stuffed Chicken Breasts

PREP: 15 MIN; GRILL: 15 MIN

MAKES 4 SERVINGS

This chicken dish has a Mexican twist with the addition of sour cream and salsa. For a supereasy sauce, mix the two together just before serving.

4 skinless boneless chicken breast halves (about 1 pound)

1/4 teaspoon salt

1/4 teaspoon pepper

3 ounces Cheddar cheese or Monterey Jack cheese with jalapeño peppers

1 tablespoon margarine or butter, melted

1/3 cup sour cream

1/4 cup salsa

Chopped fresh cilantro, if desired

1. Brush grill rack with vegetable oil. Heat coals or gas grill for direct heat (page 16).

2. Flatten each chicken breast half to 1/4-inch thickness between plastic wrap or waxed paper. Sprinkle with salt and pepper. Cut cheese into 4 slices, about 3×1×1/4 inches. Place 1 slice cheese in center of each chicken breast half. Roll chicken around cheese, folding in sides. Brush rolls with margarine.

3. Cover and grill chicken rolls, seam sides down, 4 to 5 inches from MEDIUM heat about 15 minutes, turning after 10 minutes, until juice of chicken is no longer pink when centers of thickest pieces are cut.

4. Serve chicken with sour cream and salsa. Sprinkle with cilantro.

1 Serving: Calories 280 (Calories from Fat 155); Fat 17g (Saturated 9g); Cholesterol 95mg; Sodium 420mg; Carbohydrate 2g (Dietary Fiber 0g); Protein 30g.

Chicken with Peppers and Artichokes

PREP: 20 MIN; MARINATE: 8 HR; GRILL: 15 MIN

MAKES 4 SERVINGS

1 jar (6 ounces) marinated artichoke hearts

1/3 cup white wine or white wine vinegar

4 skinless boneless chicken breast halves (1 pound)

2 medium bell peppers, each cut lengthwise into fourths

4 medium green onions, sliced (1/2 cup)

1/4 teaspoon pepper

1. Drain marinade from artichoke hearts; reserve marinade. Mix marinade and wine in shallow nonmetal dish or resealable plastic bag. Add chicken and peppers, turning to coat with marinade. Cover dish or seal bag and refrigerate at least 8 hours but no longer than 24 hours.

2. Brush grill rack with vegetable oil. Heat coals or gas grill for direct heat (page 16).

3. Remove chicken and peppers from marinade; reserve marinade. Cover and grill chicken 4 to 6 inches from MEDIUM heat 5 minutes. Turn chicken; add peppers to grill. Cover and grill 10 to 15 minutes longer or until peppers are tender and juice of chicken is no longer pink when centers of thickest pieces are cut.

4. Strain marinade. Mix marinade, artichoke hearts, onions and pepper. Heat to boiling; boil and stir 1 minute.

5. Serve artichoke sauce with chicken and peppers.

1 Serving: Calories 175 (Calories from Fat 45); Fat 5g (Saturated 2g); Cholesterol 65mg; Sodium 200mg; Carbohydrate 8g (Dietary Fiber 3g); Protein 28g.

Chicken with Peppers and Artichokes

Spicy Caribbean Chicken

PREP: 15 MIN; MARINATE: 2 HR; GRILL: 20 MIN

MAKES 6 SERVINGS

6 skinless boneless chicken breast halves (about 1 pound)

Spicy Marinade (right)

1. Prepare Spicy Marinade.

2. Place chicken in shallow nonmetal dish or resealable plastic bag. Pour marinade over chicken; turn chicken to coat with marinade. Cover and refrigerate at least 2 hours but no longer than 6 hours.

3. Brush grill rack with vegetable oil. Heat coals or gas grill for direct heat (page 16).

4. Remove chicken from marinade; reserve marinade. Cover and grill chicken 4 to 6 inches from MEDIUM heat 15 to 20 minutes, turning and brushing frequently with marinade, until juice of chicken is no longer pink when centers of thickest pieces are cut. Discard any remaining marinade.

SPICY MARINADE

4 medium green onions, sliced

2 jalapeño chilies, seeded and chopped

1/3 cup lemon juice

1/4 cup honey

2 tablespoons chopped fresh or 2 teaspoons dried thyme leaves

2 tablespoons vegetable oil

1/2 teaspoon salt

1/4 teaspoon ground allspice

1/4 teaspoon ground nutmeg

Place all ingredients in food processor or blender. Cover and process about 20 seconds or until smooth. About 1 cup.

1 Serving: Calories 190 (Calories from Fat 55); Fat 6g (Saturated 2g); Cholesterol 65mg; Sodium 160mg; Carbohydrate 8g (Dietary Fiber 0g); Protein 26g.

Parisian Chicken Salad

PREP: 20 MIN; MARINATE: 1 HR; CHILL: 2 HR; GRILL: 20 MIN

MAKES 4 SERVINGS

You'll love this sophisticated salad with its very French touches of olives, chives, Dijon mustard and brandy.

Parisian Mayonnaise (right)

1/4 cup olive or vegetable oil

2 tablespoons dry white wine or apple juice

1 teaspoon chopped fresh or 1/2 teaspoon dried thyme leaves

4 skinless boneless chicken breast halves (about 1 pound)

8 cups bite-size pieces mixed salad greens

1 medium tomato, cut into 8 wedges

1/2 medium cucumber, thinly sliced

3 tablespoons niçoise olives or small pitted ripe olives

1 tablespoon chopped fresh chives

1. Prepare Parisian Mayonnaise.

2. Mix oil, wine and thyme in shallow nonmetal dish or resealable plastic bag. Add chicken, turning to coat with marinade. Cover and refrigerate at least 1 hour but no longer than 24 hours.

3. Brush grill rack with vegetable oil. Heat coals or gas grill for direct heat (page 16).

4. Remove chicken from marinade; reserve marinade. Cover and grill chicken 4 to 5 inches from MEDIUM heat 15 to 20 minutes, turning and brushing frequently with marinade, until juice of chicken is no longer pink when centers of thickest pieces are cut. Discard any remaining marinade.

5. To serve, cut each chicken breast half diagonally into 4 pieces. Arrange salad greens on serving platter. Arrange chicken on greens. Garnish with tomato, cucumber and olives. Sprinkle with chives. Serve with Parisian Mayonnaise.

PARISIAN MAYONNAISE

3/4 cup mayonnaise or salad dressing

2 tablespoons brandy or apple juice

1 tablespoon ketchup

1 teaspoon lemon juice

1 teaspoon Dijon mustard

1/8 teaspoon ground red pepper (cayenne)

Mix all ingredients. Cover and refrigerate at least 2 hours to blend flavors. About 1 cup.

1 Serving: Calories 585 (Calories from Fat 460); Fat 51g (Saturated 8g); Cholesterol 85mg; Sodium 420mg; Carbohydrate 7g (Dietary Fiber 2g); Protein 27g.

Speedy Microwave-to-Grill Cooking

Combine the talents of your grill with those of your microwave to speed cooking—grilling time generally will be cut in half! It's a winning combination. Moistness is retained through partial microwaving, and the smoky flavor and browned appearance from grilling make the food both attractive and delicious.

Use this cooking combination when grilling bone-in chicken pieces, meaty spareribs, dense raw vegetables such as carrots and potatoes or fresh raw sausage like bratwurst, which are known to overbrown on the outside before the center is cooked. It's also a perfect combination to use if the coals are burning too hot.

While the coals are heating to the desired temperature, you can have the cooking underway in the microwave. Much of the fat cooks away from foods during microwaving, so you can count on fewer flare-ups and healthier cooking. Basic microwaving and grilling skills will be helpful when you use this cooking combination.

To Partially Microwave

Use microwavable casseroles and dishes with covers to partially cook foods most quickly. If you do not have a cover, use plastic wrap and turn back a corner to allow steam to escape. Plastic dishes are nice, if you have them, because they're lighter in weight and can be safer outdoors than glass dishes.

Meat can be brushed with 2 to 4 tablespoons of your favorite barbecue sauce or marinade before microwaving to add flavor. Add 1/4 cup of water or broth to vegetables before microwaving.

Arrange food with thickest parts to outside edge of dish.

Cover tightly and microwave on High following the Microwave-to-Grill-Guide.

Turn over, rotate or stir food after half the microwave time.

Drain well and immediately place food on the grill to complete cooking.

Note: If grilling more than 4 pounds of food, microwave in two batches.

Microwave-to-Grill-Guide

Food	Time on High	What to Look For
Chicken pieces (bone-in)	4 to 6 minutes per pound	Edges of pieces will be cooked; parts will be pink but hot.
Ribs	6 to 8 minutes per pound	No longer pink; may not be cooked through.
Sausage links, raw	4 to 6 minutes per pound	No longer pink; may not be cooked through.
Vegetable pieces (3/4- to 1-inch) such as potatoes, carrots or winter squash	4 to 6 minutes per pound	Softened

To Finish on the Grill

As a guide, grill food for about half the time recommended in the recipe. However additional time may be needed because microwave wattages vary as do grills and grilling conditions, so use the doneness test in the recipe as the final guide.

MICROWAVE-TO-GRILL FOOD SAFETY

It is especially important to plan preparation time so that food can go directly from the microwave to the grill. Do not refrigerate partially cooked meat or let it stand at room temperature before grilling. It's the perfect place for bacteria to grow. Plan to have the coals ready by the time foods are removed from the microwave. After food is microwaved, immediately place it on the grill to complete cooking.

Sesame Chicken Salad

PREP: 20 MIN; GRILL: 20 MIN

MAKES 6 SERVINGS

4 skinless boneless chicken breast halves (about 1 pound)

2 teaspoons vegetable oil

Sesame Dressing (below)

4 cups bite-size pieces romaine

1 cup thinly sliced cucumber

1 cup shredded carrots (1 1/2 medium)

1 jar (7 ounces) baby corn, drained

1. Brush grill rack with vegetable oil. Heat coals or gas grill for direct heat (page 16).

2. Brush chicken with oil. Cover and grill chicken 4 to 6 inches from MEDIUM heat 15 to 20 minutes, turning once, until juice is no longer pink when centers of thickest pieces are cut.

3. While chicken is grilling, prepare Sesame Dressing.

4. To serve, cut chicken diagonally into 1/2-inch slices. Toss dressing and remaining ingredients; divide among on 6 serving plates. Top with chicken.

SESAME DRESSING

1/3 cup vegetable oil

1/4 cup white vinegar

1 tablespoon sesame seed, toasted

1 teaspoon sesame oil

1/2 teaspoon sugar

Beat all ingredients with wire whisk. About 2/3 cup.

1 Serving: Calories 260 (Calories from Fat 160); Fat 18g (Saturated 3g); Cholesterol 45mg; Sodium 125mg; Carbohydrate 8g (Dietary Fiber 2g); Protein 19g.

Rosemary-Lemon Chicken

PREP: 15 MIN; MARINATE: 8 HR; GRILL: 35 MIN

MAKES 6 SERVINGS

To enhance the flavor of this easy chicken even more, make a "brush" of rosemary sprigs and use it to brush remaining marinade over chicken.

1/2 cup lemon juice

2 tablespoons chopped fresh or 2 teaspoons dried rosemary leaves, crushed

2 tablespoons finely chopped onion

3 tablespoons vegetable oil

1 teaspoon grated lemon peel

1/2 teaspoon salt

1/4 teaspoon pepper

3 pounds chicken thighs

1. Mix all ingredients except chicken in shallow nonmetal dish or resealable plastic bag. Add chicken, turning to coat with marinade. Cover dish or seal bag and refrigerate at least 8 hours but no longer than 24 hours

2. Brush grill rack with vegetable oil. Heat coals or gas grill for direct heat (page 16).

3. Remove chicken from marinade; reserve marinade. Cover and grill chicken, skin sides up, 4 to 6 inches from MEDIUM heat 20 minutes; turn. Brush with marinade. Cover and grill 15 to 25 minutes longer or until juice of chicken is no longer pink when centers of thickest pieces are cut.

4. Heat remaining marinade to boiling; boil and stir 1 minute. Serve with chicken.

1 Serving: Calories 345 (Calories from Fat 205); Fat 23g (Saturated 6g); Cholesterol 105mg; Sodium 300mg; Carbohydrate 2g (Dietary Fiber 0g); Protein 32g.

Coconut Drumsticks with Fruit Sauce

PREP: 20 MIN; GRILL: 20 MIN

MAKES **6** SERVINGS

1/2 cup coconut milk

2 tablespoons soy sauce

1 tablespoon vegetable oil

12 chicken legs (about 3 pounds)

1/3 cup flaked coconut

Fruit Sauce (right)

1. Brush grill rack with vegetable oil. Heat coals or gas grill for direct heat (page 16).

2. Mix coconut milk, soy sauce and oil; brush over chicken. Spread flaked coconut in 9-inch round aluminum foil pan.

3. Cover and grill chicken and coconut 4 to 6 inches from MEDIUM heat 10 minutes, stirring coconut twice. Remove flaked coconut from grill; set aside. Turn chicken; brush with coconut sauce. Cover and grill 10 to 15 minutes longer or until juice of chicken is no longer pink when centers of thickest pieces are cut.

4. While chicken is grilling, prepare Fruit Sauce.

5. To serve, spoon sauce over chicken. Sprinkle with toasted coconut.

FRUIT SAUCE

1/2 cup Nectarine Chutney (page 210) or prepared chutney

1/2 cup coconut milk

1 medium nectarine, pitted and chopped

Prepare Nectarine Chutney. Mix chutney and remaining ingredients in 1-quart saucepan. Cook over low heat about 5 minutes, stirring occasionally, until hot. About 1 1/4 cups.

1 Serving: Calories 365 (Calories from Fat 205); Fat 23g (Saturated 11g); Cholesterol 95mg; Sodium 280mg; Carbohydrate 12g (Dietary Fiber 1g); Protein 29g.

Fruity Chicken Wings

PREP: 15 MIN; MARINATE: 2 HR;
GRILL: 18 MIN; COOK: 5 MIN

MAKES 4 SERVINGS

12 chicken wings (about 2 1/2 pounds)

1 cup chicken broth

1/4 cup dry white wine or apple juice

**1 1/2 tablespoons chopped fresh
     or 1 1/2 teaspoons dried thyme leaves**

2 medium green onions, thinly sliced (1/4 cup)

2 cloves garlic, finely chopped

2 teaspoons cornstarch

1/2 teaspoon sugar

1/4 cup diced dried fruit and raisin mixture

4 cups hot cooked rice

1. Cut each chicken wing at joints to make 3 pieces; discard tip. Cut off excess skin; discard.

2. Mix broth, wine, thyme, onions and garlic in shallow nonmetal dish or resealable plastic bag. Add chicken, turning to coat with marinade. Cover dish or seal bag and refrigerate, turning chicken occasionally, at least 2 hours but no longer than 24 hours.

3. Brush grill rack with vegetable oil. Heat coals or gas grill for direct heat (page 16).

4. Remove chicken from marinade; reserve marinade. Cover and grill chicken 4 to 6 inches from MEDIUM heat 12 to 18 minutes, turning once, until juice is no longer pink when centers of thickest pieces are cut.

5. While chicken is grilling, mix 1/4 cup of the marinade, the cornstarch and sugar in 1 1/2-quart saucepan. Stir in remaining marinade and the dried fruit. Heat to boiling, stirring constantly. Boil and stir about 1 minute or until thickened.

6. Serve fruit sauce and chicken over rice.

1 Serving: Calories 545 (Calories from Fat 205); Fat 23g (Saturated 7g); Cholesterol 95mg; Sodium 190mg; Carbohydrate 53g (Dietary Fiber 1g); Protein 33g.

Firecracker Chicken Wings

PREP: 10 MIN; MARINATE: 1 HR;
GRILL: 20 MIN

MAKES 4 SERVINGS

These flavorful chicken wings also can be served as an appetizer.

12 chicken wings (2 1/2 pounds)

2 tablespoons chili powder

1 1/2 teaspoons dried oregano leaves

**1 1/4 teaspoons ground red pepper
     (cayenne)**

1 teaspoon garlic salt

1 teaspoon ground cumin

1 teaspoon pepper

Sour cream, if desired

1. Fold wing tips under opposite ends to form triangles.

2. Place remaining ingredients except sour cream in resealable plastic bag. Seal bag and shake to blend seasonings. Add chicken. Seal bag and shake until chicken is coated with seasonings. Refrigerate at least 1 hour but no longer than 24 hours.

3. Brush grill rack with vegetable oil. Heat coals or gas grill for direct heat (page 16).

4. Cover and grill chicken 4 to 6 inches from MEDIUM heat 20 to 25 minutes, turning after 10 minutes, until juice of chicken is no longer pink when centers of thickest pieces are cut.

5. Serve chicken with sour cream; sprinkle with paprika, if desired.

1 Serving: Calories 310 (Calories from Fat 200); Fat 22g (Saturated 6g); Cholesterol 90mg; Sodium 230mg; Carbohydrate 2g (Dietary Fiber 1g); Protein 27g.

Firecracker Chicken Wings

Drumsticks with Smoked Cheese Sauce

PREP: 15 MIN; GRILL: 20 MIN

MAKES 4 SERVINGS

1/3 cup chicken broth

1 tablespoon vegetable oil

2 teaspoons Worcestershire sauce

1/2 teaspoon liquid smoke

1 small onion, finely chopped (1/4 cup)

8 chicken drumsticks (about 2 pounds)

Smoked Cheese Sauce (right)

1. Brush grill rack with vegetable oil. Heat coals or gas grill for direct heat (page 16).

2. Mix broth, oil, Worcestershire sauce, liquid smoke and onion; mop or brush over chicken

3. Cover and grill chicken 4 to 6 inches from MEDIUM heat 20 to 25 minutes, turning after 10 minutes and mopping with broth mixture, until juice of chicken is no longer pink when centers of thickest pieces are cut. Discard any remaining broth mixture.

4. While chicken is grilling, prepare Smoked Cheese Sauce.

5. Serve chicken with sauce.

SMOKED CHEESE SAUCE

1 tablespoon margarine or butter

1 tablespoon all-purpose flour

1/8 teaspoon pepper

3/4 cup chicken broth

1/2 teaspoon Worcestershire sauce

1/2 cup shredded smoked Cheddar cheese (2 ounces)

2 to 3 drops red pepper sauce

Melt margarine in 1-quart saucepan over medium heat. Stir in flour and pepper. Cook, stirring constantly, until mixture is smooth and bubbly; remove from heat. Stir in broth and Worcestershire sauce. Heat to boiling, stirring constantly. Boil and stir 1 minute. Stir in cheese and pepper sauce. Cook, stirring constantly, until cheese is melted. About 1 cup.

1 Serving: Calories 360 (Calories from Fat 215); Fat 24g (Saturated 8g); Cholesterol 110mg; Sodium 390mg; Carbohydrate 3g (Dietary Fiber 0g); Protein 33g.

Turkey Breast with Plum Sauce

PREP: 10 MIN; GRILL: 1 HR 20 MIN;
COOK: 5 MIN

MAKES 8 SERVINGS

4-pound boneless whole turkey breast

1/2 teaspoon lemon pepper

1/4 cup plum or raspberry jam

Plum Sauce (below)

1. Brush grill rack with vegetable oil. Heat coals or gas grill for direct heat (page 16).

2. Sprinkle turkey with lemon pepper. Insert barbecue meat thermometer in center of turkey.

3. Cover and grill turkey, skin side down, 4 to 6 inches from MEDIUM heat 30 minutes; turn. Cover and grill 40 to 50 minutes longer, brushing occasionally with plum jam during the last 10 minutes, until thermometer reads 170°F and juice of turkey is no longer pink when center is cut. Discard any remaining jam.

4. While turkey is grilling, prepare Plum Sauce.

5. Remove turkey from grill. Cover with aluminum foil tent and let stand 10 minutes before carving. Serve turkey with sauce.

PLUM SAUCE

1 cup sliced plums

1/4 cup plum or raspberry jam

1 tablespoon white vinegar

Mix all ingredients in 1-quart saucepan. Cook over medium heat about 5 minutes, stirring occasionally, until plums are tender. About 1 1/4 cups.

1 Serving: Calories 395 (Calories from Fat 145); Fat 16g (Saturated 5g); Cholesterol 135mg; Sodium 145mg; Carbohydrate 14g (Dietary Fiber 0g); Protein 49g.

Ricotta-Basil Turkey Breast

PREP: 15 MIN; GRILL: 70 MIN; STAND: 10 MIN

MAKES 8 SERVINGS

1/2 cup ricotta cheese

**3 tablespoons chopped fresh or
    1 tablespoon dried basil leaves**

2 tablespoons grated Parmesan cheese

1 tablespoon margarine or butter, softened

1/4 teaspoon salt

2 cloves garlic, finely chopped

**2-pound boneless turkey breast half with
    untorn skin**

Vegetable oil

1/4 teaspoon salt

1/8 teaspoon pepper

1. Brush grill rack with vegetable oil. Heat coals or gas grill for indirect heat (page 16).

2. Mix ricotta cheese, basil, Parmesan cheese, margarine, 1/4 teaspoon salt and the garlic. Loosen skin on turkey in 4 or 5 places. Carefully stuff ricotta mixture evenly under skin. Rub turkey skin with oil. Sprinkle with 1/4 teaspoon salt and the pepper. Insert barbecue meat thermometer so tip is in thickest part of turkey breast.

3. Cover and grill turkey, skin side down, over drip pan and 4 to 5 inches from MEDIUM heat 20 minutes; turn. Cover and grill 40 to 50 minutes longer or until thermometer reads 170°F and juice of turkey is no longer pink when center is cut. Remove turkey from grill. Cover with aluminum foil tent and let stand 10 minutes before carving.

1 Serving: Calories 230 (Calories from Fat 115); Fat 13g (Saturated 4g); Cholesterol 75mg; Sodium 260mg; Carbohydrate 1g (Dietary Fiber 0g); Protein 27g.

Apple-Smoked Turkey Breast

PREP: 45 MIN; GRILL: 2 HR 30 MIN

MAKES **8** SERVINGS

By using this method, you'd almost believe you used a smoker! It's a great way to get smoky flavor without buying a smoker.

3 cups apple wood chips

3- to 4-pound bone-in turkey breast

1 tablespoon vegetable oil

1/4 teaspoon salt

1/4 teaspoon pepper

Peppery Apple Sauce (right)

1. Cover wood chips with water; soak 30 minutes.

2. Brush grill rack with vegetable oil. Heat coals or gas grill for indirect heat (page 16).

3. Brush turkey with oil. Sprinkle with salt and pepper. Insert barbecue meat thermometer so tip is in thickest part of turkey breast and does not touch bone.

4. Arrange hot coals around edge of firebox. Drain wood chips; place 1 cup wood chips directly on coals. Place aluminum foil pan under grilling area; fill with 3 cups water.

5. Cover and grill turkey, skin side up, over drip pan and 5 to 6 inches from LOW heat 2 1/2 to 3 hours, adding charcoal and drained wood chips every hour, until thermometer reads 170°F and juice of turkey is no longer pink when center is cut. (Add water to drip pan during cooking if necessary.)

6. While turkey is grilling, prepare Peppery Apple Sauce.

7. Remove turkey from grill; brush with sauce. Cover with aluminum foil tent and let stand 10 minutes before carving. Serve turkey with remaining sauce.

PEPPERY APPLE SAUCE

2/3 cup apple jelly

1 tablespoon cider vinegar

1/8 teaspoon ground red pepper (cayenne)

**1 tablespoon chopped fresh parsley
or 1 teaspoon dried parsley flakes**

Mix jelly, vinegar and red pepper in 1-quart saucepan. Cook over low heat about 5 minutes, stirring occasionally, until jelly is melted. Stir in parsley. About 2/3 cup.

1 Serving: Calories 315 (Calories from Fat 115); Fat 13g (Saturated 4g); Cholesterol 95mg; Sodium 160mg; Carbohydrate 16g (Dietary Fiber 0g); Protein 34g.

Greek Turkey Tenderloins

PREP: 15 MIN; MARINATE: 8 HR;
GRILL: 30 MIN; STAND: 10 MIN

MAKES 6 SERVINGS

1/2 cup plain yogurt

**2 tablespoons chopped fresh parsley
or 2 teaspoons dried parsley flakes**

**2 tablespoons chopped fresh or 2 teaspoons
dried oregano leaves**

2 tablespoons lemon juice

1/4 teaspoon pepper

1 clove garlic, finely chopped

**2 turkey breast tenderloins (each about
3/4 pound)**

Lemon slices, if desired

Parsley sprigs, if desired

1. Mix all ingredients except turkey, lemon slices and parsley in shallow nonmetal dish or resealable plastic bag. Add turkey, turning to coat with marinade. Cover dish or seal bag and refrigerate at least 8 hours but no longer than 24 hours.

2. Brush grill rack with vegetable oil. Heat coals or gas grill for direct heat (page 16).

3. Remove turkey from marinade; reserve marinade. Cover and grill turkey 4 to 5 inches from MEDIUM heat 25 to 30 minutes, brushing occasionally with marinade and turning after 15 minutes, until juice is no longer pink when center of thickest piece is cut. Discard any remaining marinade. Remove turkey from grill; let stand 10 minutes before cutting.

4. To serve, cut turkey diagonally into 1/2-inch slices. Garnish with lemon slices and parsley if desired.

1 Serving: Calories 150 (Calories from Fat 35); Fat 4g (Saturated 1g); Cholesterol 70mg; Sodium 70mg; Carbohydrate 1g (Dietary Fiber 0g); Protein 27g.

Italian Turkey Drumsticks

PREP: 15 MIN; COOK: 1 HR; GRILL: 30 MIN

MAKES 4 SERVINGS

To save time on grilling day, follow step 1 the day before, then refrigerate drumsticks until ready to grill.

4 turkey drumsticks (about 2 1/2 pounds)

1 teaspoon salt

1 clove garlic, finely chopped

1 cup chunky-style spaghetti sauce

2 tablespoons red wine or red wine vinegar

1 tablespoon olive or vegetable oil

1. Place turkey, salt and garlic in 12-inch skillet; add enough water to cover. Heat to boiling; reduce heat to low. Cover and simmer 1 to 1 1/4 hours or until turkey is tender; drain.

2. Brush grill rack with vegetable oil. Heat coals or gas grill for direct heat (page 16).

3. Mix spaghetti sauce, wine and oil; brush over turkey.

4. Cover and grill turkey 4 to 6 inches from MEDIUM heat 30 to 40 minutes, brushing occasionally with sauce mixture and turning after 20 minutes, until very tender and well browned. Discard any remaining sauce mixture.

1 Serving: Calories 445 (Calories from Fat 200); Fat 22g (Saturated 6g); Cholesterol 165mg; Sodium 640mg; Carbohydrate 3g (Dietary Fiber 0g); Protein 59g.

Italian Turkey Drumsticks

Turkey Nuggets

PREP: 15 MIN; CHILL: 1 HR; GRILL: 15 MIN

MAKES 6 SERVINGS

2 cups dry bread crumbs

1/4 cup grated Parmesan cheese

1 tablespoon chopped fresh parsley

1/4 teaspoon pepper

**1 1/2 pounds turkey breast tenderloins,
cut into 1 1/2-inch cubes**

2 eggs, beaten

Barbecue sauce, if desired

1. Mix bread crumbs, cheese, parsley and pepper. Dip turkey into eggs, then coat with bread crumb mixture. Place on plate. Cover and refrigerate 1 hour to set coating.

2. Brush grill rack with vegetable oil. Heat coals or gas grill for direct heat (page 16).

3. Grill turkey uncovered 4 to 6 inches from MEDIUM heat 12 to 15 minutes, turning frequently, until no longer pink in center.

4. Serve turkey with barbecue sauce.

1 Serving: Calories 310 (Calories from Fat 70); Fat 8g (Saturated 3g); Cholesterol 140mg; Sodium 460mg; Carbohydrate 27g (Dietary Fiber 1g); Protein 34g.

Sesame-Ginger Turkey Slices

PREP: 5 MIN; GRILL: 20 MIN

MAKES 4 SERVINGS

To toast sesame seed, heat in ungreased skillet over medium heat about 2 minutes, stirring occasionally, until golden brown.

2 tablespoons teriyaki sauce

1 tablespoon sesame seed, toasted

1 teaspoon ground ginger

1 pound turkey breast slices

4 cups hot cooked rice, if desired

1. Brush grill rack with vegetable oil. Heat coals or gas grill for direct heat (page 16).

2. Mix teriyaki sauce, sesame seed and ginger.

3. Cover and grill turkey 4 to 6 inches from MEDIUM heat 15 to 20 minutes, brushing frequently with sauce mixture and turning after 10 minutes, until no longer pink in center. Discard any remaining sauce mixture.

4. Serve turkey with rice.

1 Serving: Calories 150 (Calories from Fat 35); Fat 4g (Saturated 2g); Cholesterol 65mg; Sodium 410mg; Carbohydrate 2g (Dietary Fiber 0g); Protein 27g.

Turkey Caesar Salad

PREP: 15 MIN; MARINATE: 1 HR;
GRILL: 10 MIN

MAKES 4 SERVINGS

1/3 cup Caesar dressing

1 pound turkey breast slices, about 1/4 inch thick

Garlic Croutons (right)

8 cups coarsely torn romaine

2 tablespoons grated Parmesan cheese

1/3 cup Caesar dressing

1. Place 1/3 cup dressing in shallow nonmetal dish or resealable plastic bag. Add turkey, turning to coat with dressing. Cover dish or seal bag and refrigerate at least 1 hour but no longer than 24 hours.

2. Brush grill rack with vegetable oil. Heat coals or gas grill for direct heat (page 16).

3. Prepare Garlic Croutons.

4. Remove turkey from dressing; discard dressing. Grill turkey uncovered 4 to 5 inches from HIGH heat 10 to 12 minutes, turning once, until no longer pink in center. Add pan of croutons for last 10 minutes of grilling, stirring frequently, until golden brown.

5. To serve, cut turkey crosswise into 1-inch strips. Place romaine on serving platter. Top with turkey and croutons. Sprinkle with cheese. Drizzle with 1/3 cup dressing.

GARLIC CROUTONS

1 tablespoon margarine or butter

1/4 teaspoon garlic salt

2 slices bread, cut into 1/2-inch pieces

Place margarine and garlic salt in 9-inch round aluminum foil pan. Place pan on heated grill about 1 minute or until margarine is melted. Stir in bread to coat with margarine mixture. Grill croutons while grilling turkey about 10 minutes, stirring frequently, until golden brown.

1 Serving: Calories 315 (Calories from Fat 180); Fat 20g (Saturated 4g); Cholesterol 70mg; Sodium 400mg; Carbohydrate 5g (Dietary Fiber 1g); Protein 29g.

Flavor Boosters

For your convenience, here is a list of great-tasting marinades and sauces in this chapter.

5

Fish and Shellfish

Sizzling Appetizers

Swordfish with Tomato-Basil Butter (page 126)

Monterey Fish with Lemon Caper Sauce

PREP: 15 MIN; COOK: 5 MIN; GRILL: 20 MIN

MAKES 6 SERVINGS

Avocado slices make a mellow and attractive garnish for this tangy fish dish.

1 1/2 pounds swordfish, halibut or salmon steaks, 3/4 to 1 inch thick

1 teaspoon salt

1/4 teaspoon pepper

1/4 cup margarine or butter, melted

1 tablespoon chopped fresh or 1 teaspoon dried chervil leaves

1 tablespoon lemon juice

Lemon Caper Sauce (right)

Lemon wedges, if desired

1. Brush grill rack with vegetable oil. Heat coals or gas grill for direct heat (page 16).

2. Sprinkle fish with salt and pepper. Mix margarine, chervil and lemon juice.

3. Cover and grill fish about 4 inches from MEDIUM heat 15 to 20 minutes, brushing 2 or 3 times with margarine mixture and turning once, until fish flakes easily with fork.

4. While fish is grilling, prepare Caper Sauce.

5. Cut fish into serving pieces. Serve with sauce and lemon wedges.

LEMON CAPER SAUCE

1 lemon

1/4 cup capers, drained

1 tablespoon chopped fresh parsley

1 tablespoon margarine or butter

1/4 teaspoon salt

Peel and chop lemon, removing seeds and membrane. Mix lemon and remaining ingredients. Heat until hot. Serve warm. About 1/2 cup.

1 Serving: Calories 200 (Calories from Fat 115); Fat 13g (Saturated 3g); Cholesterol 60mg; Sodium 780mg; Carbohydrate 2g (Dietary Fiber 0g); Protein 19g.

Ginger-Lime Tuna Steaks

PREP: 15 MIN; MARINATE: 1 HR; GRILL: 20 MIN

MAKES **6** SERVINGS

Ginger-Lime Marinade (right)

1 1/2 pounds tuna, swordfish or halibut steaks, 3/4 to 1 inch thick

Lime wedges, if desired

1. Prepare Ginger-Lime Marinade.

2. If fish steaks are large, cut into 6 serving pieces. Place in shallow nonmetal dish or resealable plastic bag. Add marinade, turn fish to coat with marinade. Cover dish or seal bag and refrigerate at least 1 hour but no longer than 24 hours.

3. Brush grill rack with vegetable oil. Heat coals or gas grill for direct heat (page 16).

4. Remove fish from marinade; reserve marinade. Cover and grill fish about 4 inches from MEDIUM heat 15 to 20 minutes, brushing 2 or 3 times with marinade and turning once, until fish flakes easily with fork. Discard any remaining marinade.

5. Serve fish with lime wedges.

GINGER-LIME MARINADE

1/4 cup lime juice

2 tablespoons olive or vegetable oil

1 teaspoon finely chopped gingerroot

1/4 teaspoon salt

Dash of ground red pepper (cayenne)

1 clove garlic, crushed

Mix all ingredients. About 1/3 cup.

1 Serving: Calories 200 (Calories from Fat 90); Fat 10g (Saturated 2g); Cholesterol 45mg; Sodium 140mg; Carbohydrate 1g (Dietary Fiber 0g); Protein 26g.

Swordfish with Tomato-Basil Butter

PREP: 20 MIN; MARINATE: 15 MIN; GRILL: 15 MIN

MAKES **6** SERVINGS

To save time, you can make Tomato-Basil Butter up to one day ahead. Shape it into 1-inch balls, roll in finely chopped parsley, cover and refrigerate.

Tomato-Basil Butter (right)

1/3 cup balsamic vinegar

1 1/2 pounds swordfish, salmon or marlin steaks, 1 to 1 1/2 inches thick

Fresh basil leaves, if desired

1. Prepare Tomato-Basil Butter.

2. Place vinegar in shallow nonmetal dish or resealable plastic bag. If fish steaks are large, cut into 6 serving pieces. Add fish, turning to coat with vinegar. Cover dish or seal bag and refrigerate, turning once, at least 15 minutes but no longer than 1 hour.

3. Brush grill rack with vegetable oil. Heat coals or gas grill for direct heat (page 16).

4. Drain fish; discard vinegar. Cover and grill fish 4 inches from MEDIUM heat 10 to 15 minutes, turning once, until fish flakes easily with fork.

5. Immediately top each steak with Tomato-Basil Butter. Garnish with basil leaves.

TOMATO-BASIL BUTTER

1/4 cup margarine or butter, softened

1 tablespoon finely chopped shallots

1 tablespoon chopped fresh or 1 teaspoon dried basil leaves

1 tablespoon finely chopped drained sun-dried tomatoes in oil

Mix all ingredients. Cover and refrigerate at least 1 hour to blend flavors. About 1/3 cup.

1 Serving: Calories 195 (Calories from Fat 115); Fat 13g (Saturated 3g); Cholesterol 60mg; Sodium 150mg; Carbohydrate 1g (Dietary Fiber 0g); Protein 19g.

Tarragon Marlin Steaks with Vermouth

PREP: 10 MIN; MARINATE: 15 MIN; GRILL: 12 MIN

MAKES **6** SERVINGS

The standard cooking guide for fish of 10 minutes cooking time per 1 inch of thickness works for grilling all kinds of fish steaks. When grilling, instead of grilling the first side for half the time, try cooking the first side 1 to 2 minutes longer. Watch them carefully toward end of cooking time to avoid overcooking.

1/2 cup dry vermouth or 1/4 cup lemon juice plus 1/4 cup water

1/4 teaspoon aromatic bitters

4 large sprigs tarragon

1 1/2 pounds marlin, tuna or opah steaks, 1 to 1 1/2 inches thick

Vegetable or olive oil

1 1/2 teaspoons chopped fresh or 1/2 teaspoon dried tarragon leaves

1. Mix vermouth and bitters in shallow nonmetal dish. Add 2 sprigs tarragon. Add fish, turning to coat with marinade. Top fish with remaining 2 sprigs tarragon. Cover and let stand, turning once, at least 15 minutes but no longer than 30 minutes.

2. Brush grill rack with vegetable oil. Heat coals or gas grill for direct heat (page 16).

3. Drain fish; discard marinade but not the tarragon sprigs. Place tarragon sprigs directly on hot coals. Immediately cover and grill fish 4 inches from MEDIUM heat 10 to 15 minutes, turning once, until fish flakes easily with fork.

4. Remove fish to platter. Sprinkle with chopped tarragon.

1 Serving: Calories 160 (Calories from Fat 70); Fat 8g (Saturated 2g); Cholesterol 65mg; Sodium 60mg; Carbohydrate 0g (Dietary Fiber 0g); Protein 22g.

Trout with Rosemary

PREP: 15 MIN; GRILL: 25 MIN

MAKES **4** SERVINGS

A pan-dressed fish is all ready to cook—it's been gutted and scaled, and usually the head, tail and fins have been removed.

4 pan-dressed rainbow trout (each about 1/2 pound)

1/2 teaspoon salt

1/4 teaspoon pepper

4 sprigs rosemary (each about 3 inches long)

4 thin slices lemon

1/4 cup olive or vegetable oil

Lemon wedges, if desired

1. Heat coals or gas grill for direct heat (page 16). Brush hinged wire grill basket with vegetable oil.

2. Sprinkle cavities of fish with salt and pepper. Place 1 sprig rosemary and 1 slice lemon in each fish. Rub fish with oil. Place fish in basket.

3. Cover and grill fish about 4 inches from MEDIUM heat 20 to 25 minutes, brushing 2 or 3 times with oil and turning once, until fish flakes easily with fork.

4. Serve fish with lemon wedges.

1 Serving: Calories 405 (Calories from Fat 205); Fat 23g (Saturated 5g); Cholesterol 150mg; Sodium 430mg; Carbohydrate 1g (Dietary Fiber 0g); Protein 48g.

Sole Fillets with Spinach

PREP 15 MIN; GRILL: 10 MIN

MAKES **4** SERVINGS

1 pound spinach

1 teaspoon poultry seasoning

1/2 teaspoon chili powder

1/2 teaspoon salt

1 to 1 1/2 pounds sole, flounder or red snapper fillets, 1/4 to 1/2 inch thick

2 tablespoons margarine or butter, melted

Lemon wedges

1. Heat coals or gas grill for direct heat (page 16). Spray 13×9-inch aluminum foil pan with non-stick cooking spray.

2. Rinse spinach; shake off excess water, but do not dry. Place about three-fourths of the spinach leaves in pan, covering bottom completely.

3. Mix poultry seasoning, chili powder and salt. Lightly rub into both sides of fish. Place fish on spinach, folding thin tail ends under and, if necessary, overlapping thin edges slightly. Drizzle with margarine. Cover fish completely with remaining spinach.

4. Cover and grill fish and spinach 4 inches from MEDIUM heat 8 to 10 minutes or until fish flakes easily with fork. Check after about 3 minutes; if top layer of spinach is charring, sprinkle with about 1/4 cup water.

5. Serve fish and spinach from pan with a slotted spoon if desired. Serve with lemon wedges.

1 Serving: Calories 150 (Calories from Fat 65); Fat 7g (Saturated 2g); Cholesterol 55mg; Sodium 510mg; Carbohydrate 3g (Dietary Fiber 2g); Protein 21g.

Salmon with Cucumber Relish

PREP: 15 MIN; MARINATE: 1 HR;
GRILL: 30 MIN

MAKES **6** SERVINGS

Cucumber Relish (below)
1 large salmon fillet (about 2 pounds)
2 tablespoons olive or vegetable oil
1/4 to 1/2 teaspoon dried dill weed
1/2 teaspoon salt
1/4 teaspoon pepper

1. Prepare Cucumber Relish.

2. Heat coals or gas grill for direct heat (page 16).

3. Place fish on 24-inch piece of heavy-duty aluminum foil. Brush fish with oil. Sprinkle with dill weed, salt and pepper. Wrap foil securely around fish.

4. Cover and grill fish 4 inches from MEDIUM heat 20 to 30 minutes or until fish flakes easily with fork. Serve relish with fish.

CUCUMBER RELISH

1 medium cucumber, seeded and coarsely chopped (1 1/4 cups)
2 tablespoons chopped onion
2 tablespoons white vinegar
2 tablespoons water
1 teaspoon sugar
1/2 teaspoon salt
2 tablespoons chopped fresh parsley

Mix all ingredients in nonmetal bowl. Cover and refrigerate at least 1 hour but no longer than 8 hours. Drain relish. About 1 cup.

1 Serving: Calories 255 (Calories from Fat 115); Fat 13g (Saturated 3g); Cholesterol 100mg; Sodium 480mg; Carbohydrate 2g (Dietary Fiber 0g); Protein 32g.

Mexican Fish in Foil

PREP: 15 MIN; GRILL: 20 MIN

MAKES **6** SERVINGS

1 1/2 pounds halibut, cod or red snapper fillets, 1/2 to 3/4 inch thick
1/4 cup sliced pimiento-stuffed olives
2 teaspoons capers
3 medium green onions, thinly sliced (1/3 cup)
1 medium tomato, seeded and coarsely chopped (3/4 cup)
1 clove garlic, finely chopped
2 tablespoons lemon juice
1/4 teaspoon salt
1/8 teaspoon pepper
Lemon wedges

1. Brush grill rack with vegetable oil. Heat coals or gas grill for direct heat (page 16).

2. If fish fillets are large, cut into 6 serving pieces. Place each piece fish on 12-inch square of heavy-duty aluminum foil. Mix olives, capers, onions, tomato and garlic; spoon over fish. Drizzle with lemon juice. Sprinkle with salt and pepper. Wrap foil securely around fish.

3. Cover and grill foil packets, seam sides up, 5 to 6 inches from MEDIUM heat 15 to 20 minutes, turning once, until fish flakes easily with fork.

4. Serve fish with lemon wedges.

1 Serving: Calories 115 (Calories from Fat 20); Fat 2g (Saturated 0g); Cholesterol 60mg; Sodium 370mg; Carbohydrate 2g (Dietary Fiber 0g); Protein 22g.

Vegetable-Stuffed Fish

PREP: 25 MIN; COOK: 5 MIN; GRILL: 45 MIN

MAKES **10** TO **12** SERVINGS

Garden Vegetable Stuffing (right)

1/4 cup margarine or butter, melted

2 tablespoons lemon juice

8- to 10-pound pan-dressed fish (salmon, cod, snapper or lake trout)

1/2 teaspoon salt

1/4 teaspoon pepper

2 tablespoons vegetable oil

1. Heat coals or gas grill for direct heat (page 16). Brush hinged wire grill basket with vegetable oil.

2. Prepare Garden Vegetable Stuffing.

3. Mix margarine and lemon juice. Sprinkle cavity of fish with salt and pepper. Spoon stuffing into cavity. Close opening with skewers and lace with string. (If you have extra stuffing, place in greased foil pan; cover with aluminum foil and add to side of grill about 20 minutes before serving.) Rub fish with oil. Place fish in basket.

4. Grill fish uncovered 4 inches from MEDIUM heat 45 minutes, turning and brushing with margarine mixture 3 times, until fish flakes easily with fork. Discard any remaining margarine mixture.

GARDEN VEGETABLE STUFFING

1/4 cup margarine or butter

1 large onion, finely chopped (1 cup)

2 cups dry bread cubes

1 cup coarsely shredded carrots

3 ounces mushrooms, coarsely chopped (1 cup)

1/2 cup chopped fresh parsley

1 1/2 tablespoons lemon juice

1 teaspoon salt

1/2 teaspoon chopped fresh or 1/4 teaspoon dried marjoram leaves

1/4 teaspoon pepper

1 clove garlic, finely chopped

1 egg

Melt margarine in 10-inch skillet over medium heat. Cook onion in margarine, stirring occasionally, until onion is tender. Gently stir in remaining ingredients.

1 Serving: Calories 655 (Calories from Fat 260); Fat 29g (Saturated 8g); Cholesterol 260mg; Sodium 840mg; Carbohydrate 19g (Dietary Fiber 2g); Protein 81g.

Spicy Shrimp with Creole Sauce

PREP: 30 MIN; MARINATE: 15 MIN; GRILL: 6 MIN

MAKES 4 SERVINGS

These delicious shrimp also can be served as an appetizer. Use the Creole Sauce on the side for dipping. Make grilling the shrimp easier by using a grill screen to cook them in.

1 pound uncooked large shrimp in shells

1/2 cup olive or vegetable oil

1/2 teaspoon poultry seasoning

1/2 teaspoon dried oregano leaves (do not substitute fresh)

1/2 teaspoon chili oil or crushed red pepper

1/4 teaspoon salt

1 clove garlic, finely chopped

Creole Sauce (right)

3 cups hot cooked rice

1. Peel shrimp. (If shrimp are frozen, do not thaw; peel in cold water.) Make a shallow cut lengthwise down back of each shrimp; wash out vein.

2. Mix remaining ingredients except Creole Sauce and rice in large nonmetal bowl. Add shrimp, stirring to coat with marinade. Cover and refrigerate at least 15 minutes but no longer than 1 hour.

3. Brush grill rack with vegetable oil. Heat coals or gas grill for direct heat (page 16).

4. Prepare Creole Sauce; keep warm.

5. Drain shrimp; discard marinade. Grill shrimp uncovered 4 inches from MEDIUM heat 4 to 6 minutes, turning once, until shrimp are pink and firm.

6. Serve shrimp and Creole Sauce over rice.

CREOLE SAUCE

1 tablespoon margarine or butter

1 small green bell pepper, diced (1/2 cup)

2 cloves garlic, finely chopped

1 can (14 1/2 ounces) stewed tomatoes, undrained

1 tablespoon chopped fresh or 1 teaspoon dried thyme leaves

1/8 teaspoon pepper

1/8 teaspoon red pepper sauce

2 large bay leaves

Melt margarine in 1 1/2-quart saucepan over medium heat. Cook bell pepper and garlic in margarine, stirring occasionally, until bell pepper is crisp-tender. Stir in remaining ingredients, breaking up tomatoes. Heat to boiling; reduce heat to low. Simmer uncovered 5 to 10 minutes, stirring occasionally, until thickened. Discard bay leaves. Serve warm. About 2 cups.

1 Serving: Calories 310 (Calories from Fat 100); Fat 11g (Saturated 2g); Cholesterol 105mg; Sodium 330mg; Carbohydrate 39g (Dietary Fiber 2g); Protein 16g.

Indonesian Barbecued Shrimp

PREP: 25 MIN; MARINATE: 1 HR; GRILL: 20 MIN

MAKES 4 SERVINGS

**1 1/2 pounds uncooked large shrimp
in shells**

2 tablespoons vegetable oil

2 tablespoons water

1 tablespoon lemon juice

1 teaspoon packed brown sugar

1/2 teaspoon salt

1/4 to 1/2 teaspoon red pepper sauce

2 cloves garlic, crushed

Spicy Peanut Sauce (right)

Lime wedges, if desired

1. Peel shrimp. (If shrimp are frozen, do not thaw; peel in cold water.) Make a shallow cut lengthwise down back of each shrimp; wash out vein.

2. Mix remaining ingredients except Spicy Peanut Sauce and lime wedges in medium nonmetal bowl or resealable plastic bag. Add shrimp, stirring to coat with marinade. Cover bowl or seal bag and refrigerate at least 1 hour but no longer than 12 hours.

3. Prepare Spicy Peanut Sauce.

4. Heat coals or gas grill for direct heat (page 16).

5. Remove shrimp from marinade; reserve marinade. Thread shrimp on six 15-inch metal skewers, leaving space between each. Cover and grill shrimp about 4 inches from MEDIUM heat 10 to 20 minutes, turning and brushing with marinade 2 or 3 times, until shrimp are pink and firm. Discard any remaining marinade.

6. Serve shrimp with Spicy Peanut Sauce and lime wedges.

SPICY PEANUT SAUCE

1/2 cup peanut butter

1/2 cup water

1 tablespoon packed brown sugar

1 tablespoon lemon juice

1/2 teaspoon salt

1/2 teaspoon red pepper sauce

1 small clove garlic, crushed

Place all ingredients in food processor. Cover and process about 20 seconds or until smooth. Cover and let stand until serving. About 1 cup.

1 Serving: Calories 335 (Calories from Fat 200); Fat 22g (Saturated 5g); Cholesterol 160mg; Sodium 840mg; Carbohydrate 11g (Dietary Fiber 2g); Protein 25g.

Crab Legs with Lemon-Mustard Sauce

PREP: 20 MIN; CHILL: 1 HR; GRILL: 15 MIN

MAKES 4 SERVINGS

If possible, ask your butcher to cut the crab legs lengthwise in half for you. If you are cutting them yourself, be very careful.

Lemon-Mustard Sauce (right)

3 pounds frozen king crab legs, thawed

1/2 cup margarine or butter, melted

Lemon wedges

1. Prepare Lemon-Mustard Sauce.

2. Brush grill rack with vegetable oil. Heat coals or gas grill for direct heat (page 16).

3. Carefully cut crab legs lengthwise in half through shell with sharp knife or poultry shears, leaving narrow parts of legs whole.

4. Place crab legs, shell sides down, on grill; brush with margarine. Cover and grill 10 to 15 minutes or until shells turn red and crabmeat turns white and firm.

5. Serve crab legs with Lemon-Mustard Sauce and lemon wedges.

LEMON-MUSTARD SAUCE

3/4 cup mayonnaise or salad dressing

2 tablespoons lemon juice

1 tablespoon Dijon mustard

1/8 teaspoon ground red pepper (cayenne)

Mix all ingredients. Cover and refrigerate at least 1 hour to blend flavors. About 1 cup.

1 Serving: Calories 565 (Calories from Fat 425); Fat 47g (Saturated 8g); Cholesterol 190mg; Sodium 880mg; Carbohydrate 2g (Dietary Fiber 0g); Protein 34g.

Crab Legs with
Lemon-Mustard Sauce

Crab Cakes with Herb Mayonnaise

PREP: 20 MIN; GRILL: 20 MIN

MAKES 4 SERVINGS

Herb Mayonnaise (right)

3/4 pound cooked crabmeat

1 1/4 cups soft bread crumbs

1/4 cup mayonnaise or salad dressing

3 tablespoons finely chopped onion

1 teaspoon salt

1 teaspoon ground mustard (dry)

1/4 teaspoon red pepper sauce

Lemon wedges

1. Heat coals or gas grill for direct heat (page 16). Brush hinged wire grill basket with vegetable oil.

2. Prepare Herb Mayonnaise.

3. Mix remaining ingredients except lemon wedges. Shape mixture into 6 patties, about 3 inches in diameter. Place patties in basket.

4. Cover and grill patties 5 to 6 inches from MEDIUM heat 15 to 20 minutes, turning once, until crab cakes are golden brown and hot in center.

5. Serve crab cakes with mayonnaise and lemon wedges.

HERB MAYONNAISE

1/2 cup mayonnaise or salad dressing

1 tablespoon chopped fresh or 1 teaspoon dried dill weed or tarragon leaves

2 teaspoons chopped fresh chives

2 teaspoons chopped fresh parsley

2 teaspoons lemon juice

1 teaspoon Dijon mustard

Dash of ground red pepper (cayenne)

Mix all ingredients. Cover and refrigerate until serving. About 2/3 cup.

1 Serving: Calories 515 (Calories from Fat 325); Fat 36g (Saturated 6g); Cholesterol 110mg; Sodium 1360mg; Carbohydrate 27g (Dietary Fiber 1g); Protein 22g.

Mussels with Buttery Herb Sauce

PREP: 40 MIN; GRILL: 5 MIN

MAKES 4 SERVINGS

Place mussels on grill with rounded sides down to catch juices in the bottom half of the shell. Be careful when removing mussels from the grill—the liquid is hot! Serve the mussels in large shallow bowls with their juice and the buttery sauce. They're also great with crusty bread or served over pasta.

**2 pounds mussels in shells
  (60 to 72 mussels)**

Buttery Herb Sauce (right)

1. Discard any broken-shell or open (dead) mussels. Scrub remaining mussels in cool water, removing any barnacles with a dull paring knife. Remove beards by tugging them away from shells. Place mussels in container. Cover with cool water. Agitate water with hand, then drain and discard water. Repeat several times until water runs clear; drain.

2. Brush grill rack with vegetable oil. Heat coals or gas grill for direct heat (page 16).

3. Cover and grill mussels 4 inches from MEDIUM heat 3 to 5 minutes or until mussels open, removing mussels as they open. Discard unopened mussels.

4. Place mussels on platter, or divide among shallow soup bowls. Drizzle hot margarine mixture over mussels.

BUTTERY HERB SAUCE

1/2 cup margarine or butter, melted

**2 teaspoons dried thyme leaves
  (do not substitute fresh)**

**2 teaspoons dried sage leaves
  (do not substitute fresh)**

1 1/2 teaspoons celery salt

**1/4 teaspoon chili oil or crushed red
  peppers**

Melt margarine in small 8-inch skillet over medium heat. Stir in remaining ingredients. Reduce heat to low and cover to keep warm, or reheat just before serving.

1 Serving: Calories 180 (Calories from Fat 115); Fat 13g (Saturated 3g); Cholesterol 35mg; Sodium 330mg; Carbohydrate 3g (Dietary Fiber 0g); Protein 13g.

Sizzling Appetizers

Often grilling is part of leisurely casual entertaining. So while waiting for your main course, try popping an appetizer or two on the grill—it's a nice change from chips and dip! Enjoy great grilled flavor in favorites such as Cheesy Quesadillas (page 140) or Crispy Honey Wings (page 140). You may not have thought of cooking appetizers this way, but after trying it, you're certain to do it again!

Orange-Almond Brie

PREP: 10 MIN; GRILL: 3 MIN

MAKES **6** SERVINGS

Watch the cheese carefully during grilling to avoid overcooking. For a slightly different appetizer, substitute 2/3 cup Pear-Cranberry Chutney (page 208) for the orange mixture.

2 tablespoons sliced almonds

1/2 cup orange marmalade

1 tablespoon Dijon mustard

1 teaspoon white wine vinegar

8- to 10-ounce round cold Brie cheese (not creamy)

1 tablespoon margarine or butter, melted

Assorted crackers, if desired

Crisp apple and pear wedges, if desired

1. Brush grill rack with vegetable oil. Heat coals or gas grill for direct heat (page 16).

2. While grill is heating, spread almonds in 8-inch square aluminum foil pan. Grill uncovered 3 to 5 minutes, stirring once or twice, until almonds just start to brown.

3. Mix marmalade, mustard and vinegar. Spread marmalade mixture in 6-inch circle on serving plate.

4. Brush both sides of cheese with margarine. Cover and grill cheese 4 inches from MEDIUM-HOT heat 1 to 3 minutes, turning once, until cheese just begins to melt.

5. Place cheese on marmalade mixture. Brush lightly with about 1 teaspoon of the marmalade mixture. Sprinkle almonds over cheese and marmalade mixture.

6. Serve cheese with crackers and fruit wedges.

1 Serving: Calories 210 (Calories from Fat 110); Fat 12g (Saturated 7g); Cholesterol 25mg; Sodium 380mg; Carbohydrate 18g (Dietary Fiber 0g); Protein 8g.

Orange-Almond Brie,
Stuffed Focaccia (page 141),
Crispy Honey Wings (page 140)

Cheesy Quesadillas

PREP: 15 MIN; GRILL: 4 MIN

MAKES 4 SERVINGS

For speedier appetizers, the cheese mixture can be prepared several days ahead and refrigerated.

Fresh Tomato Salsa (page 203) or prepared salsa, if desired

1/2 cup shredded sharp Cheddar cheese (2 ounces)

1/4 cup grated Parmesan cheese

2 medium green onions, thinly sliced (1/4 cup)

1 1/2 tablespoons mayonnaise or salad dressing

1 tablespoon chopped green chilies, well drained

1 tablespoon vegetable oil

4 flour or corn tortillas (8 or 6 inches in diameter)

1. Heat coals or gas grill for direct heat (page 16).

2. Prepare Fresh Tomato Salsa.

3. Mix cheeses, onions, mayonnaise and chilies.

4. Lightly brush oil on one side of 2 tortillas. Place tortillas, oil sides down, on grill screen or work surface. Spread each with half of the cheese mixture. Top with remaining tortillas; gently press down. Brush tops with remaining oil.

5. Grill tortillas uncovered 4 inches from MEDIUM heat 2 to 4 minutes, turning once, until cheese begins to melt and tortillas begin to brown (watch carefully).

6. To serve, cut quesadillas into wedges. Serve with Fresh Tomato Salsa.

1 Serving: Calories 285 (Calories from Fat 155); Fat 17g (Saturated 6g); Cholesterol 20mg; Sodium 440mg; Carbohydrate 25g (Dietary Fiber 1g); Protein 9g.

Crispy Honey Wings

PREP: 15 MIN; GRILL: 25 MIN

MAKES 32 APPETIZERS

16 chicken wings (about 3 pounds)

3/4 cup honey

1/4 cup white Worcestershire sauce

1/2 teaspoon ground ginger

1. Brush grill rack with vegetable oil. Heat coals or gas grill for direct heat (page 16).

2. Cut each chicken wing at joints to make 3 pieces; discard tip.

3. Mix remaining ingredients.

4. Grill chicken uncovered 4 to 6 inches from MEDIUM heat 20 to 25 minutes, brushing frequently with honey mixture and turning after 10 minutes, until juice of chicken is no longer pink when centers of thickest pieces are cut. Discard any remaining honey mixture.

1 Appetizer: Calories 75 (Calories from Fat 35); Fat 4g (Saturated 1g); Cholesterol 15mg; Sodium 30mg; Carbohydrate 6g (Dietary Fiber 0g); Protein 4g.

Stuffed Focaccia

PREP: 15 MIN; GRILL: 7 MIN

MAKES **6** SERVINGS

By using a grill screen, this sandwich is a snap to move to and from the grill.

1 loaf focaccia bread (8 to 9 inches in diameter)

1/2 cup chopped drained sun-dried tomatoes in oil (reserve 2 tablespoons oil)

1 cup shredded mozzarella cheese (4 ounces)

1 1/2 teaspoons chopped fresh or 1/2 teaspoon dried rosemary leaves

1 1/2 teaspoons chopped fresh or 1/2 teaspoon dried thyme leaves

1/4 teaspoon pepper

1. Brush grill rack with vegetable oil. Heat coals or gas grill for direct heat (page 16).

2. Cut focaccia horizontally in half. Lightly brush outsides and cut sides of both halves with reserved tomato oil. Place bottom half on grill screen or work surface. Sprinkle with cheese to about 1/4 inch from edge; gently press in cheese. Top with tomatoes. Sprinkle with rosemary, thyme and pepper. Top with other focaccia half; gently press down.

3. Cover and grill focaccia 5 to 6 inches from MEDIUM heat 5 to 7 minutes, turning once, until cheese is melted and focaccia is slightly toasted (watch carefully).

4. To serve, cut focaccia into wedges. Serve warm.

1 Serving: Calories 200 (Calories from Fat 90); Fat 10g (Saturated 3g); Cholesterol 10mg; Sodium 300mg; Carbohydrate 20g (Dietary Fiber 1g); Protein 8g.

Italian Stuffed Mushrooms

PREP: 15 MIN; GRILL: 20 MIN

MAKES **4** TO **6** SERVINGS

1 pound large white mushrooms (about 2 1/2 inches in diameter)

1/2 cup soft bread crumbs

2 tablespoons chopped fresh or 2 teaspoons dried basil leaves

1 tablespoon grated Parmesan cheese

1 tablespoon olive or vegetable oil

Dash of salt

2 cloves garlic, finely chopped

1. Heat coals or gas grill for direct heat (page 16). Brush 8-inch square aluminum foil pan with vegetable oil.

2. Remove stems from mushrooms. Place mushroom tops, stem sides up, in pan. Chop mushroom stems. Mix chopped mushroom stems and remaining ingredients; spoon onto mushroom tops. Cover pan with aluminum foil, sealing edges securely.

3. Cover and grill mushrooms 4 to 6 inches from MEDIUM heat 15 to 20 minutes or until mushrooms are tender.

1 Serving: Calories 125 (Calories from Fat 45); Fat 5g (Saturated 1g); Cholesterol 0mg; Sodium 170mg; Carbohydrate 16g (Dietary Fiber 2g); Protein 4g.

Continued on next page

Roasted Garlic with French Bread

PREP: 5 MIN; GRILL: 35 MIN

MAKES 6 SERVINGS

If you like roasted garlic, double the amount and use the extra for making garlic butter or add it to mashed potatoes.

2 large bulbs garlic

2 tablespoons olive or vegetable oil

Salt and pepper, if desired

12 thin slices French bread

1. Heat coals or gas grill for direct heat (page 16).

2. Peel loose paperlike layers from garlic bulbs, but do not separate cloves. Place each garlic bulb on 12-inch square of heavy-duty aluminum foil. Brush generously with oil. Sprinkle with salt and pepper. Wrap foil securely around bulbs.

3. Cover and grill garlic 4 inches from MEDIUM heat 25 to 35 minutes or until cloves are very soft. Add bread for last 5 minutes of grilling, turning once, until golden brown.

4. To serve, squeeze garlic pulp from papery skin onto bread and spread.

1 Serving: Calories 140 (Calories from Fat 55); Fat 6g (Saturated 1g); Cholesterol 0mg; Sodium 180mg; Carbohydrate 19g (Dietary Fiber 1g); Protein 3g.

Zucchini Bites

PREP: 15 MIN; MARINATE: 15 MIN; GRILL: 4 MIN

MAKES 6 SERVINGS (ABOUT 24 PIECES)

Using a grill screen prevents the bite-size vegetables from slipping through the grill grids. If a screen is not available, use 2 layers of heavy-duty aluminum foil punched with holes; a cookie sheet is useful to transfer the foil to and from the grill.

1/2 cup Italian dressing

1/2 teaspoon Italian seasoning

1/4 teaspoon cracked black pepper

2 medium zucchini, cut into 1/2-inch slices

3/4 cup grated Parmesan cheese

1. Mix dressing, Italian seasoning and pepper in shallow nonmetal dish or resealable plastic bag. Add zucchini, turning to coat with marinade. Cover dish or seal bag and let stand at least 15 minutes but no longer than 1 hour.

2. Heat coals or gas grill for direct heat (page 16). Brush grilling screen with vegetable oil.

3. Drain zucchini; discard marinade. Toss cheese and 4 to 6 slices zucchini at a time in resealable plastic bag, coating zucchini with cheese.

4. Place zucchini on grilling screen. Grill zucchini uncovered 4 inches from MEDIUM heat 3 to 4 minutes, turning 2 or 3 times, until cheese is light brown and zucchini is crisp-tender.

1 Serving: Calories 150 (Calories from Fat 115); Fat 13g (Saturated 4g); Cholesterol 10mg; Sodium 340mg; Carbohydrate 4g (Dietary Fiber 1g); Protein 5g.

Eggplant Dip

PREP: 15 MIN; **GRILL:** 30 MIN

MAKES ABOUT $1^{1}/_{2}$ CUPS DIP

Tahini is a thick paste made from ground sesame seed, and it gives this dip Mediterranean flair.

1 medium eggplant (about 2 pounds)

4 to 5 tablespoons lemon juice

1/4 cup sesame seed paste (tahini)

1 teaspoon salt

2 cloves garlic, crushed

2 teaspoons olive or vegetable oil

2 tablespoons chopped fresh parsley

Paprika

Greek or ripe olives, if desired

Crackers or toasted pita bread wedges, if desired

1. Brush grill rack with vegetable oil. Heat coals or gas grill for direct heat (page 16).

2. Pierce eggplant in several places with long-tined fork. Cover and grill eggplant 4 inches from MEDIUM heat 20 to 30 minutes, turning frequently, until eggplant is very soft and skin is charred. Place eggplant in wire colander over bowl or in sink about 30 minutes to drain and cool.

3. Cut eggplant lengthwise in half. Scoop out and finely chop eggplant pulp. Mix eggplant, lemon juice, sesame seed paste, salt and garlic. Spoon eggplant mixture into shallow serving bowl; flatten top of mixture with back of spoon. Drizzle with oil and sprinkle with parsley and paprika.

4. Garnish eggplant dip with olives. Serve with crackers.

1 Serving: Calories 25 (Calories from Fat 20); Fat 2g (Saturated 0g); Cholesterol 0mg; Sodium 100mg; Carbohydrate 2g (Dietary Fiber 1g); Protein 1g.

Seafood Salad Vinaigrette

PREP: 20 MIN; MARINATE: 1 HR; GRILL: 20 MIN

MAKES **6** SERVINGS

Shallot-Thyme Vinaigrette (right)

12 uncooked large shrimp in shells (about 3/4 pound)

1 pound marlin, swordfish or tuna steaks, 3/4 to 1 inch thick

1 medium bulb fennel, cut crosswise into 6 slices

10 leaves romaine, coarsely shredded

1 small bunch arugula, torn into bite-size pieces

1 can (14 ounces) artichoke hearts, drained, or 5 or 6 stalks canned hearts of palm, drained and cut into 1-inch pieces

1/2 small red onion, thinly sliced

12 cherry tomatoes

12 Kalamata or ripe olives

1. Prepare Shallot-Thyme Vinaigrette.

2. Peel shrimp. (If shrimp are frozen, do not thaw; peel in cold water.) Make a shallow cut lengthwise down back of each shrimp; wash out vein. Place shrimp, fish and 1/4 cup of the vinaigrette in shallow nonmetal dish or resealable plastic bag. Turn fish and shrimp to coat with marinade or turn bag. Cover dish or seal bag and refrigerate 1 hour. Reserve remaining vinaigrette to serve with salad.

3. Brush grill rack with vegetable oil. Heat coals or gas grill for direct heat (page 16).

4. Remove fish and shrimp from marinade; reserve marinade. Cover and grill fish and fennel 5 to 6 inches from MEDIUM heat 5 minutes; brush with marinade. Add shrimp. Cover and grill 10 to 15 minutes, turning and brushing fish, fennel and shrimp with marinade 2 or 3 times, until shrimp are pink and firm, fish flakes easily with fork and fennel is tender.

5. To serve, cut fish into bite-size pieces. Arrange romaine and arugula on serving platter. Arrange fish, fennel, shrimp and remaining ingredients on top. Serve with remaining reserved vinaigrette.

SHALLOT-THYME VINAIGRETTE

1/2 cup olive or vegetable oil

1/4 cup balsamic vinegar

1 tablespoon finely chopped shallot

1 tablespoon chopped fresh or 1 teaspoon dried thyme leaves

1 tablespoon Dijon mustard

2 tablespoons white wine vinegar

1/4 teaspoon salt

Mix all ingredients. About 1 cup.

1 Serving: Calories 320 (Calories from Fat 205); Fat 23g (Saturated 4g); Cholesterol 70mg; Sodium 460mg; Carbohydrate 13g (Dietary Fiber 5g); Protein 20g.

Dilled Scallops
with Orange-Chive Mayonnaise

PREP: 20 MIN; GRILL: 10 MIN

MAKES 4 SERVINGS

Orange-Chive Mayonnaise (right)

1/4 cup margarine or butter, melted

2 tablespoons chopped fresh or 2 teaspoons dried dill weed

4 teaspoons orange-flavored liqueur or orange juice

1/4 teaspoon salt

1 pound sea scallops

1. Heat coals or gas grill for direct heat (page 16). Spray hinged wire grill basket with vegetable oil.

2. Prepare Orange-Chive Mayonnaise.

3. Mix margarine, dill weed, liqueur and salt in medium bowl. Stir in scallops until well coated with margarine mixture. Place scallops in basket.

4. Cover and grill scallops 4 inches from MEDIUM heat 8 to 10 minutes or until scallops are white.

5. Serve scallops with Orange-Chive Mayonnaise.

ORANGE-CHIVE MAYONNAISE

1/2 cup mayonnaise or salad dressing

1 tablespoon chopped fresh chives or green onion tops

1 teaspoon grated orange peel

Mix all ingredients. Cover and refrigerate no longer than 24 hours. About 1/2 cup.

1 Serving: Calories 385 (Calories from Fat 260); Fat 29g (Saturated 5g); Cholesterol 50mg; Sodium 600mg; Carbohydrate 5g (Dietary Fiber 0g); Protein 26g.

Lobster Roast

PREP: 20 MIN; GRILL: 15 MIN

MAKES 2 TO 6 SERVINGS

The number of lobsters you can grill at one time is limited only by your budget and the size of your grill!

**Live lobsters (each 1 to 1 1/4 pounds)
(see note at right)**

Margarine or butter, melted

Lemon wedges, if desired

French bread, if desired

1. Allow one lobster per person. Carefully cut lobsters lengthwise in half with sharp knife or poultry shears. Remove the dark vein that runs through the center of the body and the stomach, which is just behind the head. Leave the green liver and the coral roe, which are delicacies.

2. Brush grill rack with vegetable oil. Heat coals or gas grill for direct heat (page 16).

3. Brush lobster meat generously with margarine. Place lobster halves, shell sides down, on grill. Grill uncovered about 4 inches from MEDIUM-HOT heat 10 to 15 minutes, brushing frequently with margarine, until meat turns white. Don't turn during grilling or you'll lose the juices that collect in the shell.

4. Serve lobsters hot with lemon wedges, additional melted margarine and French bread.

Note: If you'd prefer not to cut a live lobster, parboil it in enough boiling water to cover for 5 to 10 minutes, then cut in half.

1 Serving: Calories 300 (Calories from Fat 205); Fat 23g (Saturated 5g); Cholesterol 75mg; Sodium 660mg; Carbohydrate 2g (Dietary Fiber 0g); Protein 21g.

Seafood Paella

PREP: 30 MIN; GRILL: 1 HR

MAKES 4 SERVINGS

1/2 pound uncooked large shrimp in shells (about 6)

1/2 pound bay or sea scallops

8 mussels

1/3 cup olive or vegetable oil

1 medium onion, chopped (1/2 cup)

2 cloves garlic, crushed

1 cup uncooked regular long grain rice

2 1/2 cups chicken broth

1 can (14 1/2 ounces) whole tomatoes, drained

1/2 teaspoon ground saffron or 1/4 teaspoon ground turmeric

1/4 teaspoon salt

4 crab claws

1 jar (2 ounces) sliced pimientos, drained

2 tablespoons chopped fresh parsley

Lemon wedges

1. Peel shrimp. (If shrimp are frozen, do not thaw; peel in cold water.) Make a shallow cut lengthwise down back of each shrimp; wash out vein. If using sea scallops, cut each in half.

2. Discard any broken-shell or open (dead) mussels. Scrub remaining mussels in cold water, removing any barnacles with a dull paring knife. Remove beards. Place mussels in large container. Cover with cool water. Agitate water with hand, then drain and discard water. Repeat several times until water runs clear; drain.

3. Heat coals or gas grill for direct heat (page 16).

4. Place 14-inch paella pan or ovenproof skillet about 4 inches from MEDIUM heat. Heat oil in pan. Cook shrimp in oil on grill 4 to 6 minutes, stirring frequently, just until pink and firm; remove with slotted spoon. Cook scallops in same pan 3 to 5 minutes, stirring frequently, until white; remove with slotted spoon.

5. Cook onion and garlic in same pan about 5 minutes, stirring frequently, until onion is light brown. Stir in rice. Cook 5 minutes, stirring frequently. Stir in broth, tomatoes, saffron and salt, breaking up tomatoes. Cook 10 minutes, stirring frequently. Add shrimp and scallops to rice mixture.

6. Cover and grill 10 to 15 minutes or until most of the liquid is absorbed. Place mussels and crab claws on top of mixture. Cover and grill 10 to 15 minutes, removing mussels as they open, until all mussels are open, liquid is absorbed and rice is tender. (Add small amount of water if liquid is absorbed before rice is tender.) Discard any mussels that do not open.

7. To serve, garnish paella with pimientos, parsley and lemon wedges.

1 Serving: Calories 500 (Calories from Fat 190); Fat 21g (Saturated 3g); Cholesterol 90mg; Sodium 1120mg; Carbohydrate 48g (Dietary Fiber 2g); Protein 32g.

Herbed Seafood

PREP: 20 MIN; **GRILL: 10** MIN

MAKES **4** SERVINGS

For a special touch, grill the seafood in natural baking shells, which are found at some supermarkets or kitchen specialty stores. Spray each shell with nonstick cooking spray before filling, then enclose each in a 12-inch square of aluminum foil. Cover and grill 5 to 7 minutes.

1/2 pound uncooked large shrimp in shells

1/2 pound bay or sea scallops

**1/2 pound orange roughy fillets, cut into
    1-inch pieces**

**2 tablespoons chopped fresh or 2 teaspoons
    dried marjoram leaves**

1/2 teaspoon grated lemon peel

1/8 teaspoon white pepper

3 tablespoons margarine or butter, melted

2 tablespoons lemon juice

4 cups hot cooked pasta or rice

1. Heat coals or gas grill for direct heat (page 16).

2. If shrimp, scallops or fish are frozen, do not thaw; rinse in cold water. Peel shrimp. Make a shallow cut lengthwise down back of each shrimp; wash out vein. If using sea scallops, cut each in half.

3. Spray 18-inch square piece of heavy-duty aluminum foil with nonstick cooking spray. Arrange shrimp, scallops and fish on foil, placing shrimp on top. Sprinkle with marjoram, lemon peel and white pepper. Drizzle with margarine and lemon juice. Bring corners of foil up to center and seal loosely.

4. Cover and grill foil packet 4 inches from MEDIUM heat 8 to 10 minutes or until scallops are white, fish flakes easily with fork and shrimp are pink and firm.

5. Serve seafood mixture over pasta.

1 Serving: Calories 370 (Calories from Fat 100); Fat 11g (Saturated 3g); Cholesterol 130mg; Sodium 390mg; Carbohydrate 32g (Dietary Fiber 1g); Protein 37g.

Flavor Boosters

For your convenience, here is a list of sauces in this chapter.

Lemon Caper Sauce 124

Ginger-Lime Marinade 125

Tomato-Basil Butter 126

Cucumber Relish 130

Garden Vegetable Stuffing 131

Creole Sauce 132

Spicy Peanut Sauce 133

Lemon-Mustard Sauce 134

Herb Mayonnaise 136

Buttery Herb Sauce 137

Shallot-Thyme Vinaigrette 144

Orange-Chive Mayonnaise 146

6

Pizza, Sandwiches and Bread

Italian Sausage-Spinach Pizza (page 152),
Caramelized Onion Pizza (page 153)

Italian Sausage-Spinach Pizza

PREP: 30 MIN; GRILL: 5 MIN

MAKES 6 SERVINGS

Suit your taste buds by choosing hot or mild Italian sausage.

3/4 pound bulk Italian sausage

1 medium red bell pepper, chopped (1 cup)

1 medium onion, chopped (1/2 cup)

1/2 package (10-ounce size) fresh spinach leaves, chopped (3 cups)

1-pound loaf frozen bread dough, thawed

1 tablespoon olive or vegetable oil

1 can (6 ounces) Italian-style tomato paste

1 cup shredded mozzarella cheese (4 ounces)

1. Brush grill rack with vegetable oil. Heat coals or gas grill for direct heat (page 16).

2. Cook sausage in 10-inch skillet over medium heat about 10 minutes, stirring occasionally, until no longer pink; drain. Stir in bell pepper and onion. Cook about 5 minutes, stirring occasionally, until vegetables are crisp-tender. Stir in spinach; remove from heat. Cover and set aside.

3. Divide bread dough into 6 parts. Roll or pat each part into 6-inch round on lightly floured surface. Brush top of each round with oil.

4. Grill dough rounds, oil sides down, uncovered 4 to 6 inches from HIGH heat about 2 minutes or until bottoms of crusts are light brown. Remove crusts from grill, and place brown sides up on cookie sheet.

5. Spread 2 tablespoons tomato paste on each crust. Top crusts with sausage mixture. Sprinkle with cheese.

6. Slide pizzas from cookie sheet onto grill. Cover and grill 3 to 5 minutes or until bottoms of crusts are brown and cheese is melted.

1 Serving: Calories 485 (Calories from Fat 205); Fat 23g (Saturated 9g); Cholesterol 55mg; Sodium 1280mg; Carbohydrate 48g (Dietary Fiber 4g); Protein 25g.

Pizza Mexicana

PREP: 10 MIN; GRILL: 10 MIN

MAKES 4 SERVINGS

2 cups shredded taco-seasoned cheese (8 ounces)

1 package (16 ounces) Italian bread shell or ready-to-serve pizza crust (12 to 14 inches in diameter)

2 roma (plum) tomatoes, thinly sliced

1 small jalapeño chili, seeded and finely chopped

2 tablespoons chopped fresh cilantro

1. Brush grill rack with vegetable oil. Heat coals or gas grill for direct heat (page 16).

2. Sprinkle cheese evenly over bread shell. Top with remaining ingredients.

3. Cover and grill pizza 4 to 6 inches from MEDIUM heat 8 to 10 minutes or until crust is crisp and cheese is melted. (If crust browns too quickly, place a piece of aluminum foil between crust and grill.)

1 Serving: Calories 750 (Calories from Fat 225); Fat 25g (Saturated 12g); Cholesterol 60mg; Sodium 1180mg; Carbohydrate 108g (Dietary Fiber 4g); Protein 27g.

Caramelized Onion Pizza

PREP: 15 MIN; GRILL: 20 MIN

MAKES 4 SERVINGS

Cooking the onions until they are golden brown caramelizes the natural sugars for a rich, mellow flavor.

1 container (8 ounces) soft cream cheese

1/4 cup grated Romano cheese

3 tablespoons chopped fresh or 1 tablespoon dried basil leaves

1/4 teaspoon pepper

3 tablespoons margarine or butter

2 large onions, chopped (2 cups)

1 loaf (8 ounces) or 1/2 loaf (1-pound size) unsliced French bread

2 roma (plum) tomatoes, chopped

1. Heat coals or gas grill for direct heat (page 16).

2. Mix cream cheese, Romano cheese, basil and pepper in medium bowl; set aside. Place margarine in 9-inch round aluminum foil pan.

3. Grill margarine in pan uncovered 4 to 6 inches from HIGH heat about 2 minutes or until margarine is melted. Stir in onions and coat with margarine. Grill uncovered 10 to 15 minutes, stirring occasionally, until onions are golden. Remove pan from grill.

4. Cut bread horizontally in half; cut each piece crosswise in half. Grill bread, cut sides down, 1 to 2 minutes or until toasted.

5. Stir onions into cheese mixture. Spread mixture on toasted sides of bread. Top with tomatoes.

6. Cover and grill pizzas 4 to 6 inches from MEDIUM heat 2 to 3 minutes or until hot.

1 Serving: Calories 485 (Calories from Fat 290); Fat 32g (Saturated 16g); Cholesterol 65mg; Sodium 700mg; Carbohydrate 39g (Dietary Fiber 3g); Protein 13g.

Goat Cheese-Artichoke Pizzas

PREP: 10 MIN; GRILL: 10 MIN

MAKES 4 SERVINGS

1 package (3 1/2 ounces) fresh chèvre (goat) cheese (with herbs or plain)

2 packages (8 ounces each) Italian bread shells or 4 pita breads (6 inches in diameter)

1 can (14 ounces) artichoke hearts, drained and cut in half

3 tablespoons chopped drained oil-packed sun-dried tomatoes

2 tablespoons chopped pitted Kalamata olives

1 tablespoon chopped fresh parsley

1. Brush grill rack with vegetable oil. Heat coals or gas grill for direct heat (page 16).

2. Spread cheese evenly over each bread shell. Top with remaining ingredients.

3. Cover and grill pizzas 4 to 6 inches from MEDIUM heat 5 to 10 minutes or until crusts are crisp and vegetables are hot. (If crusts brown too quickly, place a piece of aluminum foil between crusts and grill.)

1 Serving: Calories 290 (Calories from Fat 80); Fat 9g (Saturated 5g); Cholesterol 25mg; Sodium 740mg; Carbohydrate 44g (Dietary Fiber 6g); Protein 14g.

Pizza Turnovers

PREP: 20 MIN; GRILL: 20 MIN

MAKES 4 SERVINGS

1 can (10 ounces) refrigerated pizza crust dough

1/4 cup spaghetti sauce

6 ounces sliced smoked turkey

1 cup shredded provolone or mozzarella cheese (4 ounces)

4 medium green onions, sliced (1/2 cup)

2 tablespoons chopped fresh or 2 teaspoons dried basil leaves

2 teaspoons olive or vegetable oil

3/4 cup spaghetti sauce

1. Heat coals or gas grill for direct heat (page 16).

2. Roll pizza crust dough on lightly floured surface into 12-inch square. Cut dough into four 6-inch squares. Brush half of each square with 1 tablespoon of the 1/4 cup spaghetti sauce to within 1/2 inch of edges. Top with turkey, cheese, onions and basil. Fold each square in half over filling; press edges to seal. Brush both sides with oil. Place turnovers on double thickness piece of heavy-duty aluminum foil. Do not wrap foil around turnovers.

3. Cover and grill turnovers 4 to 6 inches from MEDIUM heat about 20 minutes, turning after 10 minutes, until golden brown on both sides. Place spaghetti sauce in small pan or food can with label removed and heat during last 10 minutes of grilling.

4. Serve turnovers with 3/4 cup spaghetti sauce.

1 Serving: Calories 435 (Calories from Fat 170); Fat 19g (Saturated 7g); Cholesterol 60mg; Sodium 1040mg; Carbohydrate 42g (Dietary Fiber 2g); Protein 26g.

Pizza Turnovers

Foot-Long Coney Dogs

PREP: 10 MIN; GRILL: 20 MIN

MAKES 6 SERVINGS

These foot-longs would make any kid's backyard birthday party something special!

6 long hot dogs (each about 12 inches)

1 tablespoon margarine or butter, melted

1 can (15 ounces) chili with beans

6 long hot dog buns, split

3/4 cup shredded Cheddar cheese (3 ounces)

1 large onion, chopped (1 cup)

1. Brush grill rack with vegetable oil. Heat coals or gas grill for direct heat (page 16).

2. Cut crosswise diagonal slashes 1/2 inch apart and 1/4 inch deep in each hot dog.

3. Grill hot dogs uncovered 4 to 5 inches from MEDIUM heat 15 to 20 minutes, turning frequently and brushing occasionally with margarine, until hot and slashes begin to open. Remove label and top from can of chili. Add opened can of chili to grill for last 10 minutes of grilling, stirring occasionally, until hot.

4. Serve hot dogs on buns with chili, cheese and onion.

1 Serving: Calories 630 (Calories from Fat 335); Fat 37g (Saturated 14g); Cholesterol 60mg; Sodium 1830mg; Carbohydrate 55g (Dietary Fiber 4g); Protein 23g.

Sizzling Sausage Hoagie

PREP: 10 MIN; GRILL: 12 MIN

MAKES 6 SERVINGS

A flat-bladed skewer works best for this recipe as the sausage and bell pepper won't spin on the skewer when you turn it. If you don't have a flat-bladed skewer, thread sausages and peppers on two round-bladed skewers placed side by side.

6 fully cooked sausages or hot dogs

1 large bell pepper, cut into 6 strips

About 3/4 cup Italian dressing

1 loaf (1 pound) unsliced French bread, cut horizontally in half

Spicy brown mustard, if desired

1. Brush grill rack with vegetable oil. Heat coals or gas grill for direct heat (page 16).

2. Thread whole sausages and bell pepper strips crosswise alternately on 14-inch flat metal skewer. Brush dressing on cut sides of bread.

3. Grill sausages and pepper strips uncovered about 6 inches from MEDIUM heat 8 to 12 minutes, turning and brushing frequently with dressing, until brown. Add bread, cut sides down, for last 3 to 4 minutes of grilling until golden brown.

4. To serve, place skewer of sausages and pepper strips on bottom half of bread. Top with top of bread; pull out skewer. Cut bread crosswise into 6 servings. Serve with mustard.

1 Serving: Calories 610 (Calories from Fat 370); Fat 41g (Saturated 12g); Cholesterol 60mg; Sodium 1420mg; Carbohydrate 43g (Dietary Fiber 2g); Protein 19g.

Italian Sausages with Peperonata

PREP: 20 MIN; COOK: 25 MIN; GRILL: 25 MIN

MAKES 4 SERVINGS

4 uncooked hot or mild Italian sausage links (about 1 pound)

Peperonata (right)

4 hot dog buns, split

1. Brush grill rack with vegetable oil. Heat coals or gas grill for direct heat (page 16).

2. Cover and grill sausages 4 to 5 inches from MEDIUM heat about 25 minutes, turning occasionally, until no longer pink in center. Add buns, cut sides down, for last 3 to 4 minutes of grilling or until toasted.

3. While sausages are grilling, prepare Peperonata.

4. Serve sausages on buns with Peperonata.

PEPERONATA

2 tablespoons olive or vegetable oil

2 medium onions, sliced and separated into rings

2 cloves garlic, finely chopped

1 tablespoon chopped fresh or 1 teaspoon dried basil leaves

2 teaspoons chopped fresh or 1/2 teaspoon dried oregano leaves

2 teaspoons lemon juice

1/2 teaspoon salt

1/4 teaspoon pepper

2 medium green bell peppers, cut into 1/2-inch strips

2 medium red bell peppers, cut into 1/2-inch strips

1 can (4 ounces) sliced ripe olives, drained

Heat oil in 10-inch skillet over medium heat. Cook onions and garlic in oil, stirring frequently, until onions are tender. Stir in remaining ingredients except olives; reduce heat to low. Cover and simmer 15 to 20 minutes, stirring occasionally, until peppers are very soft. Stir in olives. About 3 cups.

1 Serving: Calories 605 (Calories from Fat 370); Fat 41g (Saturated 13g); Cholesterol 90mg; Sodium 1770mg; Carbohydrate 35g (Dietary Fiber 4g); Protein 28g.

Barbecued Burritos

PREP: 25 MIN; MARINATE: 8 HR; GRILL: 35 MIN

MAKES 6 SERVINGS

Brushing the folded burritos with barbecue sauce before grilling is a bit unusual, but the wonderful flavor is well worth it!

1-pound beef boneless top round steak, about 1 inch thick

Mexican Marinade (right)

Orange-Jicama Salsa (page 203), if desired

3/4 cup Spicy Texas Barbecue Sauce (page 198) or prepared barbecue sauce

6 flour tortillas (10 inches in diameter)

1 cup shredded Cheddar cheese (4 ounces)

1 medium onion, chopped (1/2 cup)

1 medium tomato, chopped (3/4 cup)

1 medium avocado, chopped

1. Pierce beef with fork several times on both sides. Prepare Mexican Marinade. Add beef, turning to coat with marinade. Cover dish or seal bag and refrigerate, turning beef occasionally, at least 8 hours but no longer than 24 hours.

2. Prepare Orange-Jicama Salsa and Spicy Texas Barbecue Sauce.

3. Brush grill rack with vegetable oil. Heat coals or gas grill for direct heat (page 16).

4. Wrap tortillas in heavy-duty aluminum foil.

5. Remove beef from marinade; discard marinade. Cover and grill beef 4 to 5 inches from MEDIUM heat 25 to 30 minutes for medium doneness, turning once. Add packet of tortillas for last 5 minutes of grilling, turning occasionally, until warm.

6. Cut beef across grain into thin slices. Place beef, cheese, onion, tomato and avocado on center of each tortilla. Fold one end of tortilla up about 1 inch over filling; fold right and left sides over folded end, overlapping. Fold remaining end down. Brush burritos with Spicy Texas Barbecue Sauce.

7. Grill burritos uncovered 4 to 5 inches from MEDIUM heat 5 minutes, turning once, until hot.

8. Serve burritos with Orange-Jicama Salsa.

MEXICAN MARINADE

1 can (5 1/2 ounces) spicy eight-vegetable juice

2 tablespoons lime juice

1 tablespoon vegetable oil

1/4 teaspoon salt

Mix all ingredients in shallow nonmetal dish or resealable plastic bag. About 1/2 cup.

1 Serving: Calories 395 (Calories from Fat 160); Fat 18g (Saturated 7g); Cholesterol 60mg; Sodium 690mg; Carbohydrate 37g (Dietary Fiber 4g); Protein 25g.

Hearty Ham and Vegetable Sandwiches

PREP: 15 MIN; GRILL: 15 MIN

MAKES 4 SERVINGS

1/3 cup mayonnaise or salad dressing

1/4 cup chopped drained pepperoncini peppers

2 tablespoons chopped ripe olives

1-pound fully cooked ham slice, 1/2 inch thick

1 large red bell pepper, cut into 8 strips

4 slices small onion, 1/4 inch thick, separated into rings

4 whole wheat sandwich buns, split

1. Brush grill rack with vegetable oil. Heat coals or gas grill for direct heat (page 16).

2. Mix mayonnaise, pepperoncini peppers and olives; cover and refrigerate. Cut ham slice into 4 pieces.

3. Cover and grill ham, bell pepper strips and onion slices 4 to 6 inches from MEDIUM heat about 15 minutes, turning after 5 minutes, until vegetables are crisp-tender. Add buns, cut sides down, for last 2 minutes of grilling. until toasted.

4. To serve, spread cut sides of buns with mayonnaise mixture. Fill buns with ham, bell pepper and onion.

1 Serving: Calories 445 (Calories from Fat 245); Fat 27g (Saturated 7g); Cholesterol 80mg; Sodium 2060mg; Carbohydrate 24g (Dietary Fiber 4g); Protein 30g.

Cajun Chicken Sandwiches

PREP: 10 MIN; MARINATE: 1 HR; GRILL: 20 MIN

MAKES 4 OPEN-FACE SANDWICHES

1/4 cup dry sherry or apple juice

1 teaspoon Worcestershire sauce

1/4 teaspoon ground red pepper (cayenne)

1/4 teaspoon black pepper

1/8 to 1/4 teaspoon red pepper sauce

4 skinless boneless chicken breast halves (about 1 pound)

4 slices French bread, 1 inch thick

4 slices tomato

4 slices red bell pepper

1. Mix sherry, Worcestershire sauce, red pepper, black pepper and pepper sauce in shallow non-metal dish or resealable plastic bag. Add chicken, turning to coat with marinade. Cover dish or seal bag and refrigerate at least 1 hour but no longer than 24 hours.

2. Brush grill rack with vegetable oil. Heat coals or gas grill for direct heat (page 16).

3. Remove chicken from marinade; reserve marinade. Grill chicken uncovered 4 to 6 inches from MEDIUM heat 15 to 20 minutes, brushing frequently with marinade and turning once, until juice is no longer pink when centers of thickest pieces are cut. Discard any remaining marinade.

4. To serve, place chicken on bread. Top with tomato and bell pepper.

1 Serving: Calories 230 (Calories from Fat 35); Fat 4g (Saturated 2g); Cholesterol 60mg; Sodium 280mg; Carbohydrate 21g (Dietary Fiber 1g); Protein 28g.

Niçoise Sandwiches

PREP: 20 MIN; GRILL: 10 MIN

MAKES 6 OPEN-FACE SANDWICHES

Now you can have the wonderful flavor of Salade Niçoise in a grilled sandwich.

1 package (9 ounces) frozen French-style green beans, cooked and drained

1 container (6.5 ounces) herb-and-garlic spreadable cheese

1 can (6 ounces) tuna, drained

1 medium tomato, chopped (3/4 cup)

1 small onion, chopped (1/4 cup)

1 teaspoon lemon juice

6 English muffins, split

1/4 cup sliced ripe olives

1. Brush grill rack with vegetable oil. Heat coals or gas grill for direct heat (page 16).

2. Mix all ingredients except muffins and olives. Spoon onto cut sides of muffin halves.

3. Cover and grill sandwiches 4 to 6 inches from MEDIUM heat 5 to 10 minutes or until muffins are crisp and topping is hot.

4. To serve, top sandwiches with olives.

1 Sandwich: Calories 255 (Calories from Fat 80); Fat 9g (Saturated 5g); Cholesterol 30mg; Sodium 540mg; Carbohydrate 32g (Dietary Fiber 3g); Protein 15g.

Texas Toast

PREP: 5 MIN; GRILL: 6 MIN

MAKES 4 SERVINGS

Known for its hearty thickness, Texas Toast is often served with ribs and other grilled meats and barbecue sauce.

1/4 cup margarine or butter, softened

4 slices white bread, about 1 inch thick

1/2 teaspoon seasoned salt or garlic salt

1. Brush grill rack with vegetable oil. Heat coals or gas grill for direct heat (page 16).

2. Spread margarine on both sides of bread slices. Sprinkle with seasoned salt.

3. Grill bread uncovered 4 inches from MEDIUM heat 4 to 6 minutes, turning once, until golden brown.

1 Serving: Calories 230 (Calories from Fat 115); Fat 13g (Saturated 3g); Cholesterol 0mg; Sodium 570mg; Carbohydrate 25g (Dietary Fiber 1g); Protein 4g.

Bruschetta

PREP: 10 MIN; GRILL: 6 MIN

MAKES 4 SERVINGS

The name of this traditional Italian garlic bread means "to roast over coals." Olive oil is used generously, and for the best flavor, try extra-virgin oil. If you like, sprinkle the bruschetta with salt and pepper before grilling.

1/2 cup olive or vegetable oil

2 tablespoons chopped fresh or 2 teaspoons dried basil leaves

2 cloves garlic, crushed

1 loaf unsliced French bread (about 12 inches), cut horizontally in half

1. Brush grill rack with vegetable oil. Heat coals or gas grill for direct heat (page 16).

2. Mix oil, basil and garlic. Brush or drizzle on cut sides of bread.

3. Grill bread uncovered, 4 inches from MEDIUM heat about 6 minutes, turning once, until golden brown.

4. To serve, cut into 1/2-inch slices.

1 Serving: Calories 440 (Calories from Fat 270); Fat 30g (Saturated 5g); Cholesterol 0mg; Sodium 440mg; Carbohydrate 38g (Dietary Fiber 2g); Protein 7g.

Stuffed French Bread

PREP: 15 MIN; GRILL: 10 MIN

MAKES 6 SERVINGS

1/3 cup Sun-Dried Tomato Pesto (page 199) or prepared pesto

1 loaf (8 ounces) or 1/2 loaf (1-pound size) unsliced French bread

1 cup shredded mozzarella cheese (4 ounces)

1. Prepare Sun-Dried Tomato Pesto.

2. Brush grill rack with vegetable oil. Heat coals or gas grill for direct heat (page 16).

3. Cut bread loaf diagonally into 12 slices to within 1/2 inch of bottom of loaf. Spread pesto on both sides of slices. Sprinkle slices with cheese. Securely wrap loaf in 18-inch piece heavy-duty aluminum foil.

4. Grill bread uncovered 5 to 6 inches from MEDIUM heat about 10 minutes, turning once, until hot.

1 Serving: Calories 235 (Calories from Fat 115); Fat 13g (Saturated 4g); Cholesterol 10mg; Sodium 370mg; Carbohydrate 20g (Dietary Fiber 1g); Protein 10g.

Sesame-Parmesan Slices

PREP: 10 MIN; GRILL: 12 MIN

MAKES 6 SERVINGS

1/4 cup margarine or butter, softened
1/2 cup grated Parmesan cheese
6 slices French or Vienna bread, 1 inch thick
1 tablespoon sesame seed

1. Brush grill rack with vegetable oil. Heat coals or gas grill for direct heat (page 16).

2. Mix margarine and cheese. Spread on both sides of bread slices. Sprinkle both sides with sesame seed.

3. Grill bread uncovered 4 inches from MEDIUM heat 10 to 12 minutes, turning once, until golden brown.

1 Serving: Calories 200 (Calories from Fat 110); Fat 12g (Saturated 4g); Cholesterol 5mg; Sodium 420mg; Carbohydrate 18g (Dietary Fiber 1g); Protein 6g.

Blue Cheese Bread

PREP: 10 MIN; GRILL: 10 MIN

MAKES 12 SLICES

Blue Cheese Spread (below)
1 loaf (1 pound) unsliced French bread

1. Brush grill rack with vegetable oil. Heat coals or gas grill for direct heat (page 16).

2. Prepare Blue Cheese Spread. Cut bread crosswise in half; reserve one half for future use. Cut remaining half diagonally into 1-inch slices. Spread 1 side of each slice with Blue Cheese Spread. Reassemble slices into loaf; wrap securely in 14-inch piece of heavy-duty aluminum foil.

3. Cover and grill bread 5 to 6 inches from MEDIUM heat 8 to 10 minutes, turning once, until hot. Open foil. Grill bread uncovered 5 minutes longer.

BLUE CHEESE SPREAD

1/3 cup margarine or butter, softened
1/4 cup finely crumbled blue cheese
1 clove garlic, finely chopped

Mix all ingredients. About 1/2 cup.

1 Slice: Calories 150 (Calories from Fat 65); Fat 7g (Saturated 2g); Cholesterol 2mg; Sodium 320mg; Carbohydrate 19g (Dietary Fiber 1g); Protein 4g.

Herbed Polenta

PREP: 10 MIN; **COOK: 10** MIN; **REFRIGERATE: 1** HR; **GRILL: 10** MIN

MAKES **6** SERVINGS

Serve polenta with a salad for a light meal, or serve as a savory side dish with meat, poultry or fish.

**1 can (14 1/2 ounces) ready-to-serve
    vegetable broth**

1/4 cup water

1/4 teaspoon salt

1 cup cornmeal

**1 tablespoon chopped fresh or 1 teaspoon
    dried basil leaves**

**1 1/2 teaspoons chopped fresh or
    1/2 teaspoon dried oregano leaves**

**1 1/2 teaspoons chopped fresh parsley or
    1/2 teaspoon dried parsley flakes**

1 tablespoon olive or vegetable oil

1. Grease 9 1/2-inch round pan. Heat broth, water and salt to boiling in 3-quart saucepan. Gradually add cornmeal, stirring constantly with wire whisk; reduce heat to low. Cook 2 minutes, stirring constantly. Stir in basil, oregano and parsley. Spoon mixture into pan; smooth top. Refrigerate uncovered about 1 hour or until cool, stirring occasionally.

2. Brush grill rack with vegetable oil. Heat coals or gas grill for direct heat (page 16).

3. Invert pan to unmold polenta onto cutting board. Cut polenta into 6 wedges. Brush both sides of polenta with oil.

4. Cover and grill polenta 4 to 5 inches from HIGH heat about 10 minutes, turning once, until light brown.

1 Serving: Calories 105 (Calories from Fat 25); Fat 3g (Saturated 1g); Cholesterol 0mg; Sodium 320mg; Carbohydrate 18g (Dietary Fiber 1g); Protein 3g.

7

Vegetables and Fruits

Surprising Desserts

Corn with Chili-Lime Spread (page 173), Tangy Onion Flowers (172)

Spicy Potato Planks

PREP: 15 MIN; COOK: 20 MIN; GRILL: 20 MIN

MAKES 4 SERVINGS

Garam masala is an Indian spice mixture. While its recipe is variable, garam masala usually consists of cardamom, cinnamon and cloves and may also include coriander, cumin, nutmeg, mace or pepper.

3 medium potatoes (about 1 1/2 pounds)

1/3 cup margarine or butter

1/2 teaspoon salt

1/8 teaspoon ground red pepper (cayenne)

1/8 teaspoon garam masala, if desired

1 large clove garlic, crushed

1. Place potatoes in enough water to cover (salted, if desired) in 3-quart saucepan. Cover and heat to boiling. Boil about 15 minutes or until almost tender; drain. Cool slightly.

2. Brush grill rack with vegetable oil. Heat coals or gas grill for direct heat (page 16).

3. Heat remaining ingredients to boiling; remove from heat. Cut each potato lengthwise into 4 or 5 slices. Brush potatoes generously with margarine mixture.

4. Cover and grill potatoes 4 inches from MEDIUM heat about 20 minutes, turning and brushing 2 or 3 times with margarine mixture, until golden brown and tender.

1 Serving: Calories 230 (Calories from Fat 135); Fat 15g (Saturated 3g); Cholesterol 0mg; Sodium 470mg; Carbohydrate 24g (Dietary Fiber 2g); Protein 2g.

Sweet Potato Slices

PREP: 10 MIN; COOK: 20 MIN; GRILL: 20 MIN

MAKES 6 SERVINGS

For a spicy flavor, stir 1/4 teaspoon ground cinnamon or ground red pepper into the margarine mixture.

3 pounds sweet potatoes or yams

1/3 cup margarine or butter, melted

1/2 teaspoon salt

Coconut, toasted, if desired

1. Brush grill rack with vegetable oil. Heat coals or gas grill for direct heat (page 16).

2. Peel sweet potatoes; cut into 1/2-inch diagonal slices. Heat 1 inch water to boiling in 3-quart saucepan. Add sweet potatoes. Cover and heat to boiling; reduce heat to low. Simmer about 12 minutes or almost tender; drain. Mix margarine and salt in a small bowl.

3. Grill sweet potato slices uncovered 4 inches from MEDIUM heat about 20 minutes, brushing frequently with margarine mixture and turning once.

4. To serve, sprinkle sweet potatoes with coconut.

Note: For 4 servings, use 2 pounds sweet potatoes. For 2 servings, use 2 sweet potatoes, 2 tablespoons margarine or butter and 1/4 teaspoon salt.

1 Serving: Calories 255 (Calories from Fat 90); Fat 10g (Saturated 2g); Cholesterol 0mg; Sodium 330mg; Carbohydrate 43g (Dietary Fiber 5g); Protein 3g.

Potato Cakes with Goat Cheese and Chives

**PREP: 15 MIN; COOK: 5 MIN; CHILL: 1 HR;
GRILL: 15 MIN**

MAKES **6** SERVINGS

1 1/3 cups water

1/3 cup milk

2 tablespoons margarine or butter

1/2 teaspoon salt

1 1/2 cups mashed potato mix (dry)

1 egg

**2 ounces chèvre (goat) cheese (with herbs
  or plain), softened**

1 clove garlic, finely chopped

2 tablespoons chopped fresh chives

Sour cream, if desired

Chopped fresh chives, if desired

1. Heat water, milk, margarine and salt to boiling
   in 2-quart saucepan; remove from heat. Stir
   in potato mix just until moistened. Let stand
   about 30 seconds or until liquid is absorbed.
   Stir in egg, cheese, garlic and 2 tablespoons
   chives. Cover and refrigerate about 1 hour or
   until firm.

2. Heat coals or gas grill for direct heat (page 16).
   Brush hinged wire grill basket with vegetable oil.

3. Shape potato mixture into 6 patties, about
   1 inch thick, using floured hands. Place patties
   in basket.

4. Cover and grill patties 4 to 6 inches from
   MEDIUM heat 10 to 15 minutes, turning once,
   until hot.

5. Serve with sour cream and chives.

1 Serving: Calories 150 (Calories from Fat 70); Fat 8g
(Saturated 3g); Cholesterol 45mg; Sodium 320mg;
Carbohydrate 15g (Dietary Fiber 0g); Protein 5g.

Herbed Mozzarella Eggplant

PREP: 15 MIN; GRILL: 12 MIN

MAKES **8** SERVINGS

You'll like this eggplant served with lamb or pork.

1/3 cup vegetable oil

**2 tablespoons chopped fresh or 2 teaspoons
  dried oregano leaves**

2 tablespoons lemon juice

1 teaspoon salt

2 cloves garlic, crushed

2 medium eggplants (about 2 1/2 pounds)

**1 cup shredded mozzarella cheese
  (4 ounces)**

1. Brush grill rack with vegetable oil. Heat coals or
   gas grill for direct heat (page 16).

2. Mix all ingredients except eggplants and cheese.
   Cut eggplants into 1 1/2-inch slices. Dip slices
   into oil mixture, coating both sides.

3. Cover and grill eggplant slices 5 to 6 inches
   from MEDIUM heat 8 to 12 minutes, turning
   and brushing 2 or 3 times with oil mixture,
   until tender. Top slices with cheese for last
   2 minutes of grilling.

1 Serving: Calories 155 (Calories from Fat 110); Fat 12g
(Saturated 3g); Cholesterol 10mg; Sodium 370mg;
Carbohydrate 10g (Dietary Fiber 3g); Protein 5g.

Skewered Ratatouille

PREP: 40 MIN; **GRILL: 20** MIN

MAKES **6** SERVINGS

Sprinkling eggplant with salt and letting it stand 30 minutes eliminates the bitter taste often found in eggplant.

1 small eggplant (about 3/4 pound)

3/4 teaspoon salt

Vegetable oil

2 small zucchini (about 1/2 pound)

1 medium green bell pepper

1 small onion

1/3 cup Italian dressing

1 cup spaghetti sauce or Italian tomato sauce, heated

1. Cut eggplant into 1-inch chunks. Place eggplant in colander over bowl or sink. Sprinkle with salt. Let drain 30 minutes. Rinse and pat dry.

2. Brush grill rack with vegetable oil. Heat coals or gas grill for direct heat (page 16).

3. Cut zucchini, bell pepper and onion into 1-inch chunks. Thread eggplant, zucchini, bell pepper and onion alternately on each of six 10-inch metal skewers, leaving space between each. Brush with dressing.

4. Cover and grill kabobs 4 to 6 inches from MEDIUM heat 15 to 20 minutes, turning and brushing twice with dressing, until vegetables are crisp-tender.

5. Heat spaghetti sauce in small pan or can with label removed during last 10 minutes of grilling, stirring occasionally. Serve kabobs with spaghetti sauce.

1 Serving: Calories 120 (Calories from Fat 70); Fat 8g (Saturated 1g); Cholesterol 0mg; Sodium 670mg; Carbohydrate 13g (Dietary Fiber 3g); Protein 2g.

Skewered Ratatouille

Tangy Onion Flowers

PREP: 20 MIN; GRILL: 50 MIN

MAKES 4 SERVINGS

Here's a delicious and low-fat alternative to the deep-fried onion blossom featured at many restaurants.

4 medium onions (each 4 to 5 ounces)
Vegetable oil
1/4 cup balsamic or cider vinegar
1 tablespoon chopped fresh or 1 teaspoon dried oregano leaves
1 tablespoon packed brown sugar
1/4 teaspoon salt
1/4 teaspoon pepper
1/3 cup seasoned croutons, crushed

1. Heat coals or gas grill for direct heat (page 16).

2. Peel onions; cut 1/2-inch slice from top of each onion and leave root end. Cut each onion from top into 8 wedges to within 1/2 inch of root end. Gently pull wedges apart, leaving root end attached.

3. Brush four 12-inch squares of heavy-duty aluminum foil with vegetable oil. Place 1 onion on each square; loosely shape foil around onion. Sprinkle onions with vinegar, oregano, brown sugar, salt and pepper. Wrap foil securely around onions.

4. Cover and grill onions 4 inches from MEDIUM heat 50 to 60 minutes or until very tender.

5. To serve, sprinkle onions with croutons.

1 Serving: Calories 60 (Calories from Fat 0); Fat 0g (Saturated 0g); Cholesterol 0mg; Sodium 170mg; Carbohydrate 16g (Dietary Fiber 2g); Protein 1g.

Leeks with Rosemary-Garlic Butter

PREP: 15 MIN; GRILL: 20 MIN

MAKES 6 SERVINGS

2 tablespoons margarine or butter, softened
1 teaspoon chopped fresh or 1/4 teaspoon dried rosemary leaves, crushed
1 clove garlic, finely chopped
6 small leeks (about 1 1/2 pounds)

1. Brush grill rack with vegetable oil. Heat coals or gas grill for direct heat (page 16).

2. Mix margarine, rosemary and garlic.

3. Remove green tops of leeks to within 2 inches of white part. Cut leeks lengthwise in half to within 1 inch of root end. Wash leeks several times in water; drain.

4. Cover and grill leeks 4 to 6 inches from MEDIUM heat 15 to 20 minutes, turning and brushing occasionally with margarine mixture, until tender and light brown.

1 Serving: Calories 65 (Calories from Fat 35); Fat 4g (Saturated 1g); Cholesterol 0mg; Sodium 60mg; Carbohydrate 7g (Dietary Fiber 2g); Protein 2g.

Corn with Chili-Lime Spread

PREP: 15 MIN; GRILL: 30 MIN

MAKES 6 SERVINGS

Chili-Lime Spread (below)
6 ears corn (with husks)

1. Prepare Chili-Lime Spread.

2. Heat coals or gas grill for direct heat (page 16).

3. Remove large outer husks from each ear corn; turn back inner husks, and remove silk. Spread each ear corn with about 2 teaspoons Chili-Lime Spread; reserve remaining spread. Pull husks up over ears; tie with fine wire to secure.

4. Grill corn uncovered 3 inches from MEDIUM heat 20 to 30 minutes, turning frequently, until tender.

5. Serve corn with remaining spread.

CHILI-LIME SPREAD

1/2 cup margarine or butter, softened
1/2 teaspoon grated lime peel
3 tablespoons lime juice
1 to 2 teaspoons ground red chilies or chili powder

Mix all ingredients. About 2/3 cup.

1 Serving: Calories 285 (Calories from Fat 155); Fat 17g (Saturated 4g); Cholesterol 0mg; Sodium 210mg; Carbohydrate 32g (Dietary Fiber 3g); Protein 4g.

Dilled Baby Carrots

PREP: 10 MIN; GRILL: 1 HR

MAKES 4 SERVINGS

1 package (1 pound) baby-cut carrots
2 teaspoons dried dill weed
1 teaspoon sugar
1 teaspoon lemon juice
1 tablespoon margarine or butter

1. Heat coals or gas grill for direct heat (page 16).

2. Place carrots on 18×12-inch piece of heavy-duty aluminum foil. Sprinkle with dill weed, sugar and lemon juice. Dot with margarine. Wrap foil securely around carrots; punch top of foil once or twice with fork to vent steam.

3. Cover and grill foil packet, seam side up, 4 to 6 inches from MEDIUM heat about 1 hour or until carrots are tender.

1 Serving: Calories 70 (Calories from Fat 25); Fat 3g (Saturated 1g); Cholesterol 0mg; Sodium 75mg; Carbohydrate 13g (Dietary Fiber 3g); Protein 1g.

Surprising Desserts

Other than the childhood favorite S'mores, rarely do desserts come to mind when we think of grilling or "cooking out." If you haven't grilled desserts, then you're in for a treat! Grilling adds an extra-special toasted flavor while the warm fruit, gooey chocolate or melted marshmallow will soon turn these treats into a tradition. Most of these recipes take just a few minutes and can be grilled while you're eating the main course, taking advantage of the cooling coals.

Angel Food Pockets

PREP: 10 MIN; **GRILL: 2** MIN

MAKES 4 SERVINGS

Use your favorite flavor of jam or preserves in these airy pockets.

4 slices angel food cake, 1 1/2 inches thick

3 tablespoons marshmallow creme

1 tablespoon raspberry jam

1 tablespoon margarine or butter, melted

1/4 cup semisweet chocolate chips

1. Heat coals or gas grill for direct heat (page 16).

2. Make horizontal cut in side of each slice of cake, forming a pocket. Mix marshmallow creme and jam; spoon 1 tablespoon mixture into each pocket. Brush both sides of cake with margarine. Place on grilling screen.

3. Grill cake uncovered 4 to 6 inches from MEDIUM heat 1 minute. Turn; top each slice with 1 tablespoon chocolate chips. Grill uncovered about 1 minute longer or until chocolate is softened.

4. To serve, spread chocolate over tops of cake slices.

1 Serving: Calories 240 (Calories from Fat 55); Fat 6g (Saturated 3g); Cholesterol 0mg; Sodium 390mg; Carbohydrate 44g (Dietary Fiber 1g); Protein 4g.

Pound Cake S'mores

PREP: 10 MIN; GRILL: 3 MIN

MAKES 4 SERVINGS

This version of an old favorite is easy to prepare ahead so it's all ready to cook after the main course is grilled. You can vary the flavor by using different flavors of chips.

4 slices pound cake, 1 inch thick

20 miniature marshmallows (about 1/4 cup)

20 semisweet chocolate chips (about 1 tablespoon)

1. Brush grill rack with vegetable oil. Heat coals or gas grill for direct heat (page 16).

2. Make horizontal cut in side of each slice of cake, forming a pocket. Fill each pocket with 5 marshmallows and 5 chocolate chips.

3. Cover and grill cake 5 to 6 inches from MEDIUM heat 2 to 3 minutes, turning once, until golden brown.

1 Serving: Calories 465 (Calories from Fat 245); Fat 27g (Saturated 12g); Cholesterol 115mg; Sodium 90mg; Carbohydrate 51g (Dietary Fiber 1g); Protein 6g.

Toasted Butter-Rum Pound Cake

PREP: 15 MIN; GRILL: 5 MIN

MAKES 8 SERVINGS

This is a terrific combination of flavors—we like it best when made with butter.

1/2 cup sour cream

2 tablespoons packed brown sugar

1 package (10 3/4 ounces) frozen pound cake

1/4 cup rum

1/4 cup margarine or butter, softened

1/2 cup sliced almonds

1. Brush grill rack with vegetable oil. Heat coals or gas grill for direct heat (page 16).

2. Mix sour cream and brown sugar; set aside.

3. Cut frozen pound cake into 8 slices. For each side, sprinkle with rum, spread with margarine, then press almonds onto margarine. Place cake slices on grilling screen.

4. Grill cake uncovered 4 to 6 inches from MEDIUM heat about 5 minutes, turning once, until golden brown.

5. To serve, top cake with sour cream mixture.

1 Serving: Calories 295 (Calories from Fat 190); Fat 21g (Saturated 12g); Cholesterol 85mg; Sodium 140mg; Carbohydrate 23g (Dietary Fiber 1g); Protein 4g.

Continued on next page

Cinnamon Balloons with Chocolate Sauce

PREP: 20 MIN; **GRILL: 15** MIN

MAKES 5 SERVINGS

1 can (7.5 ounces) refrigerated biscuit dough

10 large marshmallows

1/3 cup sugar

1/2 teaspoon ground cinnamon

2 tablespoons margarine or butter, melted

1/3 cup chocolate-flavored syrup

1. Heat coals or gas grill for direct heat (page 16). Grease 9-inch round aluminum foil pan.

2. Roll or pat biscuit dough into ten 4-inch circles. Top each with 1 marshmallow. Fold dough around marshmallow to cover completely. Pinch seams to seal.

3. Mix sugar and cinnamon. Brush biscuits with margarine; roll in cinnamon-sugar. Place biscuits, seam sides down, in pan.

4. Cover and grill biscuits 4 to 6 inches from MEDIUM heat about 15 minutes or until light brown.

5. To serve, drizzle biscuits with chocolate syrup. Serve immediately.

1 Serving: Calories 335 (Calories from Fat 100); Fat 11g (Saturated 3g); Cholesterol 0mg; Sodium 590mg; Carbohydrate 57g (Dietary Fiber 1g); Protein 3g.

Toasted Butter-Rum Pound Cake (page 175), Cinnamon Balloons with Chocolate Sauce

Summer Cobbler

PREP: 15 MIN; GRILL: 30 MIN

MAKES 8 SERVINGS

After cobbler is baked, move it to the side of the grill to keep warm until ready to serve.

1/4 cup margarine or butter, melted

1 1/4 cups Bisquick® Original baking mix

1/2 cup sugar

1/2 cup milk

1 medium nectarine or peach, sliced (1 cup)

1 cup blueberries or blackberries

1/4 cup sugar

1/2 teaspoon ground cinnamon

1. Heat coals or gas grill for direct heat (page 16).

2. Melt margarine in 9-inch round aluminum foil pan on grill. Mix baking mix, 1/2 cup sugar and the milk; beat 30 seconds. Pour over margarine in pan. Top batter with nectarine and blueberries. Sprinkle with 1/4 cup sugar and the cinnamon.

3. Cover and grill cobbler 5 to 6 inches from MEDIUM heat about 30 minutes or until toothpick inserted in center comes out clean.

1 Serving: Calories 230 (Calories from Fat 80); Fat 9g (Saturated 2g); Cholesterol 2mg; Sodium 340mg; Carbohydrate 36g (Dietary Fiber 1g); Protein 2g.

Peanut Butter–Banana Rolls

PREP: 15 MIN; GRILL: 10 MIN

MAKES 4 SERVINGS

Kids of all ages will enjoy this clever treat!

4 flour tortillas (8 inches in diameter)

1/4 cup peanut butter

1/4 cup miniature semisweet chocolate chips

2 small bananas

2 teaspoons margarine or butter, softened

Chocolate-flavored syrup, if desired

1. Heat coals or gas grill for direct heat (page 16). Soak 4 small bamboo skewers or about 6 toothpicks in water 30 minutes.

2. Spread 1 side of each tortilla with peanut butter. Sprinkle with chocolate chips. Cut each banana lengthwise in half. Place 1 banana half on each tortilla. Roll tortilla around banana; secure with wooden skewer. Brush rolls with margarine.

3. Grill rolls uncovered 4 to 6 inches from MEDIUM heat 8 to 10 minutes, turning once, until golden brown.

4. To serve, drizzle banana rolls with chocolate syrup.

1 Serving: Calories 345 (Calories from Fat 155); Fat 17g (Saturated 5g); Cholesterol 0mg; Sodium 300mg; Carbohydrate 44g (Dietary Fiber 4g); Protein 8g.

Crunchy Peach Upside-Down Cake

PREP: 10 MIN; GRILL: 30 MIN

MAKES 8 SERVINGS

2 tablespoons margarine or butter

1/4 cup sugar

1/2 teaspoon ground cinnamon

1/4 cup chopped pecans

1 large peach, peeled and sliced

1 1/2 cups Bisquick® Original baking mix

1/2 cup milk

2 tablespoons sugar

1 egg

Whipped cream, if desired

1. Heat coals or gas grill for direct heat (page 16).

2. Melt margarine in 9-inch round aluminum foil pan on grill. Mix 1/4 cup sugar and the cinnamon; sprinkle over margarine. Sprinkle pecans over sugar mixture. Arrange peach slices in single layer on sugar mixture.

3. Mix remaining ingredients except whipped cream; beat 30 seconds. Pour over peaches.

4. Cover and grill cake 5 to 6 inches from MEDIUM heat 25 to 30 minutes or until toothpick inserted in center comes out clean.

5. Immediately invert cake onto heatproof plate. Let stand a few minutes; remove pan. Serve cake warm with whipped cream.

1 Serving: Calories 195 (Calories from Fat 80); Fat 9g (Saturated 2g); Cholesterol 30mg; Sodium 370mg; Carbohydrate 27g (Dietary Fiber 1g); Protein 3g.

Continued on next page

Pears with Raspberry Sauce

PREP: 15 MIN; GRILL: 10 MIN

MAKES 6 SERVINGS

3 large firm pears (about 1 1/2 pounds)

1 tablespoon vegetable oil

1 package (10 ounces) frozen raspberries in syrup, thawed

1 teaspoon lemon juice

3 tablespoons hot fudge sauce, heated, if desired

1. Heat coals or gas grill for direct heat (page 16).

2. Peel pears; cut lengthwise in half and remove cores. Lightly brush both sides with oil.

3. Cover and grill pears, cut sides up, 4 to 6 inches from MEDIUM heat 5 minutes; turn. Cover and grill about 5 minutes longer or until tender.

4. While pears are grilling, place raspberries and lemon juice in blender or food processor. Cover and blend on medium speed, stopping blender occasionally to scrape sides, or process about 30 seconds, until well blended. Strain raspberry mixture to remove seeds, if desired.

5. Serve hot pears with raspberry sauce. Drizzle with fudge sauce.

1 Serving: Calories 170 (Calories from Fat 35); Fat 4g (Saturated 1g); Cholesterol 2mg; Sodium 15mg; Carbohydrate 37g (Dietary Fiber 5g); Protein 1g.

Mushrooms with Herbs

PREP: 10 MIN; MARINATE: 1 HR; GRILL: 20 MIN

MAKES 4 SERVINGS

You can use smaller mushrooms—just be sure to use a grilling screen or aluminum foil pan, and check for doneness after half the grilling time.

1/2 cup olive or vegetable oil

3 tablespoons lemon juice

1 teaspoon chopped fresh or 1/4 teaspoon dried oregano leaves

1 teaspoon chopped fresh or 1/4 teaspoon dried thyme leaves

1 clove garlic, crushed

1 pound large white mushrooms (about 2 1/2 inches in diameter)

1/4 teaspoon salt

1/8 teaspoon pepper

1. Mix oil, lemon juice, oregano, thyme and garlic in large nonmetal bowl or resealable plastic bag. Add mushrooms, stirring to coat with marinade. Cover and refrigerate at least 1 hour but no longer than 8 hours.

2. Heat coals or gas grill for direct heat (page 16).

3. Remove mushrooms from marinade (mushrooms will absorb most of the marinade). Cover and grill mushrooms about 4 inches from MEDIUM heat 15 to 20 minutes, turning 2 or 3 times, until tender and golden brown. Sprinkle with salt and pepper.

1 Serving: Calories 215 (Calories from Fat 190); Fat 21g (Saturated 3g); Cholesterol 0mg; Sodium 150mg; Carbohydrate 6g (Dietary Fiber 1g); Protein 2g.

Pepper Salad

PREP: 15 MIN; STAND: 1 1/4 HR; GRILL: 20 MIN

MAKES 6 SERVINGS

This simple salad is also excellent served at room temperature. If you like more flavor, stir in 1 tablespoon chopped fresh or 1 teaspoon dried herbs such as oregano or basil or 1 clove finely chopped garlic.

1/4 cup olive or vegetable oil

6 medium bell peppers

1/2 teaspoon salt

1/4 teaspoon pepper

1. Brush grill rack with vegetable oil. Heat coals or gas grill for direct heat (page 16).

2. Cover and grill bell peppers 4 inches from MEDIUM heat 15 to 20 minutes, turning frequently, until skin is blistered on all sides. Wrap peppers in clean towel or brown paper bag; cool 15 minutes.

3. Remove skin from peppers with knife. Cut peppers lengthwise in half; remove stems and seeds. Cut peppers into 1/4- to 1/2-inch-wide strips; place in nonmetal bowl. Drizzle with oil. Sprinkle with salt and pepper. Cover and refrigerate at least 1 hour but no longer than 3 days.

1 Serving: Calories 100 (Calories from Fat 80); Fat 9g (Saturated 1g); Cholesterol 0mg; Sodium 200mg; Carbohydrate 5g (Dietary Fiber 1g); Protein 1g.

Tomato-Artichoke Kabobs

PREP: 10 MIN; GRILL: 8 MIN

MAKES 4 SERVINGS

These tasty side dish kabobs couldn't be easier! Firm ripe cherry tomatoes work best for skewering.

1 jar (6 ounces) marinated artichoke hearts

12 cherry tomatoes

1. Brush grill rack with vegetable oil. Heat coals or gas grill for direct heat (page 16).

2. Drain artichoke hearts; reserve liquid. Thread artichoke hearts and tomatoes alternately on each of four 10- to 12-inch metal skewers, leaving space between each. Brush with artichoke liquid.

3. Cover and grill kabobs about 4 inches from MEDIUM heat 6 to 8 minutes, brushing with artichoke liquid and turning 2 or 3 times, until hot.

1 Serving: Calories 30 (Calories from Fat 10); Fat 1g (Saturated 0g); Cholesterol 0mg; Sodium 105mg; Carbohydrate 6g (Dietary Fiber 2g); Protein 1g.

Maple Apple Rings

PREP: 10 MIN; GRILL: 10 MIN

MAKES 4 SERVINGS

Serve this grilled fruit as a side dish with pork or turn it into dessert with a scoop of vanilla ice cream.

4 medium unpeeled apples (such as Red or Yellow Delicious or Granny Smith)

1 tablespoon margarine or butter, melted

2 tablespoons maple-flavored syrup

1/4 teaspoon ground nutmeg

1. Brush grill rack with vegetable oil. Heat coals or gas grill for direct heat (page 16).

2. Core apples. Cut thin slice from top and bottom of each apple to expose flesh; discard. Cut each apple crosswise into 3 slices. Brush both sides of apple slices with margarine.

3. Cover and grill apple slices 4 to 6 inches from medium heat about 10 minutes, turning once, until tender.

4. To serve, drizzle apples with maple syrup. Sprinkle with nutmeg.

1 Serving: Calories 140 (Calories from Fat 25); Fat 3g (Saturated 1g); Cholesterol 0mg; Sodium 45mg; Carbohydrate 29g (Dietary Fiber 4g); Protein 0g.

Caribbean Curried Bananas

PREP: 10 MIN; GRILL: 15 MIN

MAKES 3 SERVINGS

2 tablespoons margarine or butter, melted

1 teaspoon curry powder

3 large firm bananas

Lime wedge

1. Heat coals or gas grill for direct heat (page 16).

2. Mix margarine and curry powder in 8-inch square aluminum foil pan. Cut each banana crosswise in half. Roll bananas in margarine mixture. Squeeze a few drops lime juice from lime wedge over bananas. Cover pan with aluminum foil, sealing edges securely.

3. Cover and grill bananas 4 to 6 inches from MEDIUM heat 12 to 15 minutes, turning bananas once, until golden brown and tender.

1 Serving: Calories 190 (Calories from Fat 70); Fat 8g (Saturated 2g); Cholesterol 0mg; Sodium 90mg; Carbohydrate 31g (Dietary Fiber 3g); Protein 1g.

Pineapple Slices with Ginger Cream

PREP: 20 MIN; GRILL: 15 MIN

MAKES **6** SERVINGS

Succulent fresh pineapple is delicious when grilled! If you'd rather not mix the Ginger Cream, just dollop the sour cream in the center of each slice and sprinkle with the brown sugar and ginger.

Ginger Cream (right)
1 medium pineapple (about 3 pounds)
1 tablespoon margarine or butter, melted
Maraschino cherries, if desired

1. Prepare Ginger Cream.

2. Heat coals or gas grill for direct heat (page 16).

3. Cut 1/2-inch slice off top and bottom of pineapple. Cut off rind. Cut pineapple crosswise into 6 slices. Drizzle both sides of pineapple slices with margarine.

4. Cover and grill pineapple slices 4 to 6 inches from MEDIUM heat 10 to 15 minutes, turning once, until hot and light brown.

5. To serve, top pineapple with Ginger Cream. Garnish with maraschino cherries.

GINGER CREAM

1/2 cup sour cream
1 tablespoon packed brown sugar
1 tablespoon chopped crystallized ginger

Mix all ingredients. Cover and refrigerate until serving. About 1/2 cup.

1 Serving: Calories 105 (Calories from Fat 55); Fat 6g (Saturated 3g); Cholesterol 15mg; Sodium 30mg; Carbohydrate 13g (Dietary Fiber 1g); Protein 1g.

Warm Fruit Compote with Almonds

PREP: 10 MIN; GRILL: 10 MIN

MAKES **6** SERVINGS

1 can (16 ounces) pitted Royal Anne or dark sweet cherries in heavy syrup

2 medium peaches, sliced

1 medium pear, sliced

1 tablespoon chopped fresh mint leaves

1/4 cup sliced almonds

Vanilla ice cream or yogurt, if desired

1. Heat coals or gas grill for direct heat (page 16).

2. Drain cherries, reserving 1/3 cup syrup. Mix cherries, reserved syrup, peaches, pear and mint in 9-inch round aluminum foil pan. Cover pan with aluminum foil, sealing edge securely. Place almonds in 9-inch round aluminum foil pan (do not cover pan).

3. Cover and grill fruit mixture and almonds 4 inches from MEDIUM heat 8 to 10 minutes, stirring almonds twice, until peaches and pear are tender and almonds are golden brown.

4. Sprinkle almonds over fruit. Serve with vanilla ice cream.

1 Serving: Calories 95 (Calories from Fat 25); Fat 3g (Saturated 1g); Cholesterol 0mg; Sodium 0mg; Carbohydrate 18g (Dietary Fiber 3g); Protein 2g.

Brandied Skewered Fruit

PREP: 20 MIN; GRILL: 10 MIN

MAKES **6** SERVINGS

Take advantage of fresh seasonal fruits to create your own kabob combinations.

1/2 medium pineapple (about 3-pound size), cut into chunks (3 cups)

3 medium plums, cut in half

3 medium apricots or peaches, cut in half

2 tablespoons margarine or butter, melted

2 tablespoons packed brown sugar

3 tablespoons apricot brandy or apricot nectar

1. Brush grill rack with vegetable oil. Heat coals or gas grill for direct heat (page 16).

2. Thread pineapple chunks, 1 plum half and 1 apricot half on each of six 10- to 12-inch metal skewers, leaving space between each. Brush with margarine. Sprinkle with brown sugar.

3. Grill kabobs uncovered 4 to 6 inches from MEDIUM heat about 10 minutes, turning once, until hot.

4. To serve, drizzle with brandy.

1 Serving: Calories 125 (Calories from Fat 35); Fat 4g (Saturated 1g); Cholesterol 0mg; Sodium 45mg; Carbohydrate 23g (Dietary Fiber 2g); Protein 1g.

Spiced Fruit Kabobs

PREP: 5 MIN; GRILL: 8 MIN

MAKES 6 KABOBS

Use skewers with flat blades, so the fruits won't spin on the skewer when you turn the kabobs.

1/4 cup margarine or butter

1 tablespoon sugar

1/2 teaspoon ground cinnamon

3 firm plums

3 firm nectarines

2 firm medium bananas

1. Brush grill rack with vegetable oil. Heat coals or gas grill for direct heat (page 16).

2. Heat margarine, sugar and cinnamon in small pan or food can with label removed, on grill until margarine is melted.

3. Cut plums and nectarines into 4 pieces; remove pits. Cut bananas into 6 pieces. Thread fruits alternately on each of six 10- to 12-inch metal skewers, leaving space between each.

4. Grill kabobs uncovered 5 to 6 inches from MEDIUM heat 6 to 8 minutes, brushing occasionally with margarine mixture and turning 2 or 3 times, until hot.

1 Kabob: Calories 130 (Calories from Fat 45); Fat 5g (Saturated 2g); Cholesterol 0mg; Sodium 45mg; Carbohydrate 22g (Dietary Fiber 2g); Protein 1g.

8

Marinades, Sauces, Salsas and Relishes

Zesty Barbecue Sauce (page 195), Plum Barbecue Sauce (page 198), Citrus Barbecue Sauce (page 199)

International Flavor Twist

The saying, "variety is the spice of life" certainly is true when it comes to exploring the many different ethnic or international flavors of the world! Herbs and spices, along with other indigenous ingredients, help give various countries and regions very distinctive flavors.

The international flavors that follow, offer you a culinary mini-tour of some of the most popular ethnic cuisines and show how you can create their special flavors at home. Our enticing tour will bring the flavors of the Caribbean, Mexico, North Africa, Provence (France) and Thailand to your grill with recipes for a basic seasoning mix and additional recipes to use the mix. Now, without traveling, you can head for the grill and enjoy the wonderful tastes of some of the world's most flavorful cuisines!

COOKING DIRECTIONS: Choose a flavor from the chart below to prepare 4 boneless, skinless chicken breasts halves or thighs (about 1 pound). Prepare the seasoning mix of your choice. Use as a rub or marinade as directed below. Grill chicken 4 to 6 inches from medium coals 15 to 20 minutes, turning once, until juice is no longer pink when centers of thickest pieces are cut.

These flavors can be used on other meats. For each pound of meat, use about 2 tablespoons rub or prepare about 1/2 cup Marinade. Follow meat grilling directions.

International Flavors Chart

Seasoning Mix	Rub	Marinade
Mix in storage container with tight-fitting lid. Shake or stir before each use.	Brush meat with oil and rub with seasoning mix.	Mix all ingredients; pour over meat in resealable plastic bag. Refrigerate 1 to 2 hours but no longer than 24 hours. Makes about 1/2 cup mix.
Caribbean		
1/3 cup instant minced onion 1 tablespoon dry mustard 2 teaspoons ground allspice 2 teaspoons ground cinnamon 2 teaspoons crushed red pepper 1 teaspoon garlic powder 1/2 teaspoon salt	1 tablespoon vegetable oil 2 tablespoons Caribbean Seasoning Mix	2 tablespoons Caribbean Seasoning Mix 1/2 cup pineapple juice 1 tablespoon grated orange peel 1 tablespoon vegetable oil
Store in cool, dry place up to 6 months.		

Seasoning Mix	Rub	Marinade
Mexican		
1/4 cup ground red chilies or chili powder 3 tablespoons dried oregano leaves 1 tablespoon ground cumin 2 teaspoons ground coriander 1/2 teaspoon salt	1 tablespoon vegetable oil 2 tablespoons Mexican Seasoning Mix	2 tablespoons Mexican Seasoning Mix 1/4 cup dry white wine or chicken broth 1/4 cup lime juice 1 tablespoon vegetable oil
Store in cool, dry place up to 6 months.		
North African		
1/2 cup chopped fresh cilantro 1/4 cup chopped fresh mint 1 tablespoon paprika 3/4 teaspoon salt 1/2 teaspoon saffron threads, crushed or ground turmeric	1 tablespoon olive oil 2 tablespoons North African Seasoning Mix	2 tablespoons North African Seasoning Mix 1/4 cup lemon juice 1/4 cup olive oil 2 garlic cloves, finely chopped
Refrigerate up to 5 days.		
Provençal		
1/4 cup dried tarragon leaves 3 tablespoons dried thyme leaves 2 tablespoons dried sage leaves, crumbled 2 teaspoons onion powder 3/4 teaspoon salt	1 tablespoon olive oil 2 tablespoons Provençal Seasoning Mix 1 tablespoon olive oil	2 tablespoons Provençal Seasoning Mix 1/2 cup dry red wine or chicken broth 1 garlic clove, finely chopped
Store in cool, dry place up to 6 months.		
Thai		
1/3 cup chopped fresh lemon grass 3 tablespoons grated lemon peel 1 tablespoon Chinese five spice powder 1/2 teaspoon garlic powder 3/4 teaspoon salt	1 tablespoon vegetable oil 2 tablespoons Thai Seasoning Mix	2 tablespoons Thai Seasoning Mix 1/2 cup coconut milk 1 tablespoon chili-garlic paste 1 tablespoon vegetable oil
Refrigerate up to 5 days.		

Lemon Herb Marinade

PREP: 10 MIN; MARINATE: 4 HR

MAKES ABOUT 2/3 CUP MARINADE

If you like to serve extra marinade as a sauce over cooked meats, be sure to heat it to boiling first and boil 1 minute to make it safe to eat.

1/3 cup vegetable oil

1/2 teaspoon grated lemon peel

2 tablespoons lemon juice

1 tablespoon dry vermouth, dry white wine or beef broth

1 teaspoon chopped fresh or 1/4 teaspoon crushed dried sage leaves

1 teaspoon chopped fresh or 1/4 teaspoon dried oregano leaves

1/2 teaspoon salt

1/4 teaspoon coarsely ground pepper

1. Mix all ingredients in shallow nonmetal dish or resealable plastic bag. Add up to 2 pounds beef, pork, chicken or turkey, turning to coat with marinade. Cover dish or seal bag and refrigerate, turning meat occasionally, at least 4 hours but no longer than 24 hours.

2. Remove meat from marinade; discard marinade. Grill meat as desired.

1 Serving: Calories 165 (Calories from Fat 160); Fat 18g (Saturated 3g); Cholesterol 0mg; Sodium 290mg; Carbohydrate 1g (Dietary Fiber 0g); Protein 0g.

Orange-Thyme Marinade

PREP: 15 MIN; MARINATE: 6 HR

MAKES ABOUT 3/4 CUP MARINADE

1/2 cup orange juice

2 tablespoons balsamic or red wine vinegar

1 tablespoon vegetable oil

2 medium green onions, finely chopped (2 tablespoons)

1 tablespoon chopped fresh or 1 teaspoon dried thyme leaves

1 teaspoon grated orange peel

1/4 teaspoon salt

1/8 teaspoon pepper

1. Mix all ingredients in shallow nonmetal dish or resealable plastic bag. Add 2 pounds beef or pork, turning to coat with marinade. Cover and refrigerate at least 6 hours but no longer than 24 hours.

2. Remove meat from marinade; reserve marinade. Grill meat as desired.

3. Heat remaining marinade to boiling; boil and stir 1 minute.

4. Serve marinade with grilled meat.

1/4 Cup: Calories 70 (Calories from Fat 45); Fat 5g (Saturated 1g); Cholesterol 0mg; Sodium 200mg; Carbohydrate 6g (Dietary Fiber 0g); Protein 0g.

Orange-Thyme Marinade

Lime-Honey Marinade

PREP: 15 MIN; MARINATE: 8 HR

MAKES ABOUT 1 CUP MARINADE

1/4 cup lime juice

1/4 cup dry white wine or apple juice

1 tablespoon finely chopped gingerroot

2 tablespoons soy sauce

2 tablespoons honey

2 tablespoons vegetable oil

1 teaspoon grated lime peel

1 clove garlic, finely chopped

1. Mix all ingredients in shallow nonmetal dish or resealable plastic bag. Add 1 pound boneless beef, pork, chicken or turkey, turning to coat with marinade. Cover and refrigerate at least 8 hours but no more than 24 hours.

2. Remove meat from marinade; reserve marinade. Grill meat as desired, brushing occasionally with marinade.

3. Heat remaining marinade to boiling; boil and stir 1 minute.

4. Serve marinade with grilled meat.

1/4 Cup: Calories 110 (Calories from Fat 65); Fat 7g (Saturated 1g); Cholesterol 0mg; Sodium 520mg; Carbohydrate 11g (Dietary Fiber 0g); Protein 1g.

Costa Rican Marinade

PREP: 10 MIN; MARINATE: 8 HR

MAKES ABOUT 2/3 CUP MARINADE

The grated lime peel and red pepper sauce add extra kick and South American flavor to this marinade.

1/2 teaspoon grated lime peel

1/3 cup lime juice

1/4 cup tomato juice

1 tablespoon chopped fresh cilantro or parsley

2 teaspoons vegetable oil

1/4 teaspoon salt

1/8 teaspoon red pepper sauce

2 cloves garlic, finely chopped

1. Mix all ingredients in shallow nonmetal dish or resealable plastic bag. Add up to 3 pounds chicken, pork or beef, turning to coat with marinade. Cover dish or seal bag and refrigerate, turning meat occasionally, at least 8 hours but no longer than 24 hours.

2. Remove meat from marinade; discard marinade. Grill meat as desired.

1 Serving: Calories 15 (Calories from Fat 10); Fat 1g (Saturated 0g); Cholesterol 0mg; Sodium 105mg; Carbohydrate 1g (Dietary Fiber 0g); Protein 0g.

Raspberry-Port Marinade

PREP: 15 MIN; MARINATE: 4 HR

MAKES ABOUT **1** CUP MARINADE

After being used to flavor meat, this marinade is then cooked and transformed into a beautiful sauce.

3/4 cup port wine or apple juice

1 tablespoon chopped fresh or 1/2 teaspoon dried thyme leaves

2 tablespoons vegetable oil

1/2 teaspoon salt

1/8 teaspoon pepper

2 cloves garlic, finely chopped

1 cup fresh or frozen raspberries

1. Mix all ingredients except raspberries in shallow nonmetal dish or resealable plastic bag. Add up to 2 pounds pork, lamb or turkey, turning to coat with marinade. Cover dish or seal bag and refrigerate, turning meat occasionally, at least 4 hours but no longer than 24 hours.

2. Remove meat from marinade; reserve marinade. Grill meat as desired.

3. While meat is grilling, heat marinade and raspberries to boiling in 10-inch skillet over medium heat, stirring occasionally. Boil about 10 minutes, stirring occasionally, until sauce is reduced to half.

4. Serve sauce with grilled meat.

1 Serving: Calories 115 (Calories from Fat 65); Fat 7g (Saturated 1g); Cholesterol 0mg; Sodium 300mg; Carbohydrate 10g (Dietary Fiber 2g); Protein 1g.

Zesty Barbecue Sauce

PREP: 10 MIN; COOK: 5 MIN

MAKES ABOUT **1**$\frac{1}{2}$ CUPS SAUCE

For an extra-zesty sauce, increase horseradish to 2 tablespoons.

1/2 cup ketchup

2 tablespoons red wine vinegar

1 tablespoon prepared horseradish

1 small onion, finely chopped (1/4 cup)

1 can (8 ounces) jellied cranberry sauce

1. Mix all ingredients in small 1-quart saucepan. Heat to boiling; reduce heat to low. Simmer uncovered about 5 minutes, stirring frequently, until cranberry sauce is melted.

2. Cool sauce slightly. Serve sauce with grilled beef, pork or turkey. Cover and refrigerate up to 2 weeks.

1/4 Cup: Calories 80 (Calories from Fat 0); Fat 0g (Saturated 0g); Cholesterol 0mg; Sodium 250mg; Carbohydrate 21g (Dietary Fiber 1g); Protein 0g.

From Mops to Rubs

If you're looking for big, bold flavors, marinades, mops, rubs and sauces can add that exciting touch. These additions should not mask the grilled food—they should complement or enhance it. So what are the differences between marinades, mops, rubs and sauces, and how are they used?

Marinades

A mixture of spices and herbs mixed with liquid in which foods are bathed or soaked. Marinades can play double duty: They add bold flavor, but when an acid such as tomato juice or vinegar is added, they also can tenderize. Marinating less-tender, more economical meat cuts can help them grill to tender perfection. For marinades with oil, mixing in a blender or food processor will help prevent the mixture from separating.

Marinades can add flavor in as little as 15 minutes to 2 hours. Although meats can stand at room temperature up to thirty minutes, marinating meats in the refrigerator is safest. Marinating longer than 24 hours is not recommended. The flavor will not change much, and if an acid is included, the surface meat fibers can break down, resulting in a mushy texture.

Always marinate food in a nonmetal dish, such as glass or plastic, that's just a bit larger than the food itself, or use a heavy-duty plastic bag that can be tightly sealed. Acid-based marinades can react with some metals, such as aluminum. As a general guideline, marinate delicate fish fillets and vegetables about thirty minutes; fish steaks, meat chops and chicken pieces at least 1 hour; and larger meat cuts up to 24 hours. Turn the food once or twice during the marinating time, so the marinade can reach all surfaces. Marinades are not reusable; discard any leftover marinade that is not boiled at least 1 minute and used as a sauce.

Mops

A thin basting sauce frequently brushed on meats with a clean cloth mop or brush during grilling or smoking to help keep meats moist and tender. They originally were used in large southern wood-burning barbecue pits and applied with a new, clean floor mop. Barbecue mops are available at stores specializing in outdoor cooking equipment or restaurant supplies. Fresh herb sprigs such as rosemary or thyme tied together can also be used as a mop and will add extra flavor. Most often, mops are used when cooking slowly and smoking larger cuts of meat.

Mops can be as simple as broth or beer or as complex as you can imagine! If meats are fatty, use a mop made without oil or butter. In general, you can mop meats whenever you remove the lid from a grill to turn the food. Water smokers, on the other hand, keep meats very moist, so mopping isn't needed.

Rubs

A mixture of dry or wet seasonings rubbed completely over meat, using your fingers, before grilling. Rubs traditionally were used for barbecued meats cooked in dug-out earth pits, where the pitmasters had their own "secret rub." You can add a rub and immediately grill the food or, for more flavor, cover and refrigerate about 1 hour.

Rubs may contain sugar or salt or even ground nuts. The "wet" seasonings get their name from added liquid, such as oil, mustard and reduced liquids such as wine, mixed with the dry seasonings and creating a paste. When grilled, the flavored surface provides a greater flavor contrast with the interior of the meat than do marinades, which tend to meld with the flavor of the meat.

You can easily mix together seasonings from your spice cabinet, or purchase ready-to-use rubs at the supermarket.

Rubs also can be used to flavor a wide range of dishes such as condiments, soups and stews.

Sauces

The king of sauces for grilling is barbecue sauce. For years, cooks took pride in using their own barbecue sauce recipes, which were brushed or rubbed on foods during grilling or served on top or alongside meats afterwards. Most recipes are based on ketchup, chili sauce or canned tomato products, with extra flavors added to make them special. If sauces are thick or contain sugar or ingredients that will burn, brush them on during the last 15 to 20 minutes of grilling.

In these days of "no time to cook," bottled barbecue sauces are quite popular and readily available in national and regional brands. About 75 percent of all barbecue sauces sold are tomato-based sauces in one of two varieties, either regular/original or hickory/smoke flavor. The other 25 percent are made up of specialty flavors such as Honey-Dijon, Cajun or Jamaican.

SPECIAL NOTE FOR SAFE SAUCES

Leftover marinades, mops and sauces that have been in contact with raw meat should be discarded. Or, to use as a sauce with the grilled meat, heat a leftover marinade, mop or sauce to boiling, then boil for one minute. Boiling will destroy any bacteria that may have been transferred back and forth by brushing it on the uncooked meat, and keep sauces safe.

Spicy Texas Barbecue Sauce

PREP: 15 MIN; COOK: 1 HR

MAKES ABOUT 5 CUPS SAUCE

1 cup ketchup

1/2 cup packed brown sugar

1/4 cup lime juice

2 to 3 tablespoons ground red chilies or chili powder

1 tablespoon vegetable oil

1 tablespoon Worcestershire sauce

3 medium onions, chopped (1 1/2 cups)

2 jalapeño chilies, seeded and finely chopped

2 cloves garlic, finely chopped

1 can (12 ounces) tomato paste

1 can or bottle (12 ounces) beer

1. Heat all ingredients to boiling; reduce heat to low. Cover and simmer 1 hour, stirring occasionally.

2. Serve warm sauce with grilled ribs, steak, chicken or brisket.

1 Tablespoon: Calories 15 (Calories from Fat 0); Fat 0g (Saturated 0g); Cholesterol 0mg; Sodium 75mg; Carbohydrate 4g (Dietary Fiber 0g); Protein 0g.

Plum Barbecue Sauce

PREP: 10 MIN; COOK: 20 MIN

MAKES ABOUT 2 CUPS SAUCE

For an extra-smooth sauce, before heating, whirl the pitted plums with the lemonade concentrate in a blender or food processor until smooth.

1/4 cup margarine or butter

1 small onion, finely chopped (1/4 cup)

1/4 cup chili sauce

1 tablespoon Dijon mustard

1 can (16 1/2 ounces) purple plums, drained, pitted and finely chopped

1 can (6 ounces) frozen lemonade concentrate, thawed

1. Melt margarine in 2-quart saucepan over medium heat. Cook onion in margarine about 2 minutes, stirring occasionally, until tender.

2. Stir in remaining ingredients. Heat to boiling; reduce heat to low. Simmer uncovered 15 minutes, stirring occasionally.

3. Serve warm sauce with grilled chicken, pork or beef.

1 Tablespoon: Calories 35 (Calories from Fat 10); Fat 1g (Saturated 0g); Cholesterol 0mg; Sodium 45mg; Carbohydrate 6g (Dietary Fiber 0g); Protein 0g.

Citrus Barbecue Sauce

PREP: 10 MIN; **COOK: 20** MIN

MAKES ABOUT $2^{1}/_{3}$ CUPS SAUCE

1 tablespoon vegetable oil

1 large onion, finely chopped (1 cup)

1 tablespoon ground red chilies or chili powder

1/4 teaspoon ground red pepper (cayenne)

1 ancho chili, seeded and finely chopped or 1/4 cup chopped green chilies

1 cup orange juice

1/2 cup lime juice

2 tablespoons sugar

1 tablespoon chopped fresh cilantro

2 tablespoons lemon juice

1 teaspoon salt

1. Heat oil in 2-quart saucepan over medium heat. Cook onion, ground red chilies, red pepper and ancho chili in oil about 5 minutes, stirring frequently, until onion is tender.

2. Stir in remaining ingredients. Heat to boiling; reduce heat to low. Simmer uncovered 10 minutes, stirring occasionally.

3. Serve warm sauce with grilled chicken, pork, beef or fish.

1 Tablespoon: Calories 10 (Calories from Fat 0); Fat 0g (Saturated 0g); Cholesterol 0mg; Sodium 65mg; Carbohydrate 2g (Dietary Fiber 0g); Protein 0g.

Pesto

PREP: 10 MIN

MAKES ABOUT $1^{1}/_{3}$ CUPS SAUCE

We've given you several delicious versions of this versatile sauce—you even can have wonderful pesto when basil is not in season!

2 cups firmly packed fresh basil leaves

3/4 cup grated Parmesan cheese

3/4 cup olive or vegetable oil

1/4 cup pine nuts

3 cloves garlic

1. Place all ingredients in blender or food processor. Cover and blend on medium speed about 3 minutes, stopping blender occasionally to scrape sides, until smooth.

2. Serve with grilled chicken, fish, pork or beef or tossed with hot cooked pasta.

1 Tablespoon: Calories 90 (Calories from Fat 80); Fat 9g (Saturated 2g); Cholesterol 2mg; Sodium 55mg; Carbohydrate 1g (Dietary Fiber 0g); Protein 1g.

Cilantro Pesto: Substitute 1 1/2 cups firmly packed fresh cilantro and 1/2 cup firmly packed fresh parsley for the 2 cups fresh basil.

Spinach Winter Pesto: Substitute 2 cups firmly packed fresh spinach leaves and 1/2 cup firmly packed fresh or 1/4 cup dried basil leaves for the 2 cups fresh basil.

Sun-Dried Tomato Pesto: Omit basil. Decrease oil to 1/3 cup. Add 1/2 cup oil-packed sun-dried tomatoes, undrained. Use food processor.

Mustard Cream Sauce

PREP: 5 MIN; COOK: 5 MIN

MAKES ABOUT 1 CUP SAUCE

1 tablespoon margarine or butter

1 tablespoon all-purpose flour

1/8 teaspoon pepper

3/4 cup half-and-half

2 tablespoons diced pimientos

1 tablespoon Dijon mustard

2 teaspoons capers

1. Melt margarine in 1-quart saucepan over medium heat. Stir in flour and pepper. Cook over medium heat, stirring constantly, until mixture is smooth and bubbly; remove from heat. Stir in half-and-half. Heat to boiling, stirring constantly. Boil and stir 1 minute.

2. Stir in remaining ingredients.

3. Serve warm sauce with grilled ham, pork, beef or fish.

1/4 Cup: Calories 95 (Calories from Fat 70); Fat 8g (Saturated 4g); Cholesterol 15mg; Sodium 140mg; Carbohydrate 4g (Dietary Fiber 0g); Protein 2g.

Roasted Corn Salsa

PREP: 35 MIN; GRILL: 20 MIN

MAKES ABOUT 2 1/2 CUPS SALSA

Roasting adds a special flavor to this easy salsa— it's particularly good with smoked meats such as chicken, turkey or pork.

3 ears corn, husks removed

4 medium green onions

2 teaspoons vegetable oil

1 medium red bell pepper, chopped (1 cup)

2 tablespoons finely chopped Anaheim or serrano chili

3 tablespoons lemon juice

1/4 teaspoon salt

1. Brush grill rack with vegetable oil. Heat coals or gas grill for direct heat (page 16).

2. Brush corn and onions with oil.

3. Cover and grill corn and onions 4 to 6 inches from MEDIUM-HOT heat 5 minutes. Remove onions from grill; set aside. Turn corn. Cover and grill about 15 minutes, turning twice, until tender. Remove corn from grill; cool 20 minutes.

4. Cut corn from ears. Cut onions into slices. Mix corn, onions and remaining ingredients.

5. Serve salsa with grilled chicken or fish.

1/4 Cup: Calories 35 (Calories from Fat 35); Fat 1g (Saturated 0g); Cholesterol 0mg; Sodium 65mg; Carbohydrate 7g (Dietary Fiber 1g); Protein 1g.

Roasted Corn Salsa,
Sweet-Hot Salsa (page 204)

Toasted Pecan Pesto

PREP: 10 MIN; GRILL: 10 MIN

MAKES 1 CUP SAUCE

For an easy dinner, grill shrimp or fish fillets at the same time the pecans are toasting.

1/2 cup chopped pecans

2/3 cup firmly packed fresh parsley

1/2 cup chicken broth

2 tablespoons grated Romano cheese

3 tablespoons vegetable oil

2 teaspoons lemon juice

1/4 teaspoon salt

1/8 teaspoon pepper

1. Heat coals or gas grill for direct heat (page 16).

2. Place pecans in 9-inch round aluminum foil pan.

3. Grill pecans uncovered 4 to 6 inches from MEDIUM heat about 10 minutes, stirring occasionally, until golden brown.

4. Place pecans and remaining ingredients in food processor or blender. Cover and process about 1 minute or until smooth.

5. Serve sauce with grilled seafood or chicken.

1/4 Cup: Calories 215 (Calories from Fat 190); Fat 21g (Saturated 3g); Cholesterol 2mg; Sodium 300mg; Carbohydrate 4g (Dietary Fiber 1g); Protein 3g.

Roasted Garlic Sauce

PREP: 35 MIN

MAKES ABOUT 1 1/2 CUPS SAUCE

This sauce is also delicious served as a dip for chips or fresh vegetables.

Roasted Garlic with French Bread (page 142)

1 cup sour cream

2 tablespoons chopped fresh parsley

2 tablespoons dry sherry, if desired

1/8 teaspoon pepper

1. Prepare Roasted Garlic as directed, except omit French bread. Squeeze roasted garlic from bulbs; mash. Mix garlic and remaining ingredients.

2. Serve sauce with steak or baked potatoes or stirred into hot cooked pasta. Cover and refrigerate any remaining sauce.

1/4 Cup: Calories 85 (Calories from Fat 65); Fat 7g (Saturated 5g); Cholesterol 25mg; Sodium 15mg; Carbohydrate 4g (Dietary Fiber 0g); Protein 1g.

Fresh Tomato Salsa

PREP: 20 MIN

MAKES ABOUT 3½ CUPS SALSA

3 large tomatoes, seeded and chopped (3 cups)

4 medium green onions, sliced (1/2 cup)

1 small green bell pepper, chopped (1/2 cup)

3 cloves garlic, finely chopped

2 jalapeño chilies, finely chopped (1 tablespoon)

2 tablespoons chopped fresh cilantro

2 to 3 tablespoons lime juice

1/2 teaspoon salt

1. Mix all ingredients in nonmetal bowl.

2. Serve salsa with tortilla chips, fish, chicken, chops or steak.

1/4 Cup: Calories 10 (Calories from Fat 0); Fat 0g (Saturated 0g); Cholesterol 0mg; Sodium 85mg; Carbohydrate 2g (Dietary Fiber 0g); Protein 0g.

Orange-Jicama Salsa

PREP: 20 MIN; CHILL: 2 HR

MAKES ABOUT 2 CUPS SALSA

Jicama is related to the sharp-tasting turnip, but is very mild in flavor—it packs an inviting crunch in this fresh salsa. Peel the brown outer skin and then chop the white flesh. Tomatillos are green vegetables that look like cherry tomatoes. They come in husks— remove the husks and rinse off any sticky residue before chopping.

1 medium orange, peeled and chopped

1/2 cup chopped peeled jicama

1/4 cup chopped tomatillos

1/4 cup chopped red onion

2 tablespoons chopped fresh cilantro or parsley

1 tablespoon lime juice

1 teaspoon honey

1/4 teaspoon salt

1 small serrano chili, seeded and finely chopped (1 tablespoon)

1. Mix all ingredients in nonmetal bowl. Cover and refrigerate at least 2 hours to blend flavors.

2. Serve salsa with Grilled Roast Stuffed with Smoked Sausage (page 84) or other spicy grilled meat or chicken dishes.

1/4 Cup: Calories 15 (Calories from Fat 0); Fat 0g (Saturated 0g); Cholesterol 0mg; Sodium 75mg; Carbohydrate 5g (Dietary Fiber 1g); Protein 0g.

Apricot-Rosemary Salsa

PREP: 10 MIN; COOK: 10 MIN

MAKES ABOUT 1 CUP SALSA

1 can (5 1/2 ounces) apricot nectar

1/2 cup chopped dried apricots

1 tablespoon chopped shallots

3 medium roma (plum) tomatoes, chopped (3/4 cup)

2 teaspoons chopped fresh or 1/2 teaspoon crushed dried rosemary leaves

1 teaspoon lemon juice

1/8 teaspoon ground cinnamon

1/8 teaspoon ground ginger

2 tablespoons chopped fresh parsley

1. Mix apricot nectar, apricots and shallots in 2-quart saucepan. Heat to boiling over medium heat; reduce heat to low. Simmer uncovered 3 to 5 minutes or until most of nectar is absorbed.

2. Stir in remaining ingredients except parsley; heat through. Stir in parsley.

3. Serve warm or cold salsa with grilled poultry, pork or fish steaks.

1/4 Cup: Calories 70 (Calories from Fat 0); Fat 0g (Saturated 0g); Cholesterol 0mg; Sodium 10mg; Carbohydrate 18g (Dietary Fiber 2g); Protein 1g.

Sweet-Hot Salsa

PREP: 20 MIN; CHILL: 4 HR

MAKES 2 3/4 CUPS SALSA

Leaving the seeds in the jalapeño chili creates a hotter sauce.

1 medium papaya, peeled, seeded and chopped (1 1/2 cups)

1 small cucumber, peeled and chopped (1 cup)

1 small carrot, shredded

1 small jalapeño chili, seeded and finely chopped (2 to 3 teaspoons)

1 tablespoon lime juice

1 tablespoon white vinegar

1/2 teaspoon sugar

1/4 teaspoon salt

1. Mix all ingredients in nonmetal bowl. Cover and refrigerate at least 4 hours to blend flavors but no longer than 2 days.

2. Stir salsa before serving. Serve with grilled poultry, seafood or pork.

1/4 Cup: Calories 30 (Calories from Fat 0); Fat 0g (Saturated 0g); Cholesterol 0mg; Sodium 90mg; Carbohydrate 7g (Dietary Fiber 1g); Protein 1g.

Tropical Fruit Salsa

PREP: 15 MIN; **CHILL: 1** HR

MAKES ABOUT 2 CUPS SALSA

We find this has the fullest flavor when served at room temperature. If mangoes and papayas are not available, try substituting a combination of peaches, nectarines, plums and apricots.

2 kiwifruit, peeled and chopped

1 mango, peeled, pitted and chopped

1 papaya, peeled, pitted and chopped

1 jalapeño chili, seeded and finely chopped

1 cup pineapple chunks

1 tablespoon finely chopped red onion

1 tablespoon chopped fresh cilantro

2 tablespoons lime juice

1. Mix all ingredients in nonmetal bowl. Cover and refrigerate 1 to 2 hours to blend flavors.

2. Serve with grilled poultry, pork and seafood.

1/4 Cup: Calories 50 (Calories from Fat 0); Fat 0g (Saturated 0g); Cholesterol 0mg; Sodium 5mg; Carbohydrate 14g (Dietary Fiber 2g); Protein 1g.

Red, White and Green Salsa

PREP: 20 MIN; **CHILL: 1** HR

MAKES 3 CUPS SALSA

When watermelon is not in season, substitute two crisp red apples.

2 cups chopped seeded watermelon

1 cup chopped peeled jicama

1 medium stalk celery, sliced (1/2 cup)

1/4 cup chopped fresh cilantro or parsley

2 tablespoons chopped jalapeño or serrano chilies

2 tablespoons white vinegar

1/4 teaspoon salt

1. Mix all ingredients in nonmetal bowl. Cover and refrigerate at least 1 hour to blend flavors but no longer than 2 days.

2. Stir salsa before serving. Serve with grilled fish.

1/4 Cup: Calories 10 (Calories from Fat 0); Fat 0g (Saturated 0g); Cholesterol 0mg; Sodium 55mg; Carbohydrate 3g (Dietary Fiber 1g); Protein 0g.

Black Bean Relish

PREP: 10 MIN; CHILL: 1 HR

MAKES ABOUT 2½ CUPS RELISH

If serrano chilies aren't readily available, substitute 2 tablespoons drained chopped green chilies.

1 can (15 ounces) black beans, rinsed and drained

1 large tomato, finely chopped (1 cup)

1 small red bell pepper, chopped (1/2 cup)

1 serrano chili, seeded and finely chopped

1/4 cup finely chopped red onion

2 tablespoons white wine vinegar

1 tablespoon vegetable oil

1/4 teaspoon salt

1. Mix all ingredients. Cover and refrigerate about 1 hour or until chilled.

2. Serve relish with grilled beef, pork or poultry.

1/4 Cup: Calories 65 (Calories from Fat 20); Fat 2g (Saturated 0g); Cholesterol 0mg; Sodium 150mg; Carbohydrate 12g (Dietary Fiber 3g); Protein 3g.

Crunchy Vegetable Relish

PREP: 15 MIN; CHILL: 8 HR

MAKES ABOUT 4 CUPS RELISH

2 medium carrots, coarsely shredded (1 cup)

1 medium zucchini, chopped (1 cup)

2 cups finely shredded green cabbage

1/2 cup sugar

1/4 cup chopped red onion

1/4 cup balsamic or cider vinegar

1/2 teaspoon ground mustard (dry)

1 can (11 ounces) whole kernel corn with red and green peppers, undrained

1. Mix all ingredients. Cover and refrigerate at least 8 hours but no longer than 2 days.

2. Serve relish, using slotted spoon, with grilled poultry, pork, smoked sausage or beef.

1/4 Cup: Calories 50 (Calories from Fat 0); Fat 0g (Saturated 0g); Cholesterol 0mg; Sodium 50mg; Carbohydrate 12g (Dietary Fiber 1g); Protein 1g.

Gingered Zucchini Relish

PREP: 15 MIN; **GRILL:** 5 MIN; **CHILL:** 1 HR

MAKES ABOUT 2 CUPS RELISH

2 medium zucchini

1 large onion

1 tablespoon vegetable oil

1/4 cup finely chopped Anaheim chili

3 tablespoons lemon juice

3 tablespoons maple-flavored syrup

1 teaspoon finely chopped gingerroot

1/2 teaspoon salt

1. Brush grill rack with vegetable oil. Heat coals or gas grill for direct heat (page 16).

2. Cut zucchini lengthwise into 1/2-inch slices. Cut onion crosswise into 1/2-inch slices. Brush zucchini and onion with oil.

3. Grill zucchini and onion uncovered 4 inches from HIGH heat 5 to 10 minutes, turning once, until crisp-tender. Remove vegetables from grill; cool 10 minutes.

4. Chop zucchini and onion. Mix zucchini, onion and remaining ingredients in nonmetal bowl. Cover and refrigerate at least 1 hour to blend flavors but no longer than 2 days.

5. Stir relish before serving. Serve with grilled steak.

1/4 Cup: Calories 55 (Calories from Fat 20); Fat 2g (Saturated 0g); Cholesterol 0mg; Sodium 150mg; Carbohydrate 9g (Dietary Fiber 1g); Protein 1g.

Warm Fruit Medley

PREP: 10 MIN; GRILL: 9 MIN

MAKES ABOUT 2 CUPS

1 medium peach, thinly sliced

1 plum, thinly sliced

1 1/2 teaspoons lemon juice

1 1/2 teaspoons packed brown sugar

2 tablespoons golden raisins

2 teaspoons sliced almonds

**2 teaspoons margarine or butter, cut into
    2 pieces**

Place peach and plum slices on 18-inch square of heavy-duty aluminum foil. Sprinkle with lemon juice; toss to coat fruit with juice. Top with remaining ingredients in order given. Wrap foil securely around fruit. Cover and grill foil packet 4 inches from MEDIUM heat 7 to 9 minutes or until fruit is hot and crisp-tender. Add fruit medley for last 7 to 9 minutes of grilling or until fruit is hot and crisp-tender.

1/2 Cup: Calories 65 (Calories from Fat 25); Fat 3g
(Saturated 1g); Cholesterol 0mg; Sodium 25mg;
Carbohydrate 10g (Dietary Fiber 1g); Protein 1g.

Mango Relish

PREP: 20 MIN; CHILL: 1 HR

MAKES ABOUT 1 CUP RELISH

Mango adds a tropical flavor that particularly enhances fish and chicken. If mangoes are not available, canned mango, papaya or fresh or frozen (thawed) peaches are a good substitute.

**1 mango, peeled, pitted and chopped
    (1 cup)**

1/4 cup finely chopped red onion

**2 tablespoons finely chopped fresh
    or 2 teaspoons dried mint leaves**

**1 small jalapeño chili, finely chopped
    (2 to 3 teaspoons)**

2 tablespoons lime juice

1/8 teaspoon salt

1. Mix all ingredients in nonmetal bowl. Cover and refrigerate at least 1 hour to blend flavors but no longer than 2 days.

2. Serve relish with grilled fish or chicken.

1/4 Cup: Calories 45 (Calories from Fat 0); Fat 0g
(Saturated 0g); Cholesterol 0mg; Sodium 80mg;
Carbohydrate 11g (Dietary Fiber 1g); Protein 1g.

Mango Relish

Nectarine Chutney

PREP: 20 MIN; **COOK: 30** MIN

MAKES ABOUT 2 CUPS CHUTNEY

For a slightly different chutney, substitute peaches for the nectarines and orange peel for the lemon peel.

4 nectarines, coarsely chopped (3 cups)

1 small onion, chopped (1/4 cup)

1/3 cup golden raisins

1/4 cup cider vinegar

3 tablespoons packed brown sugar

1 teaspoon grated lemon peel

1 teaspoon chopped crystallized ginger

3/4 teaspoon ground allspice

1/4 teaspoon crushed red pepper

1. Mix all ingredients in 3-quart saucepan. Heat to boiling; reduce heat to low. Simmer uncovered about 30 minutes, stirring occasionally, until thickened. Store tightly covered in refrigerator up to 2 months.

2. Serve warm or cold with grilled chicken, pork, beef or lamb.

1/4 Cup: Calories 70 (Calories from Fat 0); Fat 0g (Saturated 0g); Cholesterol 0mg; Sodium 5mg; Carbohydrate 18g (Dietary Fiber 1g); Protein 1g.

Italian Eggplant Relish

PREP: 15 MIN; MARINATE: 30 MIN;
GRILL: 10 MIN; CHILL: 1 HR

MAKES ABOUT 2 CUPS RELISH

Marinated grilled eggplant is delicious served as a vegetable side dish.

**1 small eggplant (3/4 pound), cut into
   1/2-inch slices**

1/4 cup Italian dressing

1/2 cup chopped red onion

**1/4 cup Kalamata olives, pitted and
   chopped**

**1 tablespoon chopped fresh or 1 teaspoon
   dried basil leaves**

1 tablespoon Italian dressing

2 teaspoons capers

1/4 teaspoon pepper

1. Brush eggplant on both sides with 1/4 cup dressing. Place in nonmetal dish. Cover and let stand at room temperature 30 minutes.

2. Heat coals or gas grill for direct heat (page 16).

3. Remove eggplant from dressing; discard dressing. Cover and grill eggplant 4 to 6 inches from MEDIUM-HIGH heat 8 to10 minutes, turning once, until tender. Remove eggplant from grill; cool to room temperature.

4. Coarsely chop eggplant. Mix eggplant and remaining ingredients. Cover and refrigerate at least 1 hour to blend flavors but no longer than 2 days.

5. Serve relish with grilled steak or lamb.

1/4 Cup: Calories 45 (Calories from Fat 25); Fat 3g (Saturated 0g); Cholesterol 0mg; Sodium 100mg; Carbohydrate 5g (Dietary Fiber 1g); Protein 1g.

9

Smoker Cooking

*Turkey with Chili–Corn
Bread Dressing (page 217)*

Four-Pepper Beef Brisket

PREP: 10 MIN; SMOKE: 5 HR

MAKES 12 SERVINGS

Make this brisket with your favorite homemade barbecue sauce or use bottled sauce. Looking for a great barbecue sauce? Try the delicious ones we've rounded up on pages 189–211. Whatever you choose, be sure to have plenty on hand for extra flavor to serve with the brisket.

2 cups hickory wood chips

Four-Pepper Rub (right)

5-pound well-trimmed fresh beef brisket (not corned beef)

1/2 cup prepared barbecue sauce

1. Cover wood chips with water; soak 30 minutes.

2. Drain wood chips. Prepare and heat smoker using wood chips. (For charcoal smoker, use 5 pounds charcoal briquettes.)

3. Prepare Four-Pepper Rub. Rub pepper mixture into all sides of beef.

4. Brush smoker rack with vegetable oil. Cover and smoke beef about 4 hours. Brush beef with barbecue sauce; continue smoking about 1 hour longer or until meat thermometer reads 160°F.

FOUR-PEPPER RUB

1 tablespoon cracked black pepper

1 tablespoon cracked white pepper

1 tablespoon cracked red pepper

1 tablespoon lemon pepper

Mix all ingredients. About 1/4 cup.

1 Serving: Calories 300 (Calories from Fat 125); Fat 14g (Saturated 6g); Cholesterol 110mg; Sodium 230mg; Carbohydrate 2g (Dietary Fiber 0g); Protein 41g.

Four-Pepper Beef Brisket

Apple-Smoked Pork with Pepper and Onion

PREP: 20 MIN; SMOKE: 3 HR

MAKES **8** SERVINGS

Pork tenderloins are rather small, so the bell pepper and onion pieces also need to be of similar size to fit into the slits in the pork.

4 cups apple wood chips

2 pork tenderloins (each about 1 pound)

1 teaspoon garlic salt

1 small red or green bell pepper, cut into 2 × 1/2-inch pieces

1 small onion, cut into 1/4-inch slices

1. Cover wood chips with water; soak 30 minutes.

2. Drain wood chips. Prepare and heat smoker using wood chips. (For charcoal smoker, use 5 pounds charcoal briquettes.)

3. Sprinkle pork with garlic salt. Make diagonal cuts across pork at 1-inch intervals to within 1/2 inch of bottom of pork. Insert bell pepper and onion pieces alternately in cuts in pork.

4. Cover and smoke pork about 3 hours or until meat thermometer reads 160°F.

1 Serving: Calories 135 (Calories from Fat 35); Fat 4g (Saturated 2g); Cholesterol 65mg; Sodium 170mg; Carbohydrate 1g (Dietary Fiber 0g); Protein 24g.

Hot and Spicy Ribs

PREP: 10 MIN; SMOKE: 4 1/2 TO 5 HR

MAKES **6** SERVINGS

These spicy-hot ribs are great served with your favorite coleslaw, potato salad and iced tea—or any other drink that suits your mood.

4 cups hickory wood chips

Spicy Rib Rub (below)

5 pounds pork spareribs (not cut into serving pieces)

Barbecue sauce, if desired

1. Cover wood chips with water; soak 30 minutes.

2. Drain wood chips. Prepare and heat smoker using wood chips. (For charcoal smoker, use 5 pounds charcoal briquettes.)

3. Prepare Spicy Rib Rub. Cut rack of pork in half to fit on smoker rack if necessary. Rub spice mixture into pork.

4. Cover and smoke pork 4 1/2 to 5 hours or until tender.

5. Serve pork with barbecue sauce.

SPICY RIB RUB

1 tablespoon garlic powder

1 tablespoon paprika

2 teaspoons ground red pepper (cayenne)

2 teaspoons dried thyme leaves, crumbled

1 teaspoon salt

1 teaspoon pepper

Mix all ingredients. About 3 tablespoons.

1 Serving: Calories 715 (Calories from Fat 495); Fat 55g (Saturated 20g); Cholesterol 220mg; Sodium 560mg; Carbohydrate 2g (Dietary Fiber 0g); Protein 53g.

Turkey with Chili–Corn Bread Dressing

PREP: 30 MIN; SMOKE: 6 HR

MAKES **10** SERVINGS

Cranberry Compote (page 225) is a festive accompaniment to this smoky turkey and dressing.

4 cups hickory wood chips
10- to 12-pound turkey
Chili–Corn Bread Dressing (right)

1. Cover wood chips with water; soak 30 minutes.

2. Drain wood chips. Prepare and heat smoker using wood chips. (For charcoal smoker, use 5 pounds charcoal briquettes.)

3. Fasten neck skin of turkey to back with skewer. Fold wings across back with tips touching. Tuck drumsticks under band of skin at tail, or tie or skewer to tail.

4. Brush smoker rack with vegetable oil. Place turkey, breast side up, on rack in smoker. Cover and smoke turkey 6 to 6 1/2 hours or until meat thermometer reads 180°F with tip in thickest part of inside thigh muscle and does not touch bone and juice is no longer pink when center of thigh is cut.

5. While turkey is smoking, prepare Chili–Corn Bread Dressing. Cover dressing with aluminum foil and refrigerate. Add dressing, covered, for last 2 hours of smoking or until hot.

CHILI–CORN BREAD DRESSING

1 cup water
1 cup margarine or butter, melted
1 medium green bell pepper, chopped (1 cup)
1/2 chopped red onion
2 cans (4 ounces each) chopped green chilies, drained
1 package (16 ounces) corn bread stuffing mix

Mix water, margarine, bell pepper, onion and chilies in 13×9×2-inch rectangular aluminum foil pan. Add stuffing mix; toss.

1 Serving: Calories 750 (Calories from Fat 325); Fat 36g (Saturated 10g); Cholesterol 90mg; Sodium 940mg; Carbohydrate 36g (Dietary Fiber 2g); Protein 66g.

Cajun Chicken

PREP: 15 MIN; SMOKE: 2 1/2 TO 3 HR

MAKES **6** SERVINGS

Serve this spicy chicken with grilled Sweet Potato Slices (page 168) and cooling watermelon for a refreshing twist.

2 cups hickory wood chips

Cajun Spice Rub (below)

3- to 3 1/2-pound cut-up broiler-fryer chicken

1. Cover wood chips with water; soak 30 minutes.

2. Drain wood chips. Prepare and heat smoker using wood chips. (For charcoal smoker, use 4 pounds charcoal briquettes.)

3. Prepare Cajun Spice Rub. Rub pepper mixture into all sides of chicken.

4. Place chicken, skin sides up, on rack in smoker. Cover and smoke chicken 2 1/2 to 3 hours until juice is no longer pink when thickest pieces are cut when centers of thickest pieces are cut.

CAJUN SPICE RUB

1 teaspoon black pepper

1/2 teaspoon ground red pepper (cayenne)

1/2 teaspoon white pepper

1/2 teaspoon ground cumin

1/2 teaspoon ground nutmeg

1/2 teaspoon salt

Mix all ingredients. About 1 tablespoon.

1 Serving: Calories 220 (Calories from Fat 110); Fat 12g (Saturated 4g); Cholesterol 85mg; Sodium 270mg; Carbohydrate 1g (Dietary Fiber 0g); Protein 27g.

Oriental Chicken Breasts

PREP: 5 MIN; SMOKE: 45 MIN

MAKES **8** SERVINGS

Stir-fried fresh vegetables and rice round out this meal very nicely.

1 cup mesquite wood chips

Oriental Spice Rub (below)

8 large skinless boneless chicken breast halves (about 3 pounds)

1. Cover wood chips with water; soak 30 minutes.

2. Drain wood chips. Prepare and heat smoker using wood chips. (For charcoal smoker, use 2 pounds charcoal briquettes.)

3. Prepare Oriental Spice Rub. Rub spice mixture into all sides of chicken.

4. Brush smoker rack with vegetable oil. Cover and smoke chicken about 45 minutes or until juice is no longer pink when centers of thickest pieces are cut.

ORIENTAL SPICE RUB

2 tablespoons ground coriander

2 tablespoons five-spice powder

1 tablespoon packed brown sugar

1 teaspoon garlic powder

1/4 teaspoon pepper

Mix all ingredients. About 1/3 cup.

1 Serving: Calories 205 (Calories from Fat 45); Fat 5g (Saturated 2g); Cholesterol 95mg; Sodium 105mg; Carbohydrate 4g (Dietary Fiber 1g); Protein 37g.

Cornish Hens with Berry Puree

PREP: 20 MIN; SMOKE: 4 TO 5 HR

MAKES 8 SERVINGS

4 cups apple wood chips

**4 Rock Cornish hens (each about
   1 1/2 pounds)**

1/2 teaspoon salt

1/2 teaspoon pepper

Berry Puree (right)

1. Cover wood chips with water; soak 30 minutes.

2. Drain wood chips. Prepare and heat smoker
   using wood chips. (For charcoal smoker, use
   5 pounds charcoal briquettes.)

3. Sprinkle hens with salt and pepper.

4. Place hens, breast sides up, on rack in smoker.
   Cover and smoke 4 to 5 hours or until thermometer reads 180°F and juice is no longer
   pink when center of thigh is cut.

5. While hens are smoking, prepare Berry Puree.

6. Serve hens with puree.

BERRY PUREE

**3 cups fresh or frozen raspberries
   or blackberries**

1/4 cup sugar

1/4 cup raspberry vinegar

Place all ingredients in blender. Cover and
blend on medium speed until well blended.
Strain berry mixture to remove seeds, if desired.
About 2 cups.

1 Serving: Calories 330 (Calories from Fat 190); Fat 21g
(Saturated 6g); Cholesterol 150mg; Sodium 220mg;
Carbohydrate 12g (Dietary Fiber 3g); Protein 26g.

Ducklings with Sour Cherry Sauce

PREP: 25 MIN; SMOKE: 5 TO 6 HR

MAKES 8 SERVINGS

The smoked duck is enhanced by the intense cherry flavor and beautiful color of the sauce. This is an excellent meal for entertaining and will also be a hit as a family meal.

6 cups apple wood chips

2 ducklings (each 4 to 5 pounds)

1/2 teaspoon garlic salt

Sour Cherry Sauce (right)

1. Cover wood chips with water; soak 30 minutes.

2. Drain 4 cups wood chips. Prepare and heat smoker using wood chips. (For charcoal smoker, use 5 pounds charcoal briquettes.)

3. Fasten neck skin of each duckling to back with skewer. Fold wings across back with tips touching. Pierce skin all over with fork. Tuck drumsticks under band of skin at tail, or tie or skewer to tail. Sprinkle ducklings with garlic salt.

4. Place ducklings, breast sides up, on rack in smoker. Cover and smoke ducklings 5 to 6 hours or until thermometer inserted with tip in thickest part of thigh muscle and not touching bone reads 180°F and juice is no longer pink when center of thigh is cut. (Drain remaining wood chips and add after 3 hours.)

5. While ducklings are smoking, prepare Sour Cherry Sauce.

6. Serve ducklings with warm sauce.

SOUR CHERRY SAUCE

1 1/4 cups chicken broth

1 tablespoon cornstarch

1 cup dried sour cherries or dried cranberries

1/4 cup sugar

Mix broth and cornstarch in 2-quart saucepan. Stir in cherries and sugar. Cook over medium-low heat 6 to 8 minutes, stirring constantly, until mixture thickens and boils; boil and stir 1 minute. About 1 1/2 cups.

1 Serving: Calories 690 (Calories from Fat 495); Fat 55g (Saturated 19g); Cholesterol 160mg; Sodium 290mg; Carbohydrate 13g (Dietary Fiber 1g); Protein 37g.

Let's Have A Clambake!

Clambakes have long been a summertime tradition along the shores of New England, where people were perfectly equipped with a bounty of seafood and a sandy coast. Summertime and clambakes are well-suited—many seafoods are at their best during the summer and cooking outdoors is a pleasant way to spend long summer evenings. Today, with the abundance of seafood in our markets, having a clambake is an easy and fun activity, and shorelines everywhere can host a clambake.

Getting Ready

If you are preparing a clambake on a public beach or in a park, check to be sure that digging a pit and cooking will not be in violation of any laws. Be sure to dig the pit well above the high-tide mark Bring along flashlights and plenty of insect repellent. Transport seafood in a cooler to ensure food safety, then use the cooler to keep beverages chilled throughout the party. Before you leave the beach, be sure to extinguish the fire thoroughly.

For a backyard or park clambake (check what time the park closes) be sure you have at least four hours for your clambake. Put out citronella candles to cut down on bugs. Play beach-party music or whatever makes you think of surf, sun and fun!

Don't expect people to sit down formally for this dinner—this is pure finger-food fun! You may want to provide blankets or beach towels to sit on the beach or bring along a few card tables or folding picnic tables from home. Be sure you have nutcrackers and picks on hand so the guests can eat the lobster easily. And don't forget a set of tongs, and mitts, for the cook.

For fun, purchase paper or plastic lobster bibs to protect guests' clothing. Personalize the bibs by writing your own message with a marker, or have markers available so guests can personalize their own bibs.

Let's Cook

Get hold of a 30- to 40-quart stockpot, a standard size in commercial kitchens. You might check to see if you can borrow one from your local church or school. If not, stockpots are easy to rent.

Dig a pit in dirt or sand about 20 inches in diameter and deep enough to hold 8 inches of charcoal. Secure a heavy rack about 2 inches from coals on which to place the stockpot. Let charcoal burn for about 30 minutes or until coals are glowing.

Remove the outer husks from 12 ears of corn; remove the silk. Fill the stockpot with 1 inch water.

Place 12 live lobsters, each weighing about 1 pound, in the stockpot, followed by 3 pounds peeled small white onions, the corn, 3 pounds washed red potatoes and 4 pounds washed soft-shell clams (steamers). Cover the stockpot and place it on the rack in the pit over MEDIUM-HOT heat. Cook about 30 minutes or until water is boiling. Cook with water boiling for about 30 minutes longer or until potatoes are tender.

Remove stockpot from rack. Place food on large platters and serve with melted butter and sauces.

Herbed Salmon Fillet with Cucumber Sauce

PREP: 20 MIN; SMOKE: 1 1/2 HR

MAKES **8** SERVINGS

The smoky herb flavor of the salmon pairs well with the fresh Cucumber Sauce; try serving this dish with roasted new potatoes and grilled corn.

2 cups apple wood chips

4 sprigs dill weed

4 sprigs tarragon

1 small bunch thyme

1 large salmon fillet (about 2 pounds)

Cucumber Sauce (right)

1. Cover wood chips with water; soak 30 minutes.

2. Drain wood chips. Prepare and heat smoker using wood chips. (For charcoal smoker, use 5 pounds charcoal briquettes.)

3. Place dill weed, tarragon and thyme lengthwise on top of fish fillet; secure with string.

4. Brush smoker rack with vegetable oil. Cover and smoke fish about 1 1/2 hours or until fish flakes easily with fork (160°F).

5. While fish is smoking, prepare Cucumber Sauce.

6. Serve fish with sauce.

CUCUMBER SAUCE

1 large cucumber, seeded and chopped (1 cup)

1 cup sour cream or plain yogurt

2 tablespoons chopped fresh parsley or 1 teaspoon dried parsley flakes

2 tablespoons chopped fresh or 1 teaspoon freeze-dried chives

1/4 teaspoon salt

1 clove garlic, finely chopped

Mix all ingredients. Cover and refrigerate at least 1 hour. About 2 cups.

1 Serving: Calories 190 (Calories from Fat 100); Fat 11g (Saturated 5g); Cholesterol 80mg; Sodium 140mg; Carbohydrate 2g (Dietary Fiber 0g); Protein 21g.

Herbed Salmon Fillet with Cucumber Sauce

Smoked Salmon

PREP: 15 MIN; SMOKE: 3 HR

MAKES 8 SERVINGS

3 cups hickory wood chips

2 tablespoons margarine or butter, melted

2 tablespoons lemon juice

2 tablespoons chopped fresh or 1 teaspoon dried dill weed

3-pound pan-dressed salmon

Fresh dill weed, if desired

Lemon slices, if desired

1. Cover wood chips with water; soak 30 minutes.

2. Drain wood chips. Prepare and heat smoker using 1 cup of the wood chips. (For charcoal smoker, use 5 pounds charcoal briquettes.)

3. Mix margarine, lemon juice and 2 tablespoons dill weed; brush over both sides of fish.

4. Cover and smoke fish 3 to 3 1/2 hours, brushing once or twice with lemon juice mixture, until fish flakes easily with fork (160°F). Add 1 cup wood chips and more charcoal every hour. Discard any remaining lemon juice mixture.

5. To serve, cut fish into serving pieces. Garnish with fresh dill weed and lemon slices.

1 Serving: Calories 125 (Calories from Fat 55); Fat 6g (Saturated 2g); Cholesterol 55mg; Sodium 70mg; Carbohydrate 0g (Dietary Fiber 0g); Protein 18g.

Trout with Hazelnut Stuffing

PREP: 25 MIN; SMOKE: 1 1/2 HR

MAKES 4 SERVINGS

The Hazelnut Stuffing also is excellent in pork chops or chicken breasts.

2 cups apple or other fruitwood chips

Hazelnut Stuffing (below)

4 pan-dressed rainbow trout (each about 1/2 pound)

1. Cover wood chips with water; soak 30 minutes.

2. Drain wood chips. Prepare and heat smoker using wood chips. (For charcoal smoker, use 3 pounds charcoal briquettes.)

3. Prepare Hazelnut Stuffing. Spoon about 1/4 cup stuffing mixture into cavity of each fish; secure with string.

4. Brush smoker rack with vegetable oil. Cover and smoke fish about 1 1/2 hours or until fish flakes easily with fork (160°F).

HAZELNUT STUFFING

1 cup seasoned stuffing crumbs

1/4 cup chopped hazelnuts or pecans, toasted if desired

2 tablespoons margarine or butter, melted

2 tablespoons apple juice

1/2 teaspoon dried sage leaves, crumbled

Mix all ingredients. About 1 cup.

1 Serving: Calories 405 (Calories from Fat 200); Fat 22g (Saturated 4g); Cholesterol 95mg; Sodium 420mg; Carbohydrate 15g (Dietary Fiber 1g); Protein 38g.

Swordfish with Cranberry Compote

PREP: 20 MIN; COOK: 15 MIN; COOL: 30 MIN; SMOKE: 1 HR

MAKES 8 SERVINGS

Bright red Cranberry Compote with its slightly sweet and spicy flavor is an excellent counterpoint to the mild swordfish.

1 cup hickory wood chips

**8 swordfish or whitefish steaks,
    about 1 inch thick (each 6 ounces)**

Cranberry Compote (right)

1. Cover wood chips with water; soak 30 minutes.

2. Drain wood chips. Prepare and heat smoker using wood chips. (For charcoal smoker, use 2 pounds charcoal briquettes.)

3. Brush smoker rack with vegetable oil. Cover and smoke fish about 1 hour or until fish flakes easily with fork.

4. While fish is smoking, prepare Cranberry Compote.

5. Serve fish with compote.

CRANBERRY COMPOTE

1 teaspoon vegetable oil

1 medium onion, chopped (1/2 cup)

1/2 cup sugar

1/4 cup water

1/4 teaspoon salt

1/4 teaspoon ground cloves

1 package (12 ounces) cranberries

Heat oil in 2-quart saucepan over medium heat. Cook onion in oil about 2 minutes, stirring occasionally, until softened. Stir in remaining ingredients; reduce heat to low. Cover and simmer about 12 minutes, stirring occasionally, until cranberries pop. Remove from heat; cool 30 minutes stirring occasionally. Serve warm or cold. About 2 cups.

1 Serving: Calories 255 (Calories from Fat 70); Fat 8g (Saturated 3g); Cholesterol 90mg; Sodium 150mg; Carbohydrate 19g (Dietary Fiber 2g); Protein 29g.

Dilled Garlic Corn on the Cob

PREP: 25 MIN; SMOKE: 1 1/2 HR

MAKES 8 SERVINGS

Use any leftover corn to add smoky flavor to your favorite corn relish, corn muffins or corn pudding recipes.

2 cups mesquite wood chips

2 tablespoons chopped fresh or 2 teaspoons dried dill weed

3 tablespoons olive or vegetable oil

2 cloves garlic, finely crushed

8 ears corn (with husks)

1. Cover wood chips with water; soak 30 minutes.

2. Drain wood chips. Prepare and heat smoker using wood chips. (For charcoal smoker, use 3 pounds charcoal briquettes.)

3. Mix dill weed, oil and garlic. Remove large outer husks from each ear corn; turn back inner husks, and remove silk. Brush corn with dill weed mixture. Pull husks up over ears; tie with fine wire or twist ends to secure.

4. Cover and smoke corn about 1 1/2 hours or until tender.

1 Serving: Calories 115 (Calories from Fat 35); Fat 4g (Saturated 1g); Cholesterol 0mg; Sodium 15mg; Carbohydrate 20g (Dietary Fiber 2g); Protein 2g.

Citrus Smoked Shrimp

PREP: 10 MIN; MARINATE: 30 MIN; SMOKE: 45 MIN

MAKES 6 SERVINGS

Serve this versatile shrimp as an appetizer, on salad greens as an entrée or hot and smoky with crusty bread.

1 cup hickory wood chips

1/2 cup orange juice

1 tablespoon grated lime peel

1/4 cup lime juice

1 tablespoon vegetable oil

1 tablespoon honey

2 pounds fresh or frozen large shrimp in shells (about 30), thawed if frozen

1. Cover wood chips with water; soak 30 minutes.

2. Mix remaining ingredients except shrimp in shallow nonmetal bowl or resealable plastic bag. Add shrimp, stirring to coat with marinade. Cover and refrigerate 30 minutes.

3. Drain wood chips. Prepare and heat smoker using wood chips. (For charcoal smoker, use 2 pounds charcoal briquettes.)

4. Remove shrimp from marinade; pour marinade into water pan in smoker. Add water to "fill" line in pan. Cover and smoke shrimp about 45 minutes or until pink and firm.

1 Serving: Calories 75 (Calories from Fat 10); Fat 1g (Saturated 0g); Cholesterol 140mg; Sodium 160mg; Carbohydrate 1g (Dietary Fiber 0g); Protein 15g.

Citrus Smoked Shrimp

Smoky Mushrooms

PREP: 15 MIN; SMOKE: 1 HR

MAKES 8 SERVINGS

2 cups apple wood chips

**1 pound portobello mushrooms,
    cut into 1/2-inch slices**

**1 pound regular white mushrooms,
    cut into 1/2-inch slices**

1/4 cup red wine vinegar

2 tablespoons vegetable oil

2 teaspoons Dijon mustard

1/4 teaspoon salt

1. Cover wood chips with water; soak 30 minutes.

2. Drain wood chips. Prepare and heat smoker using wood chips. (For charcoal smoker, use 2 pounds charcoal briquettes.)

3. Place mushrooms in 13×9-inch aluminum foil pan or on 18-inch square of heavy-duty aluminum foil. Mix remaining ingredients; pour over mushrooms. Cover pan loosely with foil, or wrap foil square loosely around mushrooms.

4. Cover and smoke mushrooms about 1 hour or until mushrooms are tender.

1 Serving: Calories 40 (Calories from Fat 20); Fat 2g (Saturated 0g); Cholesterol 0mg; Sodium 50mg; Carbohydrate 5g (Dietary Fiber 1g); Protein 2g.

Flavor Boosters

For your convenience, here is a list of rubs and sauces in this chapter.

Four-Pepper Rub 214

Spicy Rib Rub 216

Chili–Corn Bread Dressing 217

Cajun Spice Rub 218

Oriental Spice Rub 218

Berry Puree 219

Sour Cherry Sauce 220

Cucumber Sauce 222

Cranberry Compote 225

Helpful Nutrition and Cooking Information

Nutrition Guidelines:

We provide nutrition information for each recipe that includes calories, fat, cholesterol, sodium, carbohydrate, fiber and protein. Individual food choices can be based on this information.

Recommended intake for a daily diet of 2,000 calories as set by the Food and Drug Administration:

Total Fat	Less than 65 g
Saturated Fat	Less than 20g
Cholesterol	Less than 300mg
Sodium	Less than 2,400mg
Total Carbohydrate	300g
Dietary Fiber	25g

Criteria Used for Calculating Nutrition Information:

- The first ingredient was used wherever a choice is given (such as 1/3 cup sour cream or plain yogurt).

- The first ingredient amount was used wherever a range is given (such as 3 to 3 1/2 pound cut-up broiler-fryer chicken).

- The first serving number was used wherever a range is given (such as 4 to 6 servings).

- "If desired" ingredients (such as sprinkle with brown sugar if desired) and recipe variations are *not* included.

- Only the amount of a marinade or frying oil that is estimated to be absorbed by the food during preparation or cooking was calculated.

Cooking Terms Glossary:

Beat: Mix ingredients vigorously with spoon, fork, wire whisk, hand beater or electric mixer until smooth and uniform.

Boil: Heat liquid until bubbles rise continuously and break on the surface and steam is given off. For rolling boil, the bubbles form rapidly.

Chop: Cut into coarse or fine irregular pieces with a knife, food chopper, blender or food processor.

Cube: Cut into squares 1/2 inch or larger.

Dice: Cut into squares smaller than 1/2 inch.

Grate: Cut into tiny particles using small rough holes of grater (citrus peel or chocolate).

Grease: Rub the inside surface of a pan with shortening, using pastry brush, piece of waxed paper or paper towel, to prevent food from sticking during baking (as for some casseroles).

Julienne: Cut into thin, matchlike strips, using knife or food processor (vegetables, fruits, meats).

Mix: Combine ingredients in any way that distributes them evenly.

Sauté: Cook foods in hot oil or margarine over medium-high heat with frequent tossing and turning motion.

Shred: Cut into long thin pieces by rubbing food across the holes of a shredder, as for cheese, or by using a knife to slice very thinly, as for cabbage.

Simmer: Cook in liquid just below the boiling point on top of the stove; usually after reducing heat from a boil. Bubbles will rise slowly and break just below the surface.

Stir: Mix ingredients until uniform consistency. Stir once in a while for stirring occasionally, often for stirring frequently and continuously for stirring constantly.

Toss: Tumble ingredients lightly with a lifting motion (such as green salad), usually to coat evenly or mix with another food.

Ingredients used in recipe testing and nutrition calculations:

- Ingredients used for testing represent those that the majority of consumers use in their homes: large eggs, 2% milk, 80% lean ground beef, canned ready-to-use chicken broth, and vegetable oil spread containing *not less than 65% fat.*

- Fat-free, low-fat or low-sodium products are not used, unless otherwise indicated.

- Solid vegetable shortening (not butter, margarine, nonstick cooking sprays or vegetable oil spread as they can cause sticking problems) is used to grease pans, unless otherwise indicated.

Equipment used in Recipe Testing:

We use equipment for testing that the majority of consumers use in their homes. If a specific piece of equipment (such as a wire whisk) is necessary for recipe success, it will be listed in the recipe.

- Cookware and bakeware *without* non-stick coatings were used, unless otherwise indicated.

- No dark colored, black or insulated bakeware was used.

- When a baking *pan* is specified in a recipe, a *metal* pan was used; a baking *dish* or pie *plate* means ovenproof glass was used.

- An electric hand mixer was used for mixing *only when mixer speeds are specified* in the recipe directions. When a mixer speed is not given, a spoon or fork was used.

Metric Conversion Guide

Volume

U.S. Units	Canadian Metric	Australian Metric
1/4 teaspoon	1 mL	1 ml
1/2 teaspoon	2 mL	2 ml
1 teaspoon	5 mL	5 ml
1 tablespoon	15 mL	20 ml
1/4 cup	50 mL	60 ml
1/3 cup	75 mL	80 ml
1/2 cup	125 mL	125 ml
2/3 cup	150 mL	170 ml
3/4 cup	175 mL	190 ml
1 cup	250 mL	250 ml
1 quart	1 liter	1 liter
1 1/2 quarts	1.5 liters	1.5 liters
2 quarts	2 liters	2 liters
2 1/2 quarts	2.5 liters	2.5 liters
3 quarts	3 liters	3 liters
4 quarts	4 liters	4 liters

Weight

U.S. Units	Canadian Metric	Australian Metric
1 ounce	30 grams	30 grams
2 ounces	55 grams	60 grams
3 ounces	85 grams	90 grams
4 ounces (1/4 pound)	115 grams	125 grams
8 ounces (1/2 pound)	225 grams	225 grams
16 ounces (1 pound)	455 grams	500 grams
1 pound	455 grams	1/2 kilogram

Note: The recipes in this cookbook have not been developed or tested using metric measures. When converting recipes to metric, some variations in quality may be noted.

Measurements

Inches	Centimeters
1	2.5
2	5.0
3	7.5
4	10.0
5	12.5
6	15.0
7	17.5
8	20.5
9	23.0
10	25.5
11	28.0
12	30.5
13	33.0
14	35.5
15	38.0

Temperatures

Fahrenheit	Celsius
32°	0°
212°	100°
250°	120°
275°	140°
300°	150°
325°	160°
350°	180°
375°	190°
400°	200°
425°	220°
450°	230°
475°	240°
500°	260°

Index

Numbers in *italics* refer to photos.

Complete your cookbook library with these *Betty Crocker* titles

Betty Crocker's A Passion for Pasta
Betty Crocker's Best Bread Machine Cookbook
Betty Crocker's Best Chicken Cookbook
Betty Crocker's Best Christmas Cookbook
Betty Crocker's Best of Baking
Betty Crocker's Best of Healthy and Hearty Cooking
Betty Crocker's Best-Loved Recipes
Betty Crocker's Bisquick® Cookbook
Betty Crocker's Bread Machine Cookbook
Betty Crocker's Ultimate Cake Mix Cookbook
Betty Crocker's Cook It Quick
Betty Crocker's Cookbook, 9th Edition—*The* **BIG RED** *Cookbook*™
Betty Crocker's Cookbook, Bridal Edition
Betty Crocker's Cookie Book
Betty Crocker's Cooking for Two
Betty Crocker's Cooky Book, Facsimile Edition
Betty Crocker's Cooking Basics
Betty Crocker's Easy Slow Cooker Dinners
Betty Crocker's Eat and Lose Weight
Betty Crocker's Entertaining Basics
Betty Crocker's Flavors of Home
Betty Crocker's Healthy New Choices
Betty Crocker's Indian Home Cooking
Betty Crocker's Italian Cooking
Betty Crocker's Kids Cook!
Betty Crocker's Kitchen Library
Betty Crocker's Living with Cancer
Betty Crocker's Low-Fat Low-Cholesterol Cooking Today
Betty Crocker's New Cake Decorating
Betty Crocker's New Chinese Cookbook
Betty Crocker's Picture Cook Book, Facsimile Edition
Betty Crocker's Quick & Easy Cookbook
Betty Crocker's Slow Cooker Cookbook
Betty Crocker's Southwest Cooking
Betty Crocker's Vegetarian Cooking